# ONE WEEK LOAN

D1643920

# Educational Research in Practice

Making Sense of Methodology

Edited by Joanna Swann and John Pratt

**continuum**
LONDON • NEW YORK

**Continuum**
The Tower Building, 11 York Road, London, SE1 7NX
15 East 26th Street, New York, NY 10010

**British Library Cataloguing-in-Publication Data**
A catalogue record for this book is available from the British Library.

ISBN: 0–8264–5342–2 (hardback)

Typeset in Palatino by RefineCatch Limited, Bungay, Suffolk
Printed and bound in Great Britain by
Bookcraft (Bath) Ltd, Midsomer Norton, Somerset

We all have our philosophies, whether or not we are aware of this fact, and our philosophies are not worth very much. But the impact of our philosophies upon our actions and our lives is often devastating. This makes it necessary to try to improve our philosophies by criticism. This is the only apology for the continued existence of philosophy which I am able to offer.

Karl Popper
*Objective Knowledge: An Evolutionary Approach*

I hold that orthodoxy is the death of knowledge, since the growth of knowledge depends entirely on the existence of disagreement.

Karl Popper
*The Myth of the Framework*

The brilliance comes in your mistakes – that's how you discover new things. And the only way to make mistakes is to stretch and take chances. If you play it safe, you'll never progress.

Miles Davis
quoted in *Miles Davis: The Definitive Biography*

# Contents

*Acknowledgements*                                                    vii

**Part I: An Introduction to Educational Research in Practice**        1

1   Why you should read this book                                      3
    *Joanna Swann and John Pratt*

**Part II: Different Approaches to Educational Research**              9

2   A Popperian approach to research on learning and
    method                                                           11
    *Joanna Swann*
3   The postmodern prism: fracturing certainty in
    educational research                                             35
    *Elizabeth Atkinson*
4   A Popperian approach to policy research                          51
    *John Pratt*
5   Critical approaches to research in practice                      67
    *Michael Collins*
6   Science in educational research                                  84
    *William E. Tunmer, Jane E. Prochnow and James W. Chapman*
7   Research in a bicultural context: the case of Aotearoa/
    New Zealand                                                      98
    *Patricia Maringi G. Johnston*
8   Case study research                                             111
    *Michael Bassey*

**Part III: Dialogues from a Research Community**                    125

9   Decision-making in the real world: postmodernism
    versus fallibilist realism                                      127
    *Elizabeth Atkinson and Joanna Swann*

10   Research and social improvement: critical theory and
      the politics of change                                    141
      *Michael Collins and Joanna Swann*
11   Culture, race and discourse                                152
      *Patricia Maringi G. Johnston and John Pratt*
12   How general are generalizations?                           164
      *Michael Bassey and John Pratt*

**Part IV: Educational Research in Practice                     173**

13   Doing good research                                        175
      *John Pratt and Joanna Swann*
      Glossary: a Popperian view of some important research
      terms and their usage                                     194
      *Joanna Swann and John Pratt*

      *Contributors*                                            221
      *Index*                                                   225

# Acknowledgements

We are very grateful to the following people for providing feedback on the draft typescript: Elizabeth Atkinson, Richard Bailey, Michael Bassey, Tyrrell Burgess, Martyn Hammersley, Sarah Loader, George McNamara, Brian Marley, Eileen Piggot-Irvine and David Turner. We are also very grateful to David Miller for comments on a lengthy paper from which some of the discussion in Chapter 2 has been drawn. The range and detail of the comments we received from our reviewers enabled us to make significant improvements. Errors and limitations that remain are, of course, our responsibility.

At Continuum, our thanks go to Anthony Haynes for his genuine intellectual interest in the issues raised by *Educational Research in Practice: Making Sense of Methodology*, and for helping to get the project underway. We are also grateful to Alexandra Webster for seeing the book through to publication.

In Chapter 8, Michael Bassey's diagram of 'A model of the relationship between educational research, the practice of teaching and the making of educational policy' is reprinted, with permission, from *Case Study Research in Educational Settings*, Open University Press, Buckingham, UK, 1999.

The idea for this book was conceived by Joanna in 2000 while she was a Senior Lecturer in Educational Research at the College of Education, Massey University, New Zealand. She acknowledges the warmth and support of colleagues and postgraduate research students with whom she worked at that time. No reira, tena koutou, tena koutou, tena tatou katoa.

Joanna Swann
John Pratt

# Part I

## An Introduction to Educational Research in Practice

# —1—

# Why you should read this book

Joanna Swann, *King's College London, UK*
John Pratt, *University of East London, UK*

Research is a way of finding things out and developing new ideas. It advances knowledge. It involves the researcher in learning, and it entails both critical and creative activity. The term 'research' also implies some kind of systematic investigation, with outcomes that are presented in a publicly accessible form, for discussion and use by others.

What people do in the name of research is influenced by their assumptions about knowledge and the way in which it can be advanced. People can, and sometimes do, undertake research without thinking about such matters. But this is a mistake. It's a mistake because working on the basis of inadequate or false assumptions could result in unnecessary difficulties, delays or even invalid outcomes. For this reason, this book presents accounts of different approaches to educational research, and explores some of the assumptions on which they are based. Our own assumptions about the growth of knowledge draw on the philosophy of Karl Popper, and we take the opportunity to set out some of his key ideas and their implications for research practice.

Many texts on educational research present it in terms of mutually exclusive, competing approaches and techniques. We think this reflects erroneous assumptions about how the growth of knowledge is best advanced. Nor does it match with our experience of research in practice. In addition, few of these books help novice researchers to see themselves as members of a research community.

If you pluck from the shelves of almost any university library a set of standard texts on educational research, you can expect to find discussion that divides approaches to research into two categories, quantitative and qualitative. These categories are often then associated with two paradigms, respectively, positivism and interpretivism, which in turn may be associated with science and non-science or with natural science and social science. We appreciate that these dichotomies are offered with the intention of making research methodology easier to understand. But the use of these dichotomous categories can be misleading. For instance, we do not think that there are quantitative or qualitative methodologies as such, only quantitative and qualitative techniques. The quantitative/qualitative dichotomy leads the authors of many textbooks to present a view of educational research that does not tally with what happens in practice – in the mixing of techniques from different paradigms, in collaborations between researchers with contrasting conceptions of enquiry, and in developments in non-positivist science.

In our experience, research in practice does not fit into tightly defined categories. Techniques described by textbook authors as belonging to one paradigm are often used by researchers operating with other, allegedly conflicting paradigms. Researchers who principally use qualitative techniques almost invariably make statements that refer to quantity – phrases such as 'most people', 'a few' – and many educational researchers who use quantitative techniques employ qualitative categories such as 'more satisfied', 'less satisfied', and so on. (For a critique of the quantitative/qualitative dichotomy see Pring, 2000, pp. 43–55.)

The practice of labelling approaches to research according to various 'isms' can be a useful way of conveying information about what a person believes and does – we too do it in this book. But the trouble with the positivism/interpretivism dichotomy is that it excludes many approaches adopted by researchers. None of the nine educational researchers who contributed to this book describes her or his own approach as either positivist or interpretivist. Also, and of no little importance, the practice of equating science with positivism ignores 70 years of debate in the philosophy of science – since Karl Popper published *Logik der Forschung* in 1934 (Popper, 1972) – and disregards the diversity of scientific endeavour. Many scientists are not positivists.

In addition, many texts ignore the messy aspects of doing research – the muddling through, and the constraints of time and limited resources. One consequence is that people who undertake various kinds of small-scale investigative activities in education may not think of themselves as researchers, because what they do does not match up to the canons presented in much of the literature. The value of their research is diminished, and they may be discouraged from developing rigorous studies with the potential to contribute to the improvement of educational practice.

As editors of and contributors to *Educational Research in Practice: Making Sense of Methodology*, we have set out to present a book about research methodology that encourages a consideration of basic methodological issues, and offers an eclectic but rigorous approach to educational research.

We share with other authors the view that novice researchers should be made aware of different points of view. We do this, but not by telling the reader what we think others' viewpoints are. Rather, in Part II of the book, we allow researchers with diverse interests to present their own ideas. Elizabeth Atkinson writes lucidly and accessibly about postmodernism and educational research; Michael Bassey has developed a distinctive theory of generalization, and is known also for his work on educational case study; Michael Collins, now working in Canada, is a critical theorist and an author who is widely read; Trish Johnston is an indigenous researcher in Aotearoa/New Zealand who draws on critical theory and takes a strong line about preserving the dignity of research subjects; Bill Tunmer, Jane Prochnow and James Chapman, also based in Aotearoa/New Zealand, conduct world-renowned scientific research on reading. We, the editors, base our research on the theories of learning and the growth of knowledge developed by Karl Popper: Joanna Swann is a philosopher of learning and method; John Pratt uses a Popperian approach to analyse social policy, and to predict and evaluate its outcomes.

In order to communicate something of what it is like to be a researcher, to demystify research and to enable readers to relate it to their own experience, the authors have addressed in their chapters a set of questions about what they do, why they do it, its methodological basis and perceived outcomes. These questions are shown in Box 1.1. The questions were designed to encourage authors to discuss research theory in the context of their personal research experience. Readers may find it useful to address these questions in relation to their own research.

It is one thing to read accounts of different approaches to research, quite another to see how exponents of contrasting ideas engage in discussion with each other as members of a research community. Part III of this book comprises four dialogues, each involving one of the editors and one of the contributors. These dialogues offer readers first-hand debate between exponents of Popper's fallibilist realism and, variously, postmodernism, critical theory, indigenous

**Box 1.1:** Questions posed to the contributors to Part II

> What is the purpose of educational research? In your view: What is educational research for? What are the characteristics of good research in education? Why do you engage in research?
>
> How do you characterize your research, and yourself as a researcher? How does the way you construe research, and yourself as a researcher, affect the design and conduct of your research?
>
> Which methodological, cultural and/or ethical issues concern you most? How do rigour and originality figure in your research?
>
> Which aspects of doing research do you find most difficult?
>
> What influence has your research had on educational policy and practice? What influence might it have in future?
>
> Which key points do you wish to convey to new researchers?
>
> *Additional questions to be addressed, if possible:*
>
> What form has collaboration taken in your research work?
>
> Which theories of learning and the growth of knowledge influence your approach to research design, the conduct of fieldwork, interactions with colleagues, and the evaluation of research outcomes?

research, and an eclectic approach to case study. Each of the dialogues was conducted via email over a period of several weeks. The dialogues have been edited, but they were not based on a common set of questions. The topics were those which we, as editors, thought it would be interesting to pursue from our contributors' chapters.

As Popperian fallibilist realists we believe that (a) we inhabit a reality, shared by all of us, and that knowledge of this reality is possible, and (b) our knowledge should be treated as conjectural and provisional – there is no certain or secure knowledge. In contemporary terms, our approach comes under the umbrella of 'postpositivism', as do those of Michael Bassey, Bill Tunmer and his co-authors. A distinguishing feature of postpositivism is its acceptance of fallibilism – the idea that all scientific knowledge is potentially subject to the discovery of error and should therefore be regarded as provisional (see Phillips and Burbules, 2000, for extended discussion). Postpositivism, in contrast to positivism, is not widely discussed within texts on educational research. We stress that the term 'post-positivism' does not refer to a unified school of thought; not all postpositivists are, like ourselves, realists, and many do not accept the epistemology of Karl Popper (see Swann and Pratt, 1999).

We make no apology for drawing attention to Popper's work. He has been described as the greatest philosopher of the twentieth century, and in England scientific Nobel laureates and cabinet ministers alike have claimed to have been influenced by him (Magee, 1973, pp. 9–10). But his work has been neglected by most educationists, and even when cited it is often apparent that it has been misunderstood. The misunderstanding of Popper is perhaps unsurprising given that his ideas about learning and the growth of knowledge are radically different from the views held about these topics by most educationists and academics. We do not espouse an uncritical acceptance of Popper's ideas, but we do suggest that those who engage with published discussions about Popper should be wary of dismissing his work without reading it first hand.

In Part IV, we offer a brief Popperian analysis of the various methodological approaches adopted by the other contributors to the book. We then draw together ideas from throughout the book to provide a set of principles for good research practice. Many students are baffled by such technical terms as 'epistemology', 'realism' and 'paradigm'; but the concepts to which the terms refer are important. To help readers, we have provided, at the end of the book, a substantial glossary of research terms and their usage.

Although we hope that an outcome of *Educational Research in Practice* will be that educational researchers will pay greater attention to Popper, we do not offer a comprehensive account of the implications of Popper's work for educational research. Our discussions are merely – and, we hope, usefully – illustrative. Indeed, a general theme of the book is illustration. *Educational Research in Practice* is not designed to provide a comprehensive account of every approach used in educational research. It is intended to be read in conjunction with other texts. By drawing on the research experience and scholarly activities of the editors and the contributors, we hope the book will help the reader to make sense of methodology.

## REFERENCES

Magee, B. (1973) *Popper*, London: Fontana Press.
Phillips, D. C. and Burbules, N. C. (2000) *Postpositivism and Educational Research*, Lanham, MD: Rowman and Littlefield.

Popper, K. R. (1972) *The Logic of Scientific Discovery*, London: Hutchinson (first published in German in 1934) (first English edition 1959).

Pring, R. (2000) *Philosophy of Educational Research*, London: Continuum.

Swann, J. and Pratt, J. (eds) (1999) *Improving Education: Realist Approaches to Method and Research*, London: Cassell.

# Part II

Different Approaches to
Educational Research

# A Popperian approach to research on learning and method

Joanna Swann, *King's College London*, UK

## PURPOSES AND STANDARDS IN EDUCATIONAL RESEARCH

Educational research can serve many purposes. Some relate to the subjective experience and personal circumstances of the researcher. For example, doing research can be fun and intellectually stimulating and its outcomes may be good for one's career. Other purposes relate to wider concerns, in particular the desire to improve aspects of human experience and/or contribute to the sum of human knowledge. Personal and broader social purposes sometimes conflict, as in the seemingly rare cases in which researchers falsify findings in order to further their reputation. Mostly, however, self-centred and altruistic reasons for engaging in research can and do co-exist without major conflict.

I do research because I enjoy the intellectual stimulation that comes from experimenting with ideas, and, more importantly, because it is a means by which human experience may be improved. Research that has no obvious practical application is of little interest to me. In my view, the quality of an educational research project should be judged, at least in part, according to the extent to which its outcomes increase the potential for practical improvement in the conduct and/or organization of learning and teaching.

Of course, what counts as improvement depends on one's values. What some people regard as progress, others may consider to be a retrograde step. But even if one adopts a relativistic view of values (which, incidentally, I do not), it makes no sense to adopt such a view with regard to the evaluation of methods and courses of action designed to achieve what one desires. Whatever one considers the proper outcomes of education to be, one must surely admit that some methods of achieving these outcomes are better than others –

in terms of the effectiveness of the methods in achieving the ends, and whether the values of the methods are consistent with those of the ends. This is not to suggest that the task of judging improvement is unproblematic. Sometimes a situation appears to be better than an earlier one, but, in fact, undesirable changes have taken place about which we are, perhaps temporarily, ignorant.

I do not define educational research as an activity that is directed *per se* towards the improvement of educational practice (for a contrasting view see, for example, Desforges, 2001, and Michael Bassey in Chapter 8 of this volume). If people engage in research with the primary intention of finding out more about aspects of education (out of curiosity, perhaps) rather than improving social practice, I do not contest their right to call this educational research. Catalysts for change in social affairs come from a variety of sources, including – though perhaps not often – research that is focused on matters which appear to be wholly abstract and unrelated to practice.

However, I think it is important to distinguish in general terms between good and bad research. Broadly speaking, the best research projects exhibit one or more of the following characteristics:

- the revealing of a hitherto unrecognized mismatch between expectation and experience (actual or anticipated) that has far-reaching practical and/or theoretical implications;
- the formulation of a new and important problem;
- the production of a new and better solution to an existing problem;
- the development of a constructive way of challenging existing expectations.

Research of little or no public worth is that which does not challenge any significant theory, policy or practice; research that – by implication, if not by design – reinforces prejudices and encourages complacency. If research fails to challenge, then it fails to provoke change. Without change there is no potential for improvement. Bad research, in my view, is that which is not respectful of persons – because, for example, the researcher treats people merely as means to an end, and in the process causes psychological, social or physical harm – or in which the pursuit of truth is compromised by disingenuousness or ineptitude on the part of the researcher.

## HOW I CHARACTERIZE MY RESEARCH AND MYSELF AS A RESEARCHER

I have undertaken empirical research of various kinds, including action research. But although I am committed to promoting empirical investigation, fundamentally I am a philosopher of education. More specifically, I am a Popperian philosopher of learning and method.

In my opinion, one of the philosopher's principal tasks is to challenge common assumptions, particularly those embedded in widely adopted social practices. (See the first epigraph on p. v of this volume, taken from Popper, 1979[1972], p. 33.) My philosophical research explores assumptions about the nature of learning which underlie the practices of students, teachers and researchers, and that are implicit in the organization of teaching and the conduct of educational research. Assumptions about learning can be distinguished from assumptions about learners. The former include expectations about what happens in, and factors pertaining to, any situation in which learning can be said to have taken place. The latter include, for example, expectations about how individuals or groups respond to specific teaching practices, and about the learning of particular skills or subjects. Any psychological study of learning is predicated on philosophical assumptions. Psychological research is vital to the development of knowledge about how individuals and groups behave as would-be learners; but if consideration is not given to broader issues about the nature of learning, such research may be fundamentally flawed. See, by way of illustration, Roger James's critique of conditioning theory (James, 1980, Chapter 6).

My philosophical analyses of educational practice derive from the theory of the logic of learning (Swann, 1983, 1988, 1999b, 1999c, 2002a), which in turn draws on Karl Popper's evolutionary epistemology (1972a[1934], 1972b[1963], 1979[1972], 1983, 1992b[1974]) and the educational theory of Tyrrell Burgess (1975, 1977, 1979). I am not an uncritical Popperian, but my principal interest has been to explore the implications of Popper's work for the improvement of human experience. I am not particularly interested in defending his theories in writing, not least because other people (see, in particular, Miller, 1994, 2002) are better qualified to undertake this task.

My approach is clearly different from that adopted by most philosophers of education during the late 1960s and 1970s. At that time, philosophy in many education departments was defined as the practice of conceptual analysis: 'Philosophy . . . is concerned with questions about the analysis of concepts and with questions about the grounds of knowledge, belief, actions and activities' (Hirst and Peters, 1970, p. 3). Those who adopted a different approach, as I did, were effectively barred from many philosophical debates about education; if one wasn't analysing concepts, one was thought not to be engaging in philosophy. The focus of these debates became increasingly narrow and divorced from the concerns of practitioners and educationists in general, many of whom then tended to view all philosophy of education as an irrelevance. The situation improved during the 1990s; philosophy of education is now much more broadly conceived, and may be undergoing a resurgence.

## KARL POPPER'S EPISTEMOLOGY

Key features of Popper's evolutionary epistemology can be summarized as follows:

- We inhabit a reality which we can attempt to understand.
- The outcomes of our attempts to understand reality are always conjectural. No knowledge, not even scientific knowledge, is certain or even secure.
- We set out to represent reality by means of descriptive and argumentative language.
- In order to become better able to understand and also manipulate reality, we need to utilize the correspondence theory of truth – the idea that a statement is true if, and only if, it corresponds to the facts.
- The pursuit of truth can be distinguished from the pursuit of certainty.
- We can pursue truth – that is, try to gain knowledge of the facts about reality – as a regulative ideal without assuming that certain or secure knowledge is attainable.
- Science is concerned with the pursuit of truth.
- Scientific theories are universal theories which have been formulated in a way that makes them susceptible to falsification, and for which refuting evidence, if sought, has not been found. Scientific knowledge comprises falsifiable theories, and formulated problems and arguments which relate to such theories.
- Non-scientific theories are an important part of our knowledge; they are susceptible to criticism by means of argument even though they are not susceptible to refutation by reference to empirical evidence.

- The idea that knowledge advances through a process of induction is a myth.
- The growth of knowledge proceeds from old problems to new problems through a process of trial and error-elimination.
- A useful distinction can be made between three worlds with which we engage: physical objects and processes (world 1), subjective experience (world 2), and objective knowledge (world 3).
- The world of objective knowledge, a human construct that is no less real than the other two worlds, comprises formulated problems, descriptions, hypotheses, explanations and arguments. Many of these ideas are embedded in human artefacts (books, musical scores, paintings, films, etc.), social practices and institutions. Ideas in the public domain can be criticized, modified and developed by anyone who has access to them.

As mentioned in Swann (2003), 'Knowledge' is used by Popper as a generic term for all kinds of expectations (conscious or unconscious, inborn or acquired through development and/or learning), assumptions (explicit or implicit), and theoretical constructs (valid or invalid, true or false). This use of 'knowledge' is not commonplace within education, where more often it is used as a synonym for 'true belief'. Popper's broader usage takes into account that (a) we cannot be sure which of our beliefs are true, and (b) our beliefs, when entered into the public domain, exist independently of us.

In this chapter, as in Popper's work, 'theory' is used to refer to explicit statements of all kinds, including general and singular statements, and also to implicit assumptions and unstated expectations – that is, ideas which could in principle be formulated as statements but have yet to be given linguistic expression.

THE MYTH OF INDUCTION

The pursuit of knowledge has been construed in different ways at different times. Despite this variety, to a large extent the history of science can be viewed as the search for certainties or secure knowledge, and the history of philosophy can be characterized as the search for the sources of such knowledge. Of particular significance in modern times, at least in Western societies, has been the idea of inductive method, formulated early in the seventeenth century by the English philosopher Francis Bacon (in his *Novum Organum* 1902[1620]) as a way of achieving secure knowledge of the natural world. Bacon's theory, radical at the time, prioritized the role of experience in the pursuit of knowledge of the physical world. His theory of induction was hugely successful, in that it offered a new way of comprehending the natural world and led to an explosion of discovery and invention.

Although induction was formulated as the method for promoting the growth of knowledge about the natural world, its underlying logic is compatible with the common-sense view that ideas in general are derived from experience, whether this experience is characterized as the observation of natural phenomena, the 'observation' of ideas in books (through reading), or the 'observation' of ideas presented within a teacher's instructive talk (Swann, 1998).

Induction, put simply, is the idea that universal theories arise from a series of singular observation statements. Singular observation statements take the form 'This is a . . .', such as 'This is a five-year-old child who enjoys stories about animals'. A researcher who adopts induction as a method records a series of observations – each assumed to be, or treated as though it is, expectation-free – in the hope that eventually a universal theory will emerge, such as 'All five-year-old children enjoy stories about animals'. Once such a theory has presented itself, the discovery of confirming evidence is thought to verify it. If the confirming evidence is sufficiently strong, the theory may be accorded the status of a law.

Despite four centuries of acceptance, the theory of induction is deeply flawed. As the eighteenth-century Scottish philosopher David Hume pointed out: there is no logical reason to assume that the future will be like the past (Hume, 1999[1748]). For an inference to be logically valid, the conclusion must not go beyond the evidence presented in the premises; thus, inductive inference – reasoning from repeated instances of experience to other instances (conclusions) of which there is no experience – represents a logically invalid argument. No number of true singular observation statements of the kind, 'This is a five-year-old child who enjoys stories about animals' can entail the universal theory, 'All five-year-old children enjoy stories about animals'. A question which followed Hume's discovery of error within the theory of induction is, 'Why . . . do all reasonable people expect, and *believe*, that instances of which they have no experience will conform to those of which they have experience?' (Popper, 1979[1972], p. 4). Hume's criticism of induction was devastating, but he was unable to answer the question it raised, except to say that while repetition is powerless in terms of logical argument, people are nonetheless conditioned by dint of repetition to believe that similar instances will occur in the future.

Popper (1972a[1934]) followed Hume by accepting that the theory of induction is logically invalid, but, unlike Hume, he denied that induction ever takes place, psychologically or otherwise. Popper drew attention to an asymmetry between verification and falsification: while no number of true singular observation statements can verify or prove the truth of a universal theory, one true singular observation statement can refute it. Thus, although no number of true statements of the kind, 'This is a five-year-old child who enjoys stories about animals' will prove the truth of the universal theory, 'All five-year-old children enjoy stories about animals', the statement, 'This is a five-year-old child who does not enjoy stories about animals', if true, will refute it. A universal theory is always provisional and unverifiable; but some such theories can be refuted.

Popper's imaginative response to Hume's critique led to a new theory of how knowledge grows (see, in particular, Popper, 1979[1972]), and a new theory of what happens when an individual learns. A singular observation statement is significant insofar as it relates to a universal theory which, potentially, it may contradict, and an individual's observation is relevant and possible only in the context of an expectation that the individual holds about her- or himself or about some aspect of the physical, social or intellectual environment. And with regard to the question raised by Hume's critique, the idea of *belief in regularity* may, Popper argued, be exchanged for the idea of an inborn *need for regularity* (Popper, 1992b[1974], pp. 48–52). Regularities are needed, expected, sought, but often not found. Indeed, both learning and the growth of knowledge are prompted not by the acquisition of true or almost certainly true information, but by the discovery of error (or specific limitation) in existing expectations.

What we observe is dependent not only on what there is to be observed, but on the expectations we bring to the act of observation. Note also that the observation that some event, state of affairs or object is 'similar to what we've already observed' is itself dependent on expectations – expectations developed in the search for regularities. All observations are expectation-laden, and all are *made* rather than passively experienced (see, for example, Popper, 1979[1972], Appendix 1; 1985). Once we accept that there is no direct transfer of 'what can be known' into 'what we know', it becomes clear that our observations may be mistaken. For example, we may be wrong about whether 'This is a five-year-old child who does not enjoy stories about animals'. We may – individually and collectively – misconstrue the evidence.

Our observations are also limited. We can't observe everything that is there, and we may miss something that is of importance to us. Consider, for example, Oetzi, the mummified remains of a 5,300-year-old man, found in the Tyrolean Alps in 1991. This Stone Age corpse has been extensively studied, yet it took researchers almost a decade to discover that he had, shortly before his death, received an arrow wound. Initial speculation was that he had been caught in a storm and died of exposure. It was only when a researcher studied a new set of X-rays that the arrowhead was observed. Although the arrowhead is discernible on the original X-rays, the earlier researchers, who did not anticipate such a find, simply did not notice it.

With regard to our expectations – including explicit theories, universal and non-universal – we do, of course, have to assume that many of them are true. But although we act on assumptions of truth, and we can pursue truth, we can never know for sure that truth has been achieved. Note also that a large number of confirming instances does not make the truth of a universal theory more probable. If there is one five-year-old child who doesn't enjoy stories about animals, it makes no difference whether you have previously found ten or ten thousand who do; the universal theory which states, 'All five-year-old children enjoy stories about animals' is false. The discovery of evidence that seems to support a universal theory may be comforting to us, but it does not strengthen the theory. Such evidence may lull us, so to speak, into a mistaken sense of security.

Following Popper, it can be argued that all learning and all growth of knowledge entail a process of trial and error-elimination, conjectures and refutations. In the context of learning, this is the process referred to by Burgess (1977), and subsequently by myself (since Swann, 1983), as the logic of learning.

Despite the importance of Popper's work, comparatively few people have a sound understanding of much of what he proposed and argued. His epistemology is often considered to be a mere postscript to Hume. He is often mistakenly thought, for example, to have proposed falsification as an alternative means by which secure knowledge may be achieved – secure knowledge of what is not so. A decision as to whether or not a theory has been falsified is always a matter of judgement, and judgement is potentially flawed. The underlying theme of all Popper's work is that of how to advance our knowledge, not that of how to achieve foundational knowledge of what is or is not so. Such knowledge is, quite simply, beyond our reach.

## THE LOGIC OF LEARNING

The theory of the logic of learning[1] is summarized by Popper's oft-cited simplified schema of conjecture and refutation, which also applies to the growth of knowledge and to evolutionary processes in general (Popper, 1979[1972], p. 243):

$$P_1 \rightarrow TS \rightarrow EE \rightarrow P_2$$

In this schema, $P_1$ represents an initial problem. $TS$ is a trial solution applied to the problem. $EE$ refers to error-elimination, the process by which a flaw in the solution is revealed, leading to a new problem $P_2$.

A learning organism has a problem when it (a) discovers (or anticipates) a mismatch between expectation and experience – construed broadly to include experience of physical, personal, social and intellectual phenomena – and (b) has the desire and will to address the disequilibrium occasioned by the mismatch (Swann, 1999c, 2002a). Central to understanding a Popperian account of learning is the recognition that learning is often – indeed, mostly – an unconscious activity, implicit in situations (see, for example, Nørre-tranders, 1998[1991]). Note that in many situations:

> we become conscious of many of our expectations only when they are disappointed, owing to their being unfulfilled. An example would be the encountering of an unexpected step in one's path: it is the unexpectedness of the step which may make us conscious of the fact that we expected to encounter an even surface.
>
> (Popper, 1979[1972], p. 344)

When I refer to 'expectation' and 'desire' I'm not suggesting that the learning organism necessarily thinks 'I expected this' and 'I desire this'. Learning takes many forms, including self-conscious Eureka! moments and imperceptible adjustments of a kind which are not conscious and probably never will be. In all forms, however, the nature of the organism's learning is dependent not only on its experience but also on the expectations (and implied values and aspirations) it brings to bear on this experience. (This is a constructivist, though not a radical constructivist, theory – see Swann, 1995.) In the first instance, the expectations it has are those that are inborn, in its genetic make-up. These expectations – which are, essentially, expectations of regularity – are, as discussed in the preceding section of the chapter, fallible and potentially subject to disappointment in light of experience. In Popper's words:

> every animal is born with expectations or anticipations, which could be framed as hypotheses; a kind of hypothetical knowledge. . . . This inborn knowledge, these inborn expectations, will, if disappointed, create *our first problems*; and the ensuing growth of our knowledge may therefore be described as consisting throughout of corrections and modifications of previous knowledge.
>
> (1979[1972], pp. 258–9)

Although 'All life is problem solving' (Popper, 1999, p. 100), not all living things learn. What distinguishes a learning organism from a non-learning organism is the ability of the former to acquire new expectations, that is, expectations which are not purely the outcome of genetic inheritance (Swann, 2002a). Note that the use of 'problem' and 'problem solving' in the context of an evolutionary epistemology is rather different from the way the terms are used in education. Educationists tend to regard problems as conscious, rational and discrete – as in the idea that a teacher sets problems for students to solve. Alternatively, one can view problems as part of the stuff of life, and problem solving is the term used when accounting for the way in which all living organisms attempt to deal with disequilibrium. The educational implication of this alternative view is that the teacher's role should be construed in the context of problems that originate with the students (hence the idea of student-initiated curricula, discussed later in the chapter).

All problem solving is critical and creative. The problem-solving organism doesn't accept the mismatch between expectation and experience; in this sense it is critical. Rather it resolves, consciously or unconsciously, to do something about the mismatch, which entails at least a modicum of creativity. When problem solving involves learning, a greater degree of creativity is involved; this is true both for humans and members of other learning species. Within a process of learning, there are two points at which creativity is entailed: at $P$, when a mismatch is turned into a problem (as mentioned above), and at $TS$, when a solution to the problem is devised.

Any single mismatch can be turned into a number of different problems, all of which will be expectation-laden and value-impregnated. For example, 'The respondents didn't behave in the way I expected when I administered the questionnaire' can be formulated as a problem of 'how to change the behaviour of the respondents' or 'how to change the way the questionnaire is administered' or 'how to find a more effective way of eliciting the respondents' views'. It is misleading to say (as most authors do) that problems are identified: mismatches between expectation and experience are identified, but problems have to be created.

Devising a solution to a problem is creative in that the learning organism must invent a course of action that is entirely new to it, or it must adapt and apply a course of action that has already been developed. Although some elements of a solution may pre-exist, and may not have to be created from scratch, when learning takes place the application of a solution to a problem necessarily involves a novel element. In addition, error-elimination (*EE* in Popper's schema) can be the result of a creative act. Rather than wait for errors to be revealed through happenstance, human learners have the ability to set up test situations – that is, situations specifically designed to facilitate the search for error – and in this way increase their opportunities for discovering, and potentially eliminating, error or specific limitation.

Although the logic of learning applies equally to human learning and to the learning of creatures such as cats, dogs and chimpanzees, the scope of our learning is, of course, considerably greater than that of other creatures. Two significant features distinguish us from other animals, including other social animals: our facility for descriptive and argumentative language (Popper, 1972b[1963], 1979[1972]), and, linked to this, our creation of and interaction with a world of object-ive ideas (as mentioned earlier).

Descriptive and argumentative language considerably enhance our facility for criticism and creativity, and thus for learning. Together, these functions of language have enabled us to develop the world of objective knowledge. They also enable us to monitor and interrogate our own consciousness; that is, to be self-conscious. (See Eccles, 1990, for discussion about the distinction between consciousness and self-consciousness.) We encapsulate, criticize and develop our subjective ideas through our interactions with the world of objective knowledge. We, unlike other animals, often let our hypotheses (conjectures) 'die in our stead' (Popper, 1979[1972], p. 244). We can create thought experiments before we try something out in practice, and we can also test solutions to problems by means of prototypes, models and well-constructed empirical research.

Questions about the nature of learning – 'What happens when learning takes place?', 'What inhibits or what promotes learning?' and so on – are relevant to all human learners, not least because an individual's understanding of learning has a bearing on her or his ability to function effectively in a range of problem areas. Some misconceptions about learning – such as, 'Learning is only committing ideas to memory' – can impede learning and are therefore best corrected. Misconceptions about learning are themselves learned, and one should be mindful that not all learning is 'good' learning; what we learn may be trivial and diversionary, misleading or even harmful.

Although research projects are mostly designed to produce growth in public knowledge, they are also a means by which researchers facilitate their own learning. Indeed, the success of a research project is dependent on the ability and inclination of the researcher to learn.

## THE LOGIC-OF-LEARNING CONTROVERSY

Following Popper, it can be argued that learning does not take place in situations where the organism's expectations remain unchallenged; it occurs only in situations where at least one of its expectations is shown to be false or inadequate. Even learning that appears to be an outcome of repetition will involve a process of challenge and modification to the organism's expectations (see, in particular, Petersen, 1988, 1992). Quite simply, there is no learning without a problem and without trial and error-elimination. Popper's seminal achievement with regard to learning theory was his challenge to the common assumptions that learning can involve:

- direct instruction from the physical or social environment;
- direct copying of what we see;
- the exact replication of something we have done previously;
- the accumulation of confirming evidence.

The case in support of a Popperian position, and against the common assumptions stated above, is complex. For argument that relates specifically to learning, see Swann (1998, 1999c, 2002a); for discussion that addresses problem solving in general, see the work of Arne Friemuth Petersen (1984, 1985, 1988, 1992, 2000). The challenge for anyone who is unconvinced by the basic tenets of Popper's theory and my account of the logic of learning is to respond to the question, 'By what process, other than one of trial and error-elimination, could a learning organism acquire new expectations?' (Swann, 1998, 2002a). The identified process must be described in terms applicable to *biological* organisms. I emphasize 'biological', because existing non-trial-and-error accounts rely too heavily on analogies with inanimate objects. I also suggest that any satisfactory answer to this question must be consistent with recent developments in brain science, including Gerald Edelman's argument that artificial neural networks are not independent learning organisms (Edelman, 1992, pp. 226–7).

## PROMOTING LEARNING

In the United Kingdom there have been at least two sustained attempts to acknowledge in formal educational practice Popper's theory of learning and the growth of knowledge. The first of these was discussed in Burgess's *Education After School* (1977), an account of the rationale for setting up the School for Independent Study (1974–1991) at North East London Polytechnic (now the University of East London). The second was discussed in my doctoral thesis, 'How can classroom practice be improved?: an investigation of the logic of learning in classroom practice' (Swann, 1988), the outcome of an action research case study of teaching and learning in my own primary school classroom (working with children aged 7 to 11 years). But, in general, it seems there has been little empirical research on the implications of Popper's work for the organization and conduct of teaching. Certainly, most texts on the educational implications of his work are the outcome of primarily theoretical exploration. See, for example, the work of Henry Perkinson (1971, 1980, 1984, 1993), Ronald Swartz *et al.* (1980), John Halliday (1999), and Richard Bailey (2000).

In light of an analysis of the logic of learning, Burgess and I speculate that the following practices inhibit learning, and are thus best avoided if we wish to promote learning:

- restricting autonomous activity;
- discouraging confidence and desire;
- penalizing the discovery of error;
- offering inappropriate and inadequate criticism;
- offering 'unwanted answers to unasked questions' (Popper, 1992b[1974], p. 40);
- using objectives-based (in contrast to problem-based) planning and evaluation.

On this basis, the task of a school and its teachers is to create a safe place in which to learn, in which the discovery of error and specific limitation is relatively painless and safe. In general, learning is promoted when learners, teachers and others who wish to support it are prepared to adopt a critical attitude towards ideas, utilize argumentative language, develop educational relationships, abandon the myths of secure knowledge and 'the subject' (Popper, 1983, p. 5), and formulate and address learning problems.

A distinctive feature of the approach we have adopted in our own educational practice, and advocate in our publications, is the development of student-initiated curricula, whereby students are responsible, with tutor support, for devising their own learning programmes based on their own self-formulated learning problems. At the School for Independent Study these learning programmes were subject to formal procedures of validation and accreditation (see Stephenson, 1980, 1981); diplomas and degrees were awarded under the auspices of the Council for National Academic Awards. In effect, principles of procedure that have traditionally been applied only to study at doctoral level (in those situations in which the student exercises preference with regard to the nature and focus of the research), can be, and have been, applied with children, and with undergraduate and masters students.

A summary account of the logic-of-learning approach to teaching is provided in Swann (2002b). For a fuller discussion of learning and schooling, see Burgess and Swann (forthcoming).

## INFLUENCE AND PROSPECTS

The aspect of my research that I find most difficult is persuading other educationists that Karl Popper's philosophy of learning and the growth of knowledge has important implications for improving the organization and conduct of learning and teaching in schools, and that it constitutes a basis for the development of a programme of scientific research.

My logic-of-learning research has been conducted alongside full-time employment, initially as a school teacher, and later in various posts as a lecturer or contract researcher in higher education. Since 1997, writing about logic-of-learning ideas has been my principal 'leisure-time' activity. I have been reasonably successful in that most of what I've written for publication has been published. That, of course, says nothing about the extent to which my publications have been read or whether they have influenced readers' subsequent practice.

My greatest regret as a researcher is that, since completing my PhD in 1988, I have done very little empirical research on the logic of learning. From January 1997 to July 1998 I engaged in collaborative action research designed to help higher education lecturers improve their assessment practice (Swann and Arthurs, 1999; Swann and Ecclestone, 1999a, 1999b). This action research utilized principles for the problem-based methodology formulated and discussed in Swann (1999a, and see the summary presented at the end of this chapter). These principles have been well received by some teachers and lecturers, and I am aware that these ideas have been taken up by other academic researchers. But, apart from action research in higher education, I have not been in a position to develop my post-doctoral work through empirical means. More significantly, I have been unable to test the refutable hypothesis about the logic-of-learning approach to teaching that was first set out in my doctoral thesis.

This hypothesis in its simplest form can be expressed as: 'Students whose teachers practise in accordance with the theory of the logic of learning learn more than students whose teachers do not'. This formulation is not susceptible to testing. The following version, formulated here as a negative existential statement, is testable:

> Given that Class L is a class of between 20 and 25 children, taught for two years from the age of seven to nine by a teacher who acts in accordance with the theory of the logic of learning (as per the principles, methodology, practices and skills set out in Swann, 1988 and subsequent publications), and Class N is a comparable class taught for the same two years by a teacher who does not act in accordance with the theory of the logic of learning, then there does not exist a situation in which the progress of children (with regard to demonstrable improvements in: self-confidence; social skills; attitudes to learning; literacy and the use of oral language) in Class L will, between the beginning and the end of the specified two-year period, be less than or merely equivalent to that of children in Class N.
>
> (Modified from Swann, 1999b, pp. 118–19)

As discussed by Popper (1979[1972], pp. 360–1), the negative existential form – 'There does not exist . . .' – encourages the search for refutation.

An experiment in which the logic-of-learning theory is tested but not refuted would neither confirm the truth of the theory nor make its truth more probable. To think otherwise is to accept induction. If the hypothesis is refuted, the theory might then, depending on the nature of the refutation, be abandoned or modified. Modification might lead, for example, to a greater degree of specificity with regard to Class N and Class L children, teacher attitude, and so on. A modification of this kind would limit the scope of the hypothesis but would not make it less testable.

Alongside the testing of the hypothesis, it would be equally important to test the classroom practice contingent on conducting the experiment. Often, when assessing a practice, it is relatively easy to find evidence of some kind of benefit, specifically if we are pre-disposed to do so. But if we are genuinely committed to practical improvement we should be critical and ask, 'What are the unintended and undesirable consequences of doing things this way?' and 'Is there a better way of doing things?' Thus it is possible to conceive of a research project in which my hypothesis is not refuted, but which casts doubt on the efficacy of the Class L approach (because, for example, adopting this approach might have unexpected undesirable consequences).

Elsewhere (Swann, 1999b, p. 119) I have suggested that two teachers working in parallel classes within the same school could undertake small-scale research to test it. (In state schools in England this would require the suspension of the national curriculum.) One teacher would need to be an exponent of Class L teaching, the other an exponent of another approach. As a Popperian, I don't take the view that a project must necessarily be large-scale in order to be scientific. One well-conducted case study has the potential to cast doubt on existing assumptions. Whatever the nature of the research strategy and the scale of the experiment devised to test the hypo-thesis, the task of testing would be problematic, not least because of the difficulty of controlling variables. But it would be possible to devise an ethical test that would constructively challenge existing expectations. The research project would, I suggest, stimulate the development of new and better solutions to existing problems.

Although the prohibitive hypothesis is essentially a statement of (alleged) fact, it is not value-neutral. The decision to assess child-ren's progress in terms of self-confidence, social skills, attitudes to learning, and literacy and the use of oral language, rather than with reference to a national curriculum, is based on assumptions of value as well as those of fact (see Chapter 9, pp. 128, 134). The choice of tests of self-confidence, social skills, etc., would also be value-laden. But this values dimension does not stop us from legitimately posing questions of fact with regard to some of the learned characteristics of children in Class L in comparison to those of children in Class N.

I acknowledge that experiments are potentially risky for those involved. But leaving things as they are may be risky too. For

example, many of the assumptions that influence educational practice have not been critically tested. Moreover, although a practice
may have a long history of acceptance, attention may not have been
paid to its unintended consequences, some of which may be
undesirable. Nor does it mean there is no better alternative practice.
Thus, while it could be argued that to change practice is too risky
because matters might be made worse, the experimental application
of new practices is warranted when: existing practice is significantly
flawed; the proposed changes to existing practice have withstood
criticism; we seek to discover whether our new practices have
solved the problems they were intended to solve and whether they
have undesirable unforeseen consequences. Wherever possible we
should test rigorously the principal theories that are used to guide
the changes we make (Swann, 2003).

In England and Wales, the 1988 Education Reform Act gave the
Secretary of State for Education an extraordinary degree of power
with regard to the curriculum and the assessment of pupils in state-
funded schools – power which successive incumbents of this post
have embraced with enthusiasm. School teaching has become, to a
significant extent, a technical occupation rather than a professional
one: teachers are 'trained' rather than 'educated', and central government tells them, in considerable detail, what to do and how to go
about doing it. Some central government initiatives are advisory,
but the education system as a whole is so geared for compliance
with government diktat that many managers and practitioners feel
they must try to follow government policy to the letter, whether
or not the policy is enshrined in statute. In such a context, the adoption – not to mention testing – of the logic-of-learning approach to
teaching is difficult to countenance: the approach encourages initiative and criticality on the part of learners (it is anti-authoritarian),
and it generates a degree of curriculum diversity that would be an
anathema to most of today's politicians. Nevertheless, in recent
years there have been a number of educational initiatives for which
the Secretary of State has been prepared to suspend the national
curriculum, or aspects of it. Perhaps in the not-too-distant future it
will become possible to test my hypothesis within state-funded
schools.

## PRACTICAL AND THEORETICAL PROBLEMS

In the preceding section of the chapter a distinction was made
between testing a theory and testing a practice. This distinction

hinges on the idea that there are two significantly different kinds of problem – practical and theoretical – which require qualitatively different types of solution. The test of a solution to a practical problem involves addressing 'What happened?' or 'What is happening?', whereas the test of a solution to a theoretical problem involves addressing 'Is this theory true?' and/or 'Is this argument valid?'

As discussed in Swann (2003), a practical problem is a problem of how to get from one state of affairs to another (Krick, 1969[1965], p. 3). Its solution – successful or not – requires a new state of affairs that arises as a consequence of something having been done. Learning and teaching are practical activities, and people who engage in them are necessarily involved in addressing practical problems, whether or not they are conscious of this being so. Such problems can be formulated as 'How can . . .?' questions. Answers to such questions can also be formulated in words: for example, 'By doing . . .' and/or 'By not doing . . .' But the linguistic formulation is not a solution to the practical problem, it merely indicates what might be done. In contrast, theoretical problems are those for which the solution is a theory or set of theories. Such problems can usefully be divided into three categories: problems of value (what is good, what ought to be done, what is aesthetically pleasing), problems of fact (what is so in the world and why, what was so and why, what will be so and why), and problems of logic (what is valid and why).

If, for example, a team of teachers wishes to improve its teaching of literacy, it is insufficient for the teachers merely to learn more about literacy. At some stage they will have to implement change and evaluate the outcomes. In deciding what to do, the teachers may formulate a range of theoretical problems including, for example, one or more of the kind, 'What ought we to do?' A problem of this kind is solved (provisionally) by a statement of what should be done. This statement may influence the teachers' subsequent actions, but in itself is not a solution to a practical problem.

Note that a problem of 'How can we address the problem, "What ought we to do?" ', is itself practical. Its solution is a state of affairs in which the theoretical problem has been addressed.

Although Tyrrell Burgess (1977, 1985), John Pratt (1999, and see Chapter 4) and myself (Swann, 1999a) are not the only educationists to distinguish practical from theoretical problems (see, for example, Naish and Hartnett, 1975), more frequently researchers and other scholars focus on the analysis of theoretical problems and their solutions rather than practical problems and their solutions.[2] Practice, including policy-as-practice, is often recognized to be theory-laden, but rarely is it analysed in terms of 'Which practical problem, or set of practical problems, is this practice designed to solve? To what extent has it been successful? Have there been any unintended undesirable consequences? Might an alternative practice have been preferable?'

In general, research produces conjectural knowledge to which we can refer when we plan to act, act, and evaluate action. I have suggested that there are two broad ways in which it does this (Swann, 2000). The first requires researchers to make direct changes to practice, and to evaluate and write up the outcomes of this activity – specifically what has been learned. This is the role I conceive for action research. The second involves researchers in theoretical investigations, including philosophical, historical and ethical studies, and empirical enquiries of various kinds (including scientific enquiry – see Swann, 2003). Neither approach to research can provide us with reliable and comprehensive knowledge about 'what works'. Action necessarily involves a substantial amount of guesswork: our knowledge is always fallible and provisional, and practice will always be under-determined by explicit theory. Nevertheless, research can reveal errors and limitations in the assumptions which influence what we do, and in light of this it can help us to develop better ways of doing things.

## KEY POINTS FOR THE RESEARCHER AS LEARNER

If you wish to increase your own learning you should:

- Seek mismatches (actual or anticipated) between your expectations and experience; turn (selected) mismatches into problems; propose and test solutions to these problems.
- When formulating a problem, be clear about what type of problem it is, and thus what type of solution will be required: practical (How can I/we ...?) or theoretical (What ...?, Why ...?, and so on).
- Put into an accessible form the principal ideas which influence your policies, strategies and practices, so they can be criticized (by yourself and others) and replaced with potentially better ideas.
- Acknowledge that learning is a creative activity. You have to invent new ideas, arguments and practical processes.
- Be bold in your hypothesizing. Weak and ill-conceived ideas can subsequently be eliminated through critical discussion.
- Don't be afraid to be dogmatic in the early stages of developing an

idea, and don't abandon ideas in the face of premature criticism. But . . .

- You should eventually subject the idea to severe criticism, and engage with the implications of this process – the idea may need to be modified or even abandoned.
- Work with other people, and draw on the world of public knowledge, but bear in mind the fallibility of all sources of ideas.
- Make judgements on the basis of argument and evidence rather than whim, orthodoxy, fashion or expediency. This entails developing the art of argument.
- Recognize the value of diversity. Be open to a range of ideas that may be used in the creation of solutions to problems.
- Recognize that although it might feel good to find evidence that supports an idea, the discovery of such evidence plays no direct role in learning.
- Recognize that a critical test of a policy, strategy or practice involves addressing the questions, 'Did it solve the problem it was intended to solve?', 'What were/are the unintended and undesirable consequences?' and 'Is there a better way of doing things?'
- Try to create a safe place in which to discover error: remember that it is better to discover error and specific limitation in a theory, model, prototype or pilot study rather than in a widely distributed document or artefact, or in a far-reaching policy.
- Find ways to defend and maintain your confidence as a learner and your enthusiasm for learning.

## SUMMARY OF A PROBLEM-BASED METHODOLOGY FOR THE IMPROVEMENT OF PRACTICE

1. Address: 'What is going well in the present situation?', 'What do I/we expect to go well in the future?' and 'What is worth defending, maintaining and developing?' This may help to make you more confident about your endeavours. More importantly, recognizing what is good about the present situation can help you to avoid 'throwing the baby out with the bath water'.
2. Address: 'What is not going well?' and 'What do I/we anticipate may not go well in the future?', and, in light of this, 'What do I/we wish to change?'
3. Address: 'What seems to be stopping (or inhibiting) this desired change from taking place?' or 'What can be expected to stop (or inhibit) this desired change from taking place?' These questions

focus on the present situation and on the removal of impediments to desired change, rather than on a specified future state.
4. Address: 'Which inhibitions and impediments fall within my/
   our sphere of influence?'
5. On the basis of your answers to the above questions, formulate
   one or more practical problems using 'How can I/we . . .?'
6. Make a list of the strategies you might adopt in order to solve
   each problem, and select at least one to adopt and test in practice. (Different members of a team may be able to test different
   solutions.) At this point your underlying aims and ideals may
   provide a valuable stimulus for creative thinking. The cost
   implications (monetary and otherwise) of proposed solutions
   should be considered at this stage.
7. Decide how you will test the efficacy and worth of the solu- ✳
   tion(s) adopted. Be specific – use the following sentence open-
   ings: 'My solution to this problem will be successful insofar as it
   results in . . .', 'My solution will be a failure if it results in . . .' and
   'Success and failure will be judged, at least in part, by . . .'
8. Implement the chosen solutions, being mindful of the potential
   not only for desirable intended consequences but also for
   consequences that are unintended and potentially undesirable.
9. After allowing sufficient time for the solution to be tested properly, carry out a review by addressing: 'To what extent, if at all,
   has the initial problem been solved?', 'What unintended and
   unexpected consequences (desirable or undesirable) have
   arisen?' and 'With the benefit of hindsight, might another
   solution have been preferable?'
10. Write a formal account of what has taken place, and in particular
    what has been learned.

## NOTES

1. When referring to the logic of learning, I am not suggesting that
   people need to think logically and act rationally in order to
   learn. The logic of learning refers merely to a process that is
   implicit when learning takes place.
2. Popper also distinguished between practical and theoretical
   problems (Popper, 1974, p. 1025; 1992a[1969], pp. 132–3;
   1992b[1974], p. 66; 1994, p. 11), but the distinction remained
   relatively undeveloped in his work.

## REFERENCES

Bacon, F. (1902) *Novum Organum*, New York: P. F. Collier and Son (first published 1620).

Bailey, R. (2000) *Education in the Open Society – Karl Popper and Schooling*, Aldershot, UK: Ashgate.

Burgess, T. (1975) 'Choice is not enough – go for responsibility', *Where (the Education Magazine for Parents)*, 100, pp. 5–7.

Burgess, T. (1977) *Education After School*, London: Victor Gollancz.

Burgess, T. (1979) 'New ways to learn', *The Royal Society of Arts Journal*, CXXVII (5271), pp. 143–57.

Burgess, T. (1985) 'Applying Popper to social realities: practical solutions to practical problems', *ETC: A Review of General Semantics*, 42 (3), pp. 299–309.

Burgess, T. and Swann, J. (forthcoming) *Hope for Learning in School*, London: Kogan Page.

Desforges, C. (2001) *Familiar Challenges and New Approaches: Necessary Advances in Theory and Methods in Research on Learning and Teaching*, Nottingham, UK: British Educational Research Association.

Eccles, J. C. (1990) 'Physics of brain-mind interaction', *Behavioral and Brain Sciences*, 13 (4), pp. 662–3.

Edelman, G. M. (1992) *Bright Air, Brilliant Fire: On the Matter of the Mind*, New York: Basic Books.

Halliday, J. (1999) 'Popper and the philosophy of education', in P. Ghiraldelli, Jr, M. A. Peters and S. Accortini (eds) *Encyclopedia of Philosophy of Education*: http://www.educacao.pro.br/popper_and_the_philosophy_of_educ.htm (accessed 29 May 2001).

Hirst, P. H. and Peters, R. S. (1970) *The Logic of Education*, London: Routledge and Kegan Paul.

Hume, D. (1999) 'An enquiry concerning human understanding', in S. M. Cahn (ed.) *Classics of Western Philosophy*, 5th edn, New York: Hackett, pp. 626–96 (Hume's text first published in 1748).

James, R. (1980) *Return to Reason: Popper's Thought in Public Life*, Shepton Mallet, UK: Open Books Publishing.

Krick, E. V. (1969) *An Introduction to Engineering and Engineering Design*, New York: John Wiley and Sons (first edition 1965).

Miller, D. (1994) *Critical Rationalism: A Restatement and Defence*, Chicago, IL: Open Court Publishing.

Miller, D. (2002) 'Induction: a problem solved', in J. M. Böhm, H. Holweg and C. Hoock (eds) *Karl Poppers kritischer Rationalismus heute*, Tuebingen, Germany: Mohr Siebeck, pp. 81–106. Also available at: www.warwick.ac.uk/philosophy/dm-Induction.pdf (accessed 3 December 2002).

Naish, M. and Hartnett, A. (1975) 'What theory cannot do for teachers', *Education for Teaching*, 96, pp. 12–19.

Nørretranders, T. (1998) *The User Illusion: Cutting Consciousness Down to Size*, trans. J. Sydenham, London: Penguin Books (first published in Danish in 1991).

Perkinson, H. J. (1971) *The Possibilities of Error: An Approach to Education*, New York: David McKay.

Perkinson, H. J. (1980) *Since Socrates: Studies in the History of Western Educational Thought*, New York: Longman.

Perkinson, H. J. (1984) *Learning from our Mistakes: A Reinterpretation of Twentieth-Century Educational Thought*, Westport, CT: Greenwood Press.

Perkinson, H. J. (1993) *Teachers Without Goals/Students Without Purposes*, New York: McGraw-Hill.

Petersen, A. F. (1984) 'The role of problems and problem solving in Popper's early work on psychology', *Philosophy of the Social Sciences*, 14 (2), pp. 239–50.

Petersen, A. F. (1985) 'Toward a rational theory of the mind: lifelines in Popper's deductive approach to psychology', *ETC: A Review of General Semantics*, 42 (3), pp. 228–53.

Petersen, A. F. (1988) 'Why children and young animals play: a new theory of play and its role in problem solving', monograph of The Royal Danish Academy of Sciences and Letters, Copenhagen, *Historisk-filosofiske Meddelelser*, 54, pp. 1–57.

Petersen, A. F. (1992) 'On emergent pre-language and language evolution and transcendent feedback from language production on cognition and emotion in early man', in J. Wind, B. Chiarelli and B. Bichakjian (eds) *Language Origin: A Multidisciplinary Approach*, Dordrecht, The Netherlands: Kluwer Academic Publishers, pp. 449–64.

Petersen, A. F. (2000) 'Emergent consciousness considered as a solution to the problem of movement', in R. L. Amoroso, R. Antunes, C. Coelho, M. Farias, A. Leite and P. Soares (eds) *Science and the Primacy of Consciousness: Intimation of a 21st Century Revolution*, Orinda, CA: The Noetic Press, pp. 8–16.

Popper, K. R. (1972a) *The Logic of Scientific Discovery*, London: Hutchinson (first published in German in 1934) (first English edition 1959).

Popper, K. R. (1972b) *Conjectures and Refutations: The Growth of Scientific Knowledge*, London: Routledge (first edition 1963).

Popper, K. R. (1974) 'Replies to my critics', in P. A. Schilpp (ed.) *The Philosophy of Karl Popper, Book 2*, La Salle, IL: Open Court Publishing, pp. 961–1197.

Popper, K. R. (1979) *Objective Knowledge: An Evolutionary Approach*, Oxford, UK: Oxford University Press (first edition 1972).

Popper, K. R. (1983) *Realism and the Aim of Science*, from W. Y. Bartley III (ed.) *Postscript to the Logic of Scientific Discovery*, London: Hutchinson.

Popper, K. R. (1985) 'The problem of induction (1953, 1974)', in D. Miller (ed.) *Popper Selections*, Princeton, NJ: Princeton University Press, pp. 101–17.

Popper, K. R. (1992a) 'The logic of the social sciences', in idem. *In Search of a Better World: Lectures and Essays from Thirty Years*, trans. L. J. Bennett, with additional material by M. Mew; revised trans. K. R. Popper and M. Mew, London: Routledge (first published in German in 1969) (first published in English in 1976).

Popper, K. R. (1992b) *Unended Quest: An Intellectual Autobiography*, London: Routledge. (First published as 'Autobiography of Karl Popper', in P. A. Schilpp (ed.) (1974) *The Philosophy of Karl Popper, Book 1*, La Salle, IL: Open Court Publishing, pp. 1–204.)

Popper, K. R. (1994) *Knowledge and the Body-Mind Problem: In Defence of Interaction*, ed. M. A. Notturno, London: Routledge.

Popper, K. R. (1999) *All Life is Problem Solving*, London: Routledge (some chapters translated from the original German by P. Camiller).

Pratt, J. (1999) 'Testing policy', in J. Swann and J. Pratt (eds) *Improving Education: Realist Approaches to Method and Research*, London, Cassell, pp. 39–52.

Stephenson, J. (1980) 'Higher education: School for Independent Study', in

T. Burgess and E. A. Adams (eds) *Outcomes of Education*, London: Macmillan Education, pp. 132–49.

Stephenson, J. (1981) 'Student planned learning', in D. Boud (ed.) *Developing Student Autonomy in Learning*, London: Kogan Page, pp. 145–59.

Swann, J. (1983) 'Teaching and the logic of learning', *Higher Education Review*, 15 (2), pp. 31–57.

Swann, J. (1988) 'How can classroom practice be improved?: an investigation of the logic of learning in classroom practice', unpublished PhD thesis, London: Council for National Academic Awards.

Swann, J. (1995) 'Realism, constructivism, and the pursuit of truth', *Higher Education Review*, 27 (3), pp. 37–55.

Swann, J. (1998) 'What doesn't happen in teaching and learning?', *Oxford Review of Education*, 24 (2), pp. 211–23.

Swann, J. (1999a) 'Making better plans: problem-based versus objectives-based planning', in J. Swann and J. Pratt (eds) *Improving Education: Realist Approaches to Method and Research*, London: Cassell, pp. 53–66.

Swann, J. (1999b) 'The logic-of-learning approach to teaching: a testable theory', in J. Swann and J. Pratt (eds) *Improving Education: Realist Approaches to Method and Research*, London: Cassell, pp. 109–20.

Swann, J. (1999c) 'What happens when learning takes place?', *Interchange*, 30 (3), pp. 257–82.

Swann, J. (2000) 'How can research lead to improvement in education?', *Prospero*, 6 (3/4), pp. 130–8.

Swann, J. (2002a) 'Understanding and pursuing learning: the importance of the logic of learning', unpublished paper, King's College London. (Revised version of Swann, J. (2001) 'Understanding and pursuing learning: the value of the logic of learning', paper presented at the annual conference of the British Educational Research Association, University of Leeds, 13–15 September.)

Swann, J. (2002b) 'How to avoid giving unwanted answers to unasked questions: realising Karl Popper's educational dream', paper presented at the Karl Popper 2002 Centenary Congress, University of Vienna, 3–7 July.

Swann, J. (2003) 'How science can contribute to the improvement of educational practice', *Oxford Review of Education*, 29 (2) (in press).

Swann, J. and Arthurs, J. (1999) 'Empowering lecturers: a problem-based approach to improve assessment practice', *Higher Education Review*, 31 (2), pp. 50–74.

Swann, J. and Ecclestone, K. (1999a) 'Empowering lecturers to improve assessment practice in higher education', in J. Swann and J. Pratt (eds) *Improving Education: Realist Approaches to Method and Research*, London: Cassell, pp. 89–100.

Swann, J. and Ecclestone, K. (1999b) 'Improving lecturers' assessment practice in higher education: a problem-based approach', *Educational Action Research*, 7 (2), pp. 63–84.

Swartz, R. M., Perkinson, H. J. and Edgerton, S. G. (1980) *Knowledge and Fallibilism: Essays on Improving Education*, New York: New York University Press.

# The postmodern prism: fracturing certainty in educational research

Elizabeth Atkinson, *University of Sunderland, UK*

## INTRODUCTION

In this chapter, I identify ways in which postmodern thinking can shape educational research, and the benefits that postmodernism might provide in an educational context in which the concept of 'certainty' – about curriculum, teaching methods, quality, evidence, good practice, and the nature and purpose of educational research itself – has become a dangerous and all-too-prevalent commodity. Postmodernism already acts as a powerful critique in educational and social research, and can continue to provide a voice of challenge and dissent where there is, perhaps, an excess of certainty. My own explorations in the field to date focus on four key areas: identity and reflective practice; evidence and ideas; power, knowledge and language; social justice and social change. I outline my work in each of these areas below. First, though, I set the scene by locating my work in the broader academic context, and I identify and explain some key terms in postmodern thinking.

## BORDER-CROSSINGS

While my research is firmly situated within the context of education, one of the most fruitful and exciting aspects of this work has been the way in which I have found myself crossing discipline boundaries. Thus, while focusing on educational issues, my research – and that of other postmodern thinkers – draws on sociology, anthropology, cultural studies, literary criticism and linguistics, as well as linking with theoretical perspectives from feminism, queer theory and postcolonialism. This border-crossing (Giroux, 1993) also reflects the postmodern resistance to binary oppositions, and to

certainties regarding identity, position or fixed reference. It is
an exemplification of the postmodern concept of the growth of
knowledge as 'bricolage' – a drawing together of a range of diverse
tools for the job in hand, leading to a model of learning which, to
use Gilles Deleuze and Félix Guattari's metaphor (1987[1980]), is
rhizomatic – that is, spreading out unevenly and unpredictably in a
non-linear, non-hierarchical fashion.

## WHAT *IS* POSTMODERNISM?

As critics of postmodernism never tire of complaining, postmodernism is notoriously hard to define. This is because it is not so much a
theory or a philosophy as a collection of loosely linked ideas which
combine and recombine in numerous ways and contexts. At its
centre, if it can be said to have one, is a refusal to take things
for granted – an ironic, often playful, challenging of certainty.
While there could be no definitive list of the components of postmodernism, I have summarized some of its characteristic features
(Atkinson, 2002a) as follows:

- resistance towards certainty and resolution;
- rejection of fixed notions of reality, knowledge, or method;
- acceptance of complexity, lack of clarity, and multiplicity;
- acknowledgement of subjectivity, contradiction and irony;
- irreverence for traditions of philosophy or morality;
- deliberate intent to unsettle assumptions and presuppositions;
- refusal to accept boundaries or hierarchies in ways of thinking;
- disruption of binaries which define things as either/or.

The disruption of binaries was a particular preoccupation of
Jacques Derrida, who was also responsible for stating that 'there is
nothing outside the text' (1976[1967], p. 158): a statement which is
variously used to characterize and to ridicule postmodernism. This
statement is not a naïve denial of the real world, but a reminder of
the way in which the reality we perceive is socially and culturally
constructed. The postmodern process of *deconstruction* is one which
seeks to interrogate these constructed 'texts'. The process might
involve the deconstruction of language, drawing on linguistics and
literary theory; of actions, drawing on anthropology and cultural
studies; or of social patterns and constructs, drawing on sociology
and social psychology. In all these fields, postmodern thinking is
much more advanced than in the field of education; the particular
value of applying it to educational practices and contexts is the way

in which it takes apart 'common-sense' notions which teachers, researchers and policy-makers may have come to take too easily for granted. The effect of a deconstructive approach is to question the assumed educational, theoretical or moral superiority of particular world-views or dominant paradigms in educational research and practice. While postmodernism does not have a single agenda for social justice (I will return to this point later) it inevitably questions the assumed justice of, for example, the 'modernist projects' of contemporary social, educational or legal systems. It recognizes multiple views and multiple voices, and turns its attention to the 'margins' rather than the 'centre' in order to redress what Elizabeth St Pierre (1997a) calls the 'vicious binaries' by which society is constructed and defined. Thus, it can serve research as a tool for reshaping our world-view, for reinterpreting what 'is', and for challenging social or political hegemonies.

## POSTMODERNISM AND POSTMODERNITY

It is useful, at the outset, to make a distinction between 'postmodernism' and 'postmodernity'. The latter term is often used to describe the current condition of the developed (and, to some extent, the developing) world: market-led; computer-mediated; a world where time and distance are compressed by extraordinary advances in transport and communications; a world where cultural globalization may seem to result in a sense of displacement and a loss of identity; a world which is 'more modern than modern' (Woods, 1999, p. 3) – post-industrial, post-traditional, decentred and eclectic. 'Optimistic' postmodernists (such as myself) are likely to see the diversity and eclecticism of postmodernity as a valuable questioning of dominant paradigms; while pessimistic postmodernists are more inclined to 'stand at the edge of the abyss – that fearful and terrible chaos created by the loss of transcendent meaning – and struggle with [their] loss' (St Pierre, 1997a, p. 176).

## POSTMODERNISM AND POST-STRUCTURALISM

There is continuing debate as to how the terms 'postmodernism' and 'post-structuralism' differ in meaning, and interpretations differ from one source to another. Post-structuralism is generally considered to have its roots in the French philosophy of the 1960s onwards, which challenged the work of structuralists such as Claude Levi-Strauss, whose interpretations of societies had

superseded earlier functionalist views in anthropology and sociology. Although much of my work draws strongly on the thinking
of contemporary feminist post-structuralists such as Elizabeth St
Pierre, Patti Lather, Jane Flax and Judith Butler, I prefer to use the
term 'postmodernism' to describe the mode of thinking which characterizes my research (and that of other British writers working in
the same field, such as Maggie MacLure and Ian Stronach), as it
reflects the diverse and eclectic writings of the wide range of theorists whose work informs, illuminates and enriches the growing body
of work in the 'postmodern embrace' (see: Stronach and MacLure,
1997; Woods, 1999).

## INTERSECTIONS WITH FEMINISM, POSTCOLONIALISM
## AND QUEER THEORY

Postmodern thinking has found particularly rich inspiration in the
areas of feminism, postcolonialism and queer theory, although the
writers and researchers whose work forms the sources of such
inspiration would not necessarily consider themselves 'postmodern'. The disruption of normative social, cultural and academic
assumptions proposed by queer theorists (see, for example: Honeychurch, 1996; Tierney, 1997) can be seen as a process of deconstruction; and 'queering' certainties about knowledge, truth and identity
is an apt metaphor for postmodernism to adopt. Queer theory
articulates powerfully with feminist post-structuralism in the work
of Butler (1992, 1993), whose focus on the body and sexuality brings
the 'margins' into the centre of enquiry. Postcolonial theorists (see,
for example: Trinh, 1989; Bhabha, 1994; Spivak, 1996) take marginality as their starting point, not only offering perspectives from what
have been considered in imperialist/colonialist thought to be 'the
margins', but shifting the concepts of centre and margins altogether.
Again, this critique of binaries – centre/margin, inside/outside,
Self/Other – forms a valuable component in postmodern thinking.
My own work draws in particular on queer theory and feminist
post-structuralism (Atkinson, 2000b, 2001a), and on postcolonial
thinking (Atkinson, 2001b, 2002b).

The articulation between feminism and postmodernism continues
to be contested (see Nicholson, 1990). For example, while Susan
Bordo (1990), Nancy Hartsock (1990) and Jenny Bourne (1999) argue
that postmodernism's emphasis on uncertainty and multiplicity
destroys the very identity for which feminism fights, Flax (1992)
suggests that postmodernism brings a much needed loss of

innocence to feminist critique and enquiry, a loss of the naïveté which assumes that the way forward can be found through some all-embracing truth or unitary identity. Butler (1992), taking up the challenge that postmodern perspectives threaten to destroy identities, stresses that *deconstruction* is not the same as *destruction*, and that postmodern thinking brings about previously unimagined ways of thinking about the world and the language we use to describe it: a view echoed strongly by Lather (1991, 1993, 1996).

## POSTMODERNISM, WRITING AND RESEARCH

One of the criticisms often made of postmodernism, which I have taken up at length (Atkinson, 2002a), is that it is nothing more than an intellectual plaything: a way of thinking, of messing about with ideas. This leads critics to deride postmodern statements like 'producing different knowledge and producing knowledge differently' (St Pierre, 1997a, p. 175) or 'opening up new imaginaries' in research and interpretation (Scheurich, 1996, p. 49) as meaningless wordplay. Yet these concepts – and the language in which they are couched – suggest possibilities for which more formal research paradigms may have no language at all; the possibility, for example, of allowing unpredictability and uncertainty to be recognized as crucial aspects of the research situation; or the possibility of recognizing multiple and contradictory findings as valid research outcomes. Lather (1993) explores the implications of these possibilities in depth, pointing to 'transgressive' forms of validity which acknowledge the contradictions and uncertainties that are inherent in all research, but which are made invisible in more traditional research paradigms.

Postmodernism is not a research method; it is more like a prism which refracts multiple images of 'reality', reflects complexity, and fractures certainty. To the extent that it is a methodology at all, a postmodern approach to research is a methodology of ideas, and the deconstruction and reconstruction of ideas. As such, it links significantly with the views of contemporary critics who refuse to offer easy answers to educational and policy problems; critics such as Stephen Ball (1995, p. 268) who suggests a view of 'the educational theorist as a cultural critic offering perspective rather than truth', or Ivor Goodson (1999) who sees the academic as 'public intellectual' rather than the servant of the state. Stronach and MacLure (1997, p. 98) paint a picture of the 'responsible anarchist ... standing against the fantasies of grand narratives, recoverable pasts, and predictable futures', and Lather (1999, p. 6) proposes a view of research as a way of being at risk, rather than a way of being sure or finding answers. There are profound implications too for the way in which research might be written or written about. Erica McWilliam (1999, p. 1), drawing on the work of Richard Rorty (1989), describes postmodern texts as 'writing that refuses to tidy up, to provide the vision splendid, to advocate, to condemn, to redeem'.

## A POSTMODERN TOOLBOX

Michel Foucault wrote of using ideas like a set of tools with which to unmask the silent power of apparently neutral institutions, such as education, the penal system and health care (see Rabinow, 1984). Postmodernism has developed a considerable toolbox of ideas, compressed into terminology which, like any other, can seem exclusive or unnecessary to the uninitiated. Like any specialist terminology, however, it provides a valuable shorthand with which to communicate complex concepts. I have selected from this toolbox the terms which I have found most useful in opening up research, policy and practice in education, and I offer brief definitions below, identifying ways in which these concepts have been used in my own work.

*Grand Narratives:*    These are the 'big stories' by which history has explained itself, such as modernism, patriarchy, science and the Enlightenment. The term was most famously used by Jean-François Lyotard (1984[1979]), who saw the replacement of Grand Narratives with a multiplicity of diverse 'little narratives' as characterizing 'the postmodern condition'. Postmodernism is often accused of creating its own Grand Narratives in opposition to those it critiques. Postmodernists are acutely aware of this apparent contradiction, and postmodern thinking is therefore as concerned to read the silences in its own texts as in those of others. (For an example of this, see 'The mourning after the knight before', in Stronach and MacLure, 1997.)

*Regimes of truth:*    These relate closely to Lyotard's Grand Narratives. Coined by Foucault, the phrase refers to the self-perpetuating systems by which dominant ways of understanding create and maintain power, so that 'truth' and 'knowledge' become products and 'effects' of power. As Foucault put it (1984[1972], p. 74):

> 'Truth' is to be understood as a system of ordered procedures
> for the production, regulation, distribution, circulation and

operation of statements. 'Truth' is linked in a circular relation with systems of power which produce and sustain it, and to effects of power which it induces and which extend it. A regime of truth.

In Atkinson (2000c), I consider the introduction of a compulsory curriculum for initial teacher training in the UK, coupled with the implementation of all-but-compulsory approaches to the teaching of literacy and numeracy, and enforced by a punitive inspection system, as the creation of regimes of truth from which it is virtually impossible for teachers, teacher trainers and researchers to break away.

*Discourse:* Foucault's 'regimes of truth' are constructed through discourse: linguistic and textual interactions which can create and maintain meanings, or can suppress marginalized voices. The concept of discourse is by no means unique to postmodernism; it is central, for example, to the work of Jürgen Habermas (1984[1981], 1987[1981]). However, while Habermas sees discourse as the means of achieving an 'ideal speech community' through mutual understanding, postmodernism aims to challenge dominant discourses, and to discover the diverse, complex and contesting discourses which pattern individual and social action. In Atkinson (2000d), I critique the dominant discourse of 'evidence-based practice' and 'what works' in UK educational policy, arguing that other discourses, contained in ideas rather than 'evidence', are more powerful in shaping and changing educational practice. I interrogate these discourses further in Atkinson (2000c, 2000e).

*Hegemony:* Coming primarily from Antonio Gramsci (1971), and having its roots in Marxism, this term is used in some postmodern writing to mean the dominance of an idea or a set of ideas. Moreover, it locates this dominance in what Gramsci calls 'the organization of consent', a process by which dominance is achieved 'from underneath' by enlisting the consent of the dominated. I have linked this in my writing to the way in which Foucault describes the means by which power is wielded in a democracy – not by oppression, but by consent and self-discipline or self-surveillance. While some postmodern thinkers find the concept of hegemony too strongly redolent of a form of conspiracy theory, I find 'the organization of consent' an apt image for ways in which teaching, teacher training and, to some extent, educational research might be seen to be regulated and controlled currently in the UK. I explore the implications of this in

Atkinson (2000c, 2000e), while the hegemony of heterosexuality in the context of schooling is a focus of enquiry in Atkinson (2002b).

*Governmentality:* This concept illustrates the means by which hegemony, 'the organization of consent', is achieved. It is a form of government in which the subject controls her or his own behaviour in accordance with the norms of the dominant power. I have drawn in particular on the work of Thomas Popkewitz (for example: Popkewitz, 2000; Popkewitz and Lindblad, 2000) and of McCarthy and Dimitriades (2000) in relation to governmentality in Atkinson (2002a) where I consider the potential of postmodern thinking to bring about social change.

*Contingency:* This is the uncertainty, the provisionality, which marks all forms of 'knowing' from a postmodern perspective: all knowledge is partial, provisional, contingent upon certain contexts and conditions. Furthermore, meanings are permanently dependent on the meanings of the terms to which they refer; in Derrida's terms, meanings are 'endlessly deferred' – never fixed, always related to prior connotations and definitions. For a pessimistic postmodernist, this is the path to despair and 'the abyss', but optimistic post-modernists prefer to work *with* contingent meanings as a way of reflecting multiple realities. I have drawn in particular on the work of Lather (1993) and St Pierre (1997a, 1997b) to explore contingent knowledge and its implications for identity, policy and research (Atkinson, 2000a, 2000b, 2001a).

*Writing sous-rature:*   Contingent knowledge and endlessly deferred meanings, together with a dissatisfaction with the dominance of certain terms over others, leads postmodernists towards an impasse in which they are obliged to use the very language which attempts to fix and secure the meanings they are trying to deconstruct. Derrida (1976[1967]) proposes a solution to this, which is to place terms 'sous-rature', or under-erasure; terms are written but crossed out, to indicate the necessity of using them while acknowledging their limitations. I have used this strategy in Atkinson (2001a) where I place various aspects of my multiple identities 'sous-rature' (e.g. ~~mother~~, ~~earner, lecturer, researcher, lesbian~~) in order both to examine and to question their significance.

*Marginality:* Postmodern writers are concerned with the way in which the visible, present, privileged 'centre' depends for its existence and its power on the absent Other: that which is at the margin, the edges; that which is invisible and powerless. It is by 'working the margins' (Fine, 1994; MacLure, 1996) that postmodernists aim to deconstruct the binary oppositions upon which this play of power depends. Drawing on the work of postcolonial theorists such as Trinh Minh-Ha (1989), Homi Bhabha (1994) and Gayatri Spivak (1996), postmodernists consider the implications of focusing on the 'liminal spaces', the interstices, in human experience as a means of displacing and disrupting the centre. In Atkinson (2001a) I use the concept of working the margins in my exploration of identity, and follow Stronach's reworking (1996) of Deleuze's image of 'the fold' (1993[1988]) as a metaphor for the place that is not either/or but which is 'both' and 'in-between'. In Atkinson (2001b, 2002b), Othering and marginality are central concepts, forming the starting point for a critique of prejudice and discrimination in education and society.

These concepts, then, constitute the toolbox which I have put to work in exploring the four key areas described below. Along with the work of other postmodern researchers, these interrogations of policy and practice provide a critical intellectual challenge to the 'common-sense' notions which drive educational decision-making, and set out new grounds on which to explore the principles of educational research and practice. As with any approach which is based fundamentally on ideas, it is impossible to chart a straightforward relationship between the research and practical 'outcomes' on the ground – a point I have discussed at length (Atkinson, 2000d). Moreover, the effects of such research are often the more subtle, because the ideas which change people's thinking often lose their theoretical labels as they become more widely disseminated. Thus, we are unlikely to hear either teachers or politicians discussing the relative merits of postmodern thinking; however, its existence as a way of challenging educational and social certainties – like the existence of feminism, Marxism, and more recently postcolonialism and queer theory – nevertheless makes itself felt in the public discourses which shape social and educational action.

## EXPLORING IDENTITY AND REFLECTIVE PRACTICE

My first exploration of postmodernism came with the discovery that my focus, in a small-scale classroom research project, was not on motivation (as I had thought) but on 'being good'. This led to an exploration of my own internal contradictions as a teacher and researcher, and the conflict between my supposedly liberal philosophy and my apparent preoccupation with conformity and authority. This forms the subject of Atkinson (2000b) in which I overlay my original reflections (which already identified the internal contradictions in my researcher identity) with further explorations arising from postmodern thinking, drawing in particular on the work of St Pierre (1997a, 1997b) and Deborah Britzman (1995). These reflections are pursued in greater depth in Atkinson (2001a), in which I investigate my own multiple and conflicting identities, and explore the way in which I have crossed, yet remained on both sides of, social, sexual and academic boundaries. The paper draws in particular on the work of MacLure (1996) and Stronach (1996), adopting MacLure's position of 'resisting resolution ... preventing solutions to the problem of getting safely across the boundaries' (p. 283) and Stronach's use of the concept of the fold as a metaphor for an identity that is neither 'inside' nor 'outside', which has not left one identity for another, but instead refuses to relinquish either.

I take up the theme of identity again in two further papers. Atkinson (2001b) draws strongly on postcolonial thinking as well as on the postmodern concept of 'constitutive otherness' (Cahoone, 1996, p. 16), by which Self is defined by the absence of the Other, the centre by the margins. Using my own deep-seated prejudices as a starting point, I explore the ways in which Othering permeates educational and social life, and give examples of how I use the concept of Othering to introduce issues of equality and diversity to the student teachers with whom I work. In Atkinson (2002b) I explore one particular form of Othering: the normative heterosexuality of the school, and its construction of a society in which images of non-heterosexual lifestyles are perpetuated as alien.

## EXPLORING EVIDENCE AND IDEAS IN EDUCATIONAL RESEARCH AND PRACTICE

Two papers (Atkinson, 2000a, 2000d) challenge the current research and policy rhetoric around evidence-based practice in education. Both question the authority of established research paradigms, and of the 'common-sense' mentality which suggests that finding out 'what works' is the simple and uncontroversial goal of educational research. Both challenge the myth, described by Britzman (1995, p. 232), 'that "reality" is out there waiting to be captured by language'.

Atkinson (2000d) centres on a critique of a series of recent reports funded directly or indirectly by the UK government, all of which criticize educational research as being of little relevance to teaching, and propose instead a direct link between empirical data and classroom practice. The paper suggests that there is a more complex relationship between research and practice than these reports suggest, and proposes that it is ideas, not evidence, which are the prime factors in shaping and changing practice, suggesting that postmodern thinking provides a powerful contemporary source of new ideas in educational and social research. Atkinson (2000a) focuses on four specific areas in which postmodernism can challenge existing research paradigms: the areas of certainty, objectivity, validity and truth. Taking each in turn, the paper draws on existing postmodern writing to challenge these pillars of the research establishment, and to open up new possibilities for investigation and interpretation.

## EXPLORING POWER, KNOWLEDGE AND LANGUAGE

Two papers focus in particular on my own professional field: the initial training of primary teachers. Atkinson (2000c) offers a challenge to four areas of authority in teaching and initial teacher training. The paper questions the authority of the power/knowledge nexus through which educational 'knowledge' is claimed and owned by politicians and policy-makers; the authority of the models of learning against which education is devised and measured; the authority of the assumed identities of 'teacher', 'pupil' and 'researcher' within the educational context; and the authority of the language through which educational practices are created and defined. It considers the textual silences in the new national curriculum for initial teacher training in England and Wales and the recently adopted national literacy and numeracy strategies, and suggests that these initiatives constitute regimes of truth which define and perpetuate a fixed model of knowing, learning and teaching. In Atkinson (2000e) I draw on the work of Stronach (1999) in considering contemporary initiatives in education as forms of cultural performance, and link this to the work of Debbie Epstein and Richard Johnson (1998) in which the subtexts of schooling are closely identified with discourses of nationhood. I argue that the national literacy strategy presents a model of learning in which to be English is to be literate and to be literate is to be English, and suggest that this discourse, like others, suppresses and silences less dominant voices.

## EXPLORING SOCIAL JUSTICE AND SOCIAL CHANGE: CAN POSTMODERNISTS 'DO GOOD'?

In Atkinson (2001b, 2002b) I explore ways in which rethinking Othering through the lenses of postmodernism and postcolonialism can lead to real changes in educational and social practice. I take up the theme of social change as the specific focus of another paper (Atkinson, 2002a), and in my response (Atkinson, 2001c) to Mike Cole's critique of it (Cole, 2001). My paper addresses the criticisms of postmodernism, particularly those coming from a Marxist perspective, which suggest that postmodernism can have no agenda for social justice; that it disempowers those to whom it claims to give voice; that it is nothing more than a plaything for intellectuals; and that it colludes with the status quo in its refusal to act. I address each of these criticisms in turn, countering them with the arguments that, by disrupting fixed notions of society and justice, postmodernism can force us to rethink the basis on which these concepts are founded; that the recognition of multiple identities is empowering, not disempowering, to social groups loosely linked by labels such as 'gender' or 'race'; that exploring ideas and language, far from being nothing more than intellectual play, can lead to profound shifts in the way society is perceived; and that, far from colluding with the status quo, postmodern thinking disrupts and deconstructs the apparent neutrality of social policy and practice.

## SUMMARY AND CONCLUSION

In my work I have aimed to show that postmodernism questions established research paradigms; creates new and multiple identities for research, researched and researcher; raises ethical issues about knowledge, power and the dominance of linguistic, epistemological and methodological certainties; and proposes a view of learning and the growth of knowledge which is rhizomatic, unpredictable and multifaceted. It suggests an awareness of the complexity of the apparently simple, and uncovers textual silences beneath the noise and splendour of social, political and educational rhetoric. It offers interpretations that are diverse, uncertain and polyvocal, and which do not necessarily lead to clear directions or sure answers, but it is this very uncertainty which makes it both challenging and exciting. I have attempted to demonstrate that a postmodern approach to research in education and the social sciences cannot deliver specified outcomes or lead to predetermined goals, but that its effect on ways of thinking, seeing and doing may nevertheless change the world.

## POINTS FOR RESEARCHERS

- Postmodernism is not a method: it is a way of looking, or, as Maggie MacLure put it (in comments on this chapter), a way of engaging or entangling. It is neither comfortable nor predictable, but it is productive and provocative.
- A postmodern research perspective is more likely to raise questions – before, during and after the research – than to provide answers. It is this fact, however, which gives it such potential in enabling researchers to rethink assumptions – about focus, methodology and interpretations.
- Postmodern thinking is by no means confined to the boundaries of education. For this reason, researchers adopting a postmodern perspective will find themselves in the fields of sociology, literature and the arts almost without realizing it. This can have surprising and rewarding effects on educational and social research.
- Finally, postmodernism is a playful, ironic, irritating thorn in the flesh for researchers who wish to feel they are on firm ground when they are planning, conducting and interpreting research, whether empirical or theoretical. But this very playfulness can in itself lead to a serious rethinking of much of the basis on which education and society – and the ways in which they might be researched – are based.

## ACKNOWLEDGEMENTS

Warm thanks to Professor Maggie MacLure of the University of East Anglia for her comments on an earlier draft of this chapter. It is Maggie who warned me against making postmodernism into another Grand Narrative, who reminded me of postmodernism's entanglement with 'the complexities at the surface', and who linked this to Lacan's concept of things being 'out in the open where no-one can see them'. What I have done with Maggie's advice, of course, remains entirely my responsibility. Where my work has not entered the fields of which she speaks, I have not made *post hoc* alterations to my argument; but I would like to acknowledge my debt to her, and my eagerness to explore further.

## REFERENCES

Atkinson, E. (2000a) 'What can postmodern thinking do for educational research?', paper presented at the annual meeting of the American Educational Research Association, New Orleans, 24–28 April.

Atkinson, E. (2000b) 'Behind the inquiring mind: exploring the transition from external to internal inquiry', *Reflective Practice*, 1 (2), pp. 149–64.

Atkinson, E. (2000c) 'The promise of uncertainty: education, postmodernism and the politics of possibility', *International Studies in Sociology of Education*, 10 (1), pp. 81–99.

Atkinson, E. (2000d) 'In defence of ideas, or why "what works" is not enough', *British Journal of Sociology of Education*, 21 (3), pp. 317–30.

Atkinson, E. (2000e) 'The National Literacy Strategy as cultural performance: some reflections on the meaning(s) of literacy in English primary classrooms', paper presented at the joint meeting of the European Council for Educational Research and the Scottish Educational Research Association, University of Edinburgh, 20–23 September.

Atkinson, E. (2001a) 'Deconstructing boundaries: out on the inside?', *International Journal of Qualitative Studies in Education*, 14 (3), pp. 307–16.

Atkinson, E. (2001b) 'Diversity and the "Other": what are we afraid of?', paper presented at the annual meeting of the American Educational Research Association, Seattle, 10–14 April.

Atkinson, E. (2001c) 'A response to Mike Cole's "Educational postmodernism, social justice and societal change: an incompatible ménage-à-trois"', *The School Field: International Journal of Theory and Research in Education*, 12 (1/2), pp. 87–94.

Atkinson, E. (2002a) 'The responsible anarchist: postmodernism and social change', *British Journal of Sociology of Education*, 23 (1), pp. 73–87.

Atkinson, E. (2002b) 'Education for diversity in a multisexual society', *Sex Education*, 2 (2), pp. 121–34.

Ball, S. (1995) 'Intellectuals or technicians? The urgent role of theory in educational studies', *British Journal of Educational Studies*, 43 (3), pp. 255–71.

Bhabha, H. K. (1994) *The Location of Culture*, London: Routledge.

Bordo, S. (1990) 'Feminism, postmodernism, and gender-scepticism', in L. J. Nicholson (ed.) *Feminism/Postmodernism*, London: Routledge, pp. 133–56.

Bourne, J. (1999) 'Racism, postmodernism and the flight from class', in D. Hill, P. McLaren, M. Cole and G. Rikowski (eds) *Postmodernism in Educational Theory: Education and the Politics of Human Resistance*, London: Tufnell Press, pp. 131–46.

Britzman, D. P. (1995) '"The question of belief": writing post-structural ethnography', *International Journal of Qualitative Studies in Education*, 8 (3), pp. 229–38.

Butler, J. (1992) 'Contingent foundations: feminism and the question of "postmodernism"', in J. Butler and J. Scott (eds) *Feminists Theorize the Political*, New York: Routledge, pp. 3–21.

Butler, J. (1993) *Bodies that Matter*, New York: Routledge.

Cahoone, L. (1996) 'Introduction', in idem (ed.) *From Modernism to Postmodernism: An Anthology*, Oxford, UK: Blackwell, pp. 1–23.

Cole, M. (2001) 'Educational postmodernism, social justice and societal change:

an incompatible ménage-à-trois', *The School Field: International Journal of Theory and Research in Education*, 12 (1/2), pp. 69–85.

Deleuze, G. (1993) *The Fold: Leibniz and the Baroque*, trans. T. Conley, Minneapolis, MN: University of Minnesota Press (first published in French in 1988).

Deleuze, G. and Guattari, F. (1987) 'Introduction: rhizome', in G. Deleuze and F. Guattari, *A Thousand Plateaus: Capitalism and Schizophrenia*, trans. B. Massumi, Minneapolis, MN: University of Minnesota Press, pp. 3–25 (first published in French in 1980).

Derrida, J. (1976) *Of Grammatology*, trans. G. C. Spivak, Baltimore, MD: Johns Hopkins University Press (first published in French in 1967).

Epstein, D. and Johnson, R. (1998) *Schooling Sexualities*, Buckingham, UK: Open University Press.

Fine, M. (1994) 'Working the hyphens: reinventing self and other in qualitative research', in N. K. Denzin and Y. S. Lincoln (eds) *Handbook of Qualitative Research*, Thousand Oaks, CA: Sage, pp. 70–82.

Flax, J. (1992) 'The end of innocence', in J. Butler and J. Scott (eds) *Feminists Theorize the Political*, New York, Routledge, pp. 445–63.

Foucault, M. (1984) 'Truth and power', in P. Rabinow (ed.) *The Foucault Reader*, trans. C. Gordon, New York: Pantheon, pp. 51–75 (first published in French in 1972).

Giroux, H. A. (1993) *Border Crossings: Cultural Workers and the Politics of Education*, New York: Routledge.

Goodson, I. (1999) 'The educational researcher as a public intellectual', *British Educational Research Journal*, 25 (3), pp. 277–98.

Gramsci, A. (1971) *Selections from the Prison Notebooks*, trans. from Italian and ed. Q. Hoare and G. Nowell Smith, New York: International Publishers.

Habermas, J. (1984, 1987) *Theory of Communicative Action, Volumes 1 and 2*, trans. T. McCarthy, Boston, MA: Beacon Press (first published in German in 1981).

Hartsock, N. (1990) 'Foucault on power: a theory for women?', in L. J. Nicholson (ed.) *Feminism/Postmodernism*, London, Routledge, pp. 157–75.

Honeychurch, K. G. (1996) 'Researching dissident subjectivities: queering the grounds of theory and practice', *Harvard Educational Review*, 66 (2), pp. 339–55.

Lather, P. (1991) *Getting Smart: Feminist Research and Pedagogy With/In the Postmodern*, New York, Routledge.

Lather, P. (1993) 'Fertile obsession: validity after poststructuralism', *The Sociological Quarterly*, 34 (4), pp. 673–93.

Lather, P. (1996) 'Troubling clarity: the politics of accessible language', *Harvard Educational Review*, 66 (3), pp. 525–82.

Lather, P. (1999) 'Authorship, ownership, methods and ethics in research on teaching and teacher education', paper presented at the annual meeting of the American Educational Research Association, Montreal, 19–23 April.

Lyotard, J.-F. (1984) *The Postmodern Condition: A Report on Knowledge*, trans. G. Bennington and B. Massumi, Manchester, UK: Manchester University Press (first published in French in 1979).

McCarthy, C. and Dimitriades, G. (2000) 'Governmentality and the sociology of education: media, education policy and the politics of resentment', *British Journal of Sociology of Education*, 21 (2), pp. 169–85.

MacLure, M. (1996) 'Exploring the transitions: boundary work in the lives of teacher-researchers', *British Educational Research Journal*, 22 (3), pp. 273–86.

McWilliam, E. (1999) 'Irony deficiency and vitamin B', paper presented at the annual meeting of the American Educational Research Association, Montreal, 19–23 April.

Nicholson, L. (ed.) (1990) *Feminism/Postmodernism*, London: Routledge.

Popkewitz, T. S. (2000) 'The denial of change in educational change: systems of ideas in the construction of national policy and evaluation', *Educational Researcher*, 29 (1), pp. 19–29.

Popkewitz, T. S. and Lindblad, S. (2000) 'Educational governance and social inclusion and exclusion: some conceptual difficulties and problematics in policy and research', *Discourse*, 21 (1), pp. 5–44.

Rabinow, P. (ed.) (1984) *The Foucault Reader*, New York: Pantheon.

Rorty, R. (1989) *Contingency, Irony and Solidarity*, New York: Cambridge University Press.

St Pierre, E. A. (1997a) 'Methodology in the fold and the irruption of transgressive data', *International Journal of Qualitative Studies in Education*, 10 (2), pp. 175–89.

St Pierre, E. A. (1997b) 'An introduction to figurations – a poststructural practice of inquiry', *International Journal of Qualitative Studies in Education*, 10 (3), pp. 279–84.

Scheurich, J. J. (1996) 'The masks of validity: a deconstructive investigation', *International Journal of Qualitative Studies in Education*, 9 (1), pp. 49–60.

Spivak, G. (1996) *The Spivak Reader: Selected Works of Gayatri Chakravorty Spivak*, New York: Routledge.

Stronach, I. (1996) 'Fashioning post-modernism, finishing modernism: tales from the fitting room', *British Educational Research Journal*, 22 (3), pp. 359–75.

Stronach, I. (1999) 'On being the nation again', Scottish Educational Research Association Lecture, annual conference of the Scottish Educational Research Association, University of Dundee, 30 September to 2 October.

Stronach, I. and MacLure, M. (1997) *Educational Research Undone. The Postmodern Embrace*, Buckingham, UK: Open University Press.

Tierney, W. G. (1997) *Academic Outlaws: Queer Theory and Cultural Studies in the Academy*, Thousand Oaks, CA: Sage.

Trinh, M. T. (1989) *Woman, Native, Other: Writing Postcoloniality and Feminism*, Bloomington, IN: Indiana University Press.

Woods, T. (1999) *Beginning Postmodernism*, Manchester, UK: Manchester University Press.

# —4

# A Popperian approach to policy research

John Pratt, *University of East London, UK*

## THE PURPOSE OF MY RESEARCH

My research is characterized by two main concerns. The first is about purpose. I have one overriding interest in engaging in research. It is to change the world. Put like this, it seems absurdly over-ambitious; certainly it condemns me to a lifetime of disappointment. All right, so I can't change the whole world, but certainly I hope to affect bits of it in which I have developed an interest and to which I am committed. Change is integral to research. Research is a way of finding out things that were not previously known. Even if you did not intend to change anything by so doing, change of some kind has taken place – we now know something new or different – and other changes will often, sooner or (perhaps much) later, ensue. Even 'ivory tower' research can still have consequences. But because policy is one of the most important ways of achieving change, my research is research into policy.

My second concern is about method. Research is a particular way of finding things out. It seeks to produce knowledge of a particular kind; meeting particular criteria. It is necessarily an expensive activity. If the knowledge we seek were easy to find, research would not be needed; if it did not have to conform to exacting standards, it would be cheaper and easier to gain. I explicitly set about my research within an epistemological framework based mainly on the work of Karl Popper (though not all the philosophical ideas mentioned below originated with Popper). Put briefly, this involves a problem-based approach to the generation of knowledge. Popper describes the advance of knowledge as a succession of attempts to solve problems. Knowledge is always provisional; it advances by subjecting hypotheses to test. (A fuller account of this approach is found in Chapter 2 of this book and Swann and Pratt, 1999). This has a number of implications for both method and purpose.

## METHODOLOGICAL ISSUES

As noted in Chapter 1 of this book, there is a long-standing debate in the social sciences about different paradigms, usually associated with different techniques and methods, and even about different kinds of 'knowledges' (Lyotard, 1984[1979]). The different paradigms are often associated with research for different purposes. An Organisation for Economic Co-operation and Development report into educational research (OECD, 1995) distinguished a 'positivist' view of knowledge – independent of context, value-neutral and generalizable – and 'locally embedded' knowledge, arising from reflection on experience and the 'art of practice'. 'Positivist' research is characterized as using 'hard' data and techniques such as statistical analysis. The 'qualitative' paradigm is seen as using 'soft' techniques such as interviews, ethnography or auto/biographical data. It is often extended to the 'postmodern', 'relativist' argument that, as Richard Bailey summarizes, objectivity cannot be achieved: knowledge consists of an 'interpretation of "meanings" [which we, individually, ascribe to things]. No interpretation can claim final authority, since it must, in turn, be dependent upon other interpretations, which are further dependent on others' (1999, p. 32).

In my view, this distinction between two broad approaches is misleading, and much of the discussion it raises is sterile. It is not clear to me that the dichotomy even exists; the two approaches are not necessarily incompatible. Reflection and locally embedded knowledge can still, and indeed do, inevitably, embody general propositions. So-called 'positivist' research cannot be value-free – for example in the choice of propositions for testing, and because all evidence depends on the perception of the observer. Much research that seeks to test general propositions uses locally embedded knowledge and the qualitative techniques associated with the opposing paradigm.

The framework within which I work adopts a realist epistemology which recognizes that our knowledge of the world is a human construct – an interpretation, conjecture, theory – though it accepts that there is a world which exists 'out there', independent of our knowledge of it. We cannot be sure whether our construction (set of theories) accurately describes reality. Our observations are theory-laden and, in any case, no number of observations can prove the truth of a theory (as Hume showed nearly 300 years ago). But this subjectivity of observation or interpretation does not mean that truth is 'relative'. 'If an assertion is true, it is true for ever' (Popper, 1966[1945], p. 221). Propositions are either true or false (Flew, 1975). Although we can never prove the truth of a theory, as Popper (1972[1934]) showed, we can have some understanding of the validity of our conjectures by subjecting them to test. Those theories which have withstood rigorous testing are still provisional; but, within known limits, we can accept them as a basis for action or further exploration or scrutiny. What this means, incidentally, is that a Popperian approach, despite frequent accusations to the contrary, is *not* 'positivist'. It seeks not to verify and produce certainty, but instead to test and to approach the truth.

Remarkably, and most often conveniently unnoticed by his critics, Popper put forward these views about knowledge as conjectural nearly 70 years ago (ibid.), well before most of the debate about relativism and 'postmodern' approaches. Popper's approach anticipates and rebuts many of the criticisms made later. By adopting a hypothesis-testing approach, Popper accepted that the choice of hypothesis is value-bound. He took no interest in the way in which a hypothesis is derived or invented; generating one by 'induction' (by seeking patterns in an array of data, for example) has as much logical validity as dreaming up one in the bath. Hypotheses are, of their nature, interpretations of the world.

It is thus unexceptional that hypotheses are conditioned by the circumstances – whether social, economic or individual – of their formulation. It is no surprise that power structures in society may affect or control which hypotheses are selected for test, and which achieve prominence. This is, however, a social rather than a methodological problem (though it is a methodological problem if the number of hypotheses is large and the resources for testing them are limited). As researchers, we should be wary of the intentions and machinations of those who set the research agenda, and we may wish to resist particular pressures and decide to undertake or promote research into hypotheses or use methods that conflict with the dominant paradigm. We can, however, take advantage of a multiplicity of interpretations to generate – and test – a multiplicity of hypotheses. Interpretations of reality are the building blocks of science.

Popper accepted, too, the problem of the 'relativity' of observation: 'there is no doubt that we are all suffering under our own system of prejudices' (1966[1945], p. 217). He noted that all observation is theory-laden. First, we choose the thing we observe, selecting it from other things. Then, what we observe depends on unreliable and personal sense perception, and how we understand and use what we see depends on our interpretation. Popper offered a way, nevertheless, of securing objectivity, by not only accepting, but by taking advantage of this plurality of view. Generating knowledge is a social activity and it relies on the 'public character of scientific method' (ibid., p. 218). Hypotheses and evidence are subject to 'something approaching free criticism' (ibid.). It is this, he said, which 'constitutes scientific objectivity' (ibid.). Working with others in a wider community, as well as with immediate colleagues, is central to research. Their criticism is often uncomfortable, but it makes the outcome better. The criticism will inevitably reflect others' interpretations, but it is none the worse for this, indeed it is enhanced by it. Hypotheses and evidence, once made public, are no longer only the products of the individual. Hypotheses can be tested *inter-subjectively*. They are constructs, what Popper elsewhere (1979[1972]) calls world 3 objects, which can be scrutinized independently of their source. 'Scientific objectivity can be described as the inter-subjectivity of scientific method' (Popper, 1966[1945], p. 217). What results from this (continuing) process is always provisional knowledge, but knowledge which has been subject to test.

The approach thus acknowledges, without difficulty, many of the criticisms of the 'relativists', yet it still offers a way of producing knowledge with some assurance about its validity and limitations: it is the public, social, process of testing that gives it 'objectivity'. There is a distinction between different kinds of 'knowledges'. One of the starting points for Popper's work was the problem of distinguishing scientific theories from other kinds of theories, particularly 'pseudo-science' (Popper, 1992[1974], p. 41). What is important about scientific knowledge, particularly for policy, is that we know something about its nature, origins and reliability.

## RESEARCH AND POLICY

A Popperian approach has an important benefit for research into policy. Policy is concerned with doing things. In policy, it is important to do the right things. Policy-makers need to choose policies that are likely to be successful. Merely to experiment is dangerous, and, in this context, even immoral. Research can contribute to policy choice, as the British government has eventually recognized by its interest in evidence-based policy; perhaps more importantly, it can offer an independent view of the policy options and their likely consequences, and provide a check on what policy-makers are doing. As Jenny Ozga (2000, p. 1) argues, policy research is 'contested terrain'.

The approach discussed above – unlike relativism, in which all points of view are equally valid – seeks preference for one proposition over another; some explanations are more successful than others. As Popper put it (1992[1974], p. 86):

> we may speak of 'better' and of 'worse' theories . . . the better theories are those with the greater content and the greater explanatory power. . . . And these . . . are also the better testable theories; and – if they stand up to tests – the better tested theories.

In policy, this is crucial; we should have some grounds for believing that the outcomes of policy will be what we hope; ideally, policy should be based on theories which are not only testable but also tested.

Policy-makers also need theories of a particular kind – those which offer courses of action rather than simply explain phenomena. For policy is much concerned with a particular kind of question or problem. I and others (Burgess, 1977; Swann, 1999, and see Chapter 2 of this book) have gone beyond Popper in distinguishing between the kinds of questions that research may address. What we have called 'what is the case' and 'why' questions are concerned with 'pure' theory, seeking to add to our understanding of the world. Those undertaking such research add to knowledge 'for its own sake'. They may not be interested in changing what happens outside the academy. They may, for example, explore and explain the relationship between social background and attainment, or develop the idea of human capital as an explanation of differential national economic development. The products of this work may lie mouldering in journals for decades. They may or may not be seized on by others to affect educational practice.

My own work typifies a different concern – with 'how to' questions. Policy is quintessentially concerned with practical problems, such as how best to teach children of different abilities, how to pay teachers in order to motivate them, how to deal with the disparities of opportunity arising from class, sex or race. The object of research into policy is to find out how to change things.

As these examples make clear, policy is found at various levels in any society, from national, government policy (about a national curriculum, for example) to the 'personal policies' of an individual (for example, about grouping children in a class). Policy of all of these kinds or levels affects education, and it can be – and should be – subject to research. It is as important, perhaps more important, to know about the impact of a teacher's personal policy about grouping on the children in her class as it is to conduct a large-scale evaluation of national policy.

In distinguishing between practical and theoretical problems, there is an obvious danger of creating another unhelpful – and potentially false – dichotomy. The two kinds of questions are inter-connected as well as distinct. Finding out how to do things also adds to theoretical knowledge; theory can underpin action. Yet the distinction between them is important, because attempting to solve one kind of question does not necessarily lead to solutions to the other. There is a tension between the two. Understanding why things happen may be important. Uninformed or ill-informed action is unwise and dangerous. It is useful to know, for example, why some children learn more quickly than others. This knowledge may direct us to different ways of teaching. But while knowing why things happen *may* help to change them, it is not a necessary condition for change. Knowing why does not infallibly lead to solutions to practical problems. Deep-seated social or environmental factors that inhibit learning may not be remediable within the time-scale in which a teacher has to operate. It may be better, on occasion, to attempt different solutions and see which one works. Sometimes indeed, as I have argued elsewhere (Pratt, 1999), attempting to answer 'why' questions before acting can be a diversion. We cannot wait for complete theoretical understanding of a social ill before acting to diminish it.

What form should, or does, research into policy take? My answer to this question depends, again, on my basic epistemological approach. It involves treating policy as an attempt to solve problems. All policy involves or embodies a proposed solution to a problem, though it is not often expressed in this way. Although some policies may appear to be answers in search of questions, my argument is that knowledge about them, and about their success or failure, is best gained if they are so expressed. Policy statements can all be put into the form: 'If we do this, then that will happen'. Examples might be: 'If we teach children this way, they will learn better' (an attempt to solve the problem of children's under-performance); 'If we relate teachers' pay to their performance they will work harder and feel valued' (an attempt to solve the problem of under-performing teachers). These are propositional statements: they are either true or false. They can be tested. As Bryan Magee (1973, p. 75) noted, 'All government policies, indeed all executive and administrative decisions, involve empirical predictions.' As Magee went on, 'A policy is a hypothesis.' One of the tasks of research into policy is to formulate these hypotheses and predictions and to test them.

In my view, 'good' research in education policy generates tested policy hypotheses. At best, it identifies what works and what doesn't, and it can offer explanation and understanding of why things work. Policy, of course, is set in the 'real world' of messy problems and complex interactions of uncontrolled variables. There are few mono-causal explanations of complex phenomena (in either the physical or social world). However, one of the things research into policy can do is to identify limitations and circumstances within which policies work. It can help to identify unintended and undesirable consequences of policy. Equipped with this knowledge, it is possible to create new, and better, policy.

How does this work out in practice? One way of researching into policy is to take the policy as stated and test if its aims have been achieved. Nowadays, this is a less exceptional activity than it was when I started my research career. Then, as Tyrrell Burgess and I wrote:

> In government and administration decisions are taken and implemented, needs are met and obstacles surmounted; then new circumstances arise and new pressures impinge, other policies are evolved, new decisions are taken – and only rarely does anyone ask what became of the old ones.
>
> (Burgess and Pratt, 1970, p. 168)

In those days, the subject of 'policy studies' was largely unknown in British universities, there were no government 'think-tanks' and few independent ones, and the elaborate mechanisms of the 'audit society' that now call all kinds of public and social institutions to account had yet to be created. One result was that 'the same or similar policies are tried over and over again. They meet similar difficulties, involve similar mistakes and lie equally discarded, until the next time' (ibid.). It is, sadly, not clear that much has changed since then, despite these developments.

In the book from which these quotations come, we reported on the first research project on which I worked, which attempted to prevent this repetitive folly in higher education. It was a study of the development of the colleges of advanced technology (CATs) from 1956 to 1966. After the Second World War, the government sought an increased output of highly qualified technologists, and eight (later ten) CATs were established from the leading technical colleges. In 1966, the CATs became universities. Our study initially sought to trace the impact of these institutional changes on the colleges, and we duly collected a comprehensive range of data on their courses, students, staff and the changes to them. But what had started out as an account of a piece of social history soon changed.

For the CATs had been established as an alternative to universities, to offer a distinctive kind of higher education, yet within a decade they had become universities. Moreover, a change of government in 1964 led to a further set of policies to create, again, an explicitly separate and distinctive 'public sector' of higher education with 30 polytechnics as its leading institutions. In the 1970s and 1980s, more changes occurred as colleges of education were closed and merged, and a new sector of colleges of higher education emerged. Then, in 1992, the government 'unified' higher education by permitting the polytechnics and some other colleges to acquire the title of 'university' and to award their own degrees.

In the study of the CATs, we quickly found ourselves asking whether the policy was a success or a failure, and why this historical process of institutional change seemed inevitable. Soon after, we embarked on similar studies of the new polytechnics (Pratt and Burgess, 1974) and, later, of the emerging colleges of higher education (Locke *et al.*, 1985) and of the history of the polytechnics (Pratt, 1997). In each case, the aim was to test the extent to which the policy was successful and to identify the factors that led to failure.

## DIFFICULTIES AND SOME SOLUTIONS

The studies raised a number of issues that are common in policy research. First, the aims of policy are rarely stated clearly. Politicians have a vested interest in being right; identifying the terms by which they can be judged is dangerous, as the UK's New Labour government found, even with modest policy pledges, at the 2001 general election. But even if aims are stated, this does not mean that the problems to which policy is meant to be a solution have been clearly formulated. Policy documents typically offer vague and value-laden generalizations and then set out actions that will be taken. The White Paper announcing the creation of the CATs in 1956 was concerned about the apparently low output, by international standards, of British engineers, and about meeting the 'demand' for technical education. But the international comparisons were not of like with like, and student demand for places was declining (Burgess and Pratt, 1970, p. 38). In the event, most of the expansion took place in the colleges that did not become CATs. A similar vagueness prefaced the 1992 changes in higher education. The 1991 White Paper (Department of Education and Science, 1991) was much concerned with maintaining 'diversity' in the unified system, but offered no statement of what that meant; its detailed specifications of governance, funding and quality assurance mechanisms offered no indication of how they would specifically promote this desired outcome. In both cases, had the problems been more clearly formulated, and that formulation itself tested against the evidence, the nature of the proposed solution and the outcomes might have been different.

Of course, as relativists would perhaps point out, the government's stated formulation of a problem is only one view. There may be other, covert, intentions, and there are other ways of looking at any situation. The approach espoused here does not limit the researcher to official statements of policy. It is pluralist. Alternative formulations can be offered, and tested against the outcomes. In higher education, it is possible to test such hypotheses as: the polytechnics were intended to offer higher education 'on the cheap' (the evidence is that they achieved this, whether or not it was an explicit aim – Pratt, 1997), or: the creation of a unified system of higher education diminishes the class distinction of a binary system (the evidence mostly refutes the theory – see: Rustin, 2000; Pratt, 2000).

Problem formulation is important in policy and research, because a policy or a theory can only be tested in terms of the extent to which it solves the problem. As noted above, it is in testing that objectivity lies. Policy which consists largely of a statement of actions to be taken can be assessed only in terms of whether or not those actions have been taken, and, perhaps, of their consequences. Implementing the solution is not the same as solving the problem. Most of the now fashionable 'evaluations' of policy assess only whether or not the solution was implemented. The question, however, is whether it solved the problem. Unifying higher education in 1992, for example, has not been much help in sustaining institutional diversity (except of wealth and privilege) nor in increasing participation, certainly by comparison with the 'binary system' that existed previously.

The typically vague statements of policy and the problems to be tackled make the task of testing policy difficult, but not insurmountable. One of the characteristic activities of my own research has been to construct, from the statements and context of policy, propositions that can be tested. This offers an interesting analogy, but also contrast, to other approaches, for example critical theory or the process of 'deconstruction' favoured by postmodern social theorists. The aim in all cases is to produce interpretations of events. But, for me, the process is a starting point, not an end in itself, and the interpretations need to be scrutinized rather than confirmed. My intention is to produce propositions for public scrutiny, and for testing, with a view to identifying a preference in use, not to generate equally valid interpretations of reality.

In the case of higher education since the mid-1950s, for example, it was possible to formulate a number of problems to which the various policy measures can be seen as solutions. Some of these are more or less explicit in policy statements; others have to be derived from research into the origins of the policy and its political, social or economic contexts. The 1956 CAT policy and the binary and polytechnic policies of the late 1960s clearly had their roots in a longer historical and social process of educational development. From the middle of the nineteenth century, higher education had developed broadly along class lines, with vocationally oriented institutions set up separately from the established universities. The vocational colleges developed higher education as the aspirations and achievements of their students increased, and offered an important route for social mobility for (mostly male) working and working class students. Tackling the problem of social stratification was not a stated aim in any of the policy documents (though it was mentioned in a speech, *post hoc*, by one minister after prompting by researchers), but it was a relevant and testable theory.

Testing whether or not it was achieved was a matter of collecting and analysing data on social background. The research showed that the contribution to social mobility of the CATs and polytechnics was diminished, indicating that giving institutions higher status was inimical to this policy aim (Burgess and Pratt, 1970; Pratt and Burgess, 1974; Pratt, 1997).

Another example of the derivation of hypotheses from the policy context arose with the more explicit aim of the 1966 policy that the polytechnics should be 'comprehensive academic communities' (Department of Education and Science, 1966). Although the White Paper did not spell out what this meant, it was not difficult to formulate some dimensions of comprehensiveness, and test whether or not these were achieved. The researcher's task is often to ask: 'What would it look like if it were happening?' In this case, indicators of comprehensiveness included the age range, sex, entry qualifications and (as noted above) social class of students, the characteristics of staff, the range of courses and subjects on offer, etc. Research into the context helped to identify which of these were likely to be vulnerable to diminution or increase, and thus especially worth studying.

It is worth noting here that most of the data needed were already in existence. The world is chock-full of data; institutions collect all kinds of information about their operations; most of it is never used, least of all to assess the outcomes of policy. Research is an expensive activity, so minimizing the cost of it is important. Using naturally occurring data is an (often overlooked) way of doing this. I have rarely had to undertake surveys.

It is also worth noting, as in the examples above, that not all of the indicators are quantitative – the different kinds of courses and subjects are examples of qualitative changes that can, nonetheless, be used to test policy. 'Soft' qualitative data, for example the views of staff or students, could similarly be used to assess the achievement of particular policy aims – for example, in changing the culture of an institution. My experience, as I hope these brief examples make clear, is that the choice of method is contingent upon the issues being examined and the kinds of evidence that would best serve to test the policy/theory. The key point is: method comes last. Moreover, the methods may well be associated with different research 'paradigms'.

The kind of testing described above helps to answer the question, 'Did the policy work?', or perhaps, 'To what extent did it work?' When such research has been completed, we know *that* something happened (or didn't, as the case may be). Since one of the aims of research into policy (or, at least, one of my aims) is to change things, knowing that events have happened, even though in a more informed, rigorous and detailed way than would have been achieved without research, is not enough. To create policy, as well as to change policy, or prevent or avoid undesirable or unnecessary change, we need to know how and why some things work and why others do not, and to what extent they work under different circumstances. We need both explanatory and predictive knowledge. These questions raise a number of further methodological issues. Here again, I find a Popperian approach helpful.

Policy is more than just a statement of problems or aims. It involves resources, people as agents, and, typically, it is implemented through institutions. I have characterized these as 'people plus rules'. They include physical institutions such as schools and colleges, but also institutional arrangements such as salary scales, or the designation by title of physical institutions, such as polytechnics. If policy is to work, the appropriate institutions must be used and used effectively. One of the foci of my research has been the use of institutions as instruments of policy. This extends the test of a policy formulated as, 'If we do this then that will happen', to examine whether the 'this' was actually done and whether other actions are needed to ensure that 'that' actually occurs. The research into the CATs, the polytechnics and the 1992 unified system of higher education, all showed that the government neglected to use some of the instruments of policy available to it to enhance the success of the policy. For example, in the case of the polytechnics, it continued to pay teachers less because they were not all engaged in university-level work; in the 1992 unification, it offered no institutional means of maintaining diversity.

To understand why and how individuals and institutions work, I have used Popper's idea of 'situational logic'. Popper formulated this idea as part of his analysis of historical explanation, to understand the actions of an agent in any situation. Briefly, this involves conjecturing what would happen if people followed the logic of their situation.

> [We] can try, conjecturally, to give an idealized reconstruction of the *problem situation* in which the agent found himself, and to that extent make the action 'understandable' (or 'rationally understandable'), that is to say, *adequate to his situation as he saw it*.
> (Popper, 1979[1972], p. 179)

There is much debate – in the literature on both policy and social science – about 'rationality'. It is often argued that you cannot study social phenomena in the same way as the physical world, because people do not behave rationally. In policy, by contrast, a substantial literature about policy-making offers 'rational models' (for example: Simon, 1947; Lindblom, 1959). A further literature identifies the various ways in which this ideal eludes human endeavour, by flawed decision-making and imperfect implementation (for example, Barrett and Fudge, 1981). Further analysis has added wider social, organizational, political and economic factors to explain the failings (for example, Shore and Wright, 1997). Despite this, the approach is evident in the current managerialist approach to policy (Farnham and Horton, 1996[1993]). Buzzwords like 'mission' and 'vision' are now commonplace. The problem with this is that all real events are measured against some unattainable ideal.

Situational logic helps to avoid this. It explains the actions of individuals and institutions by understanding *their* rationality, not in terms of some ideal. The conjectures resulting from situational analysis form testable hypotheses (Popper, 1992[1974], p. 118); actual behaviours can be examined to test whether our constructions of their problem situation are accurate. In policy it is of little use saying 'people *should* act like this' (for example, polytechnic teachers should sustain non-degree work) when from their point of view it is rational to act otherwise (by dropping it to seek increased pay). The tested conjectures can be used to inform policy-makers about the steps they will need to take to increase the probability that policy is successful.

Even if there is no previous empirical experience to go on, situational logic can offer reasonable foresight about the possible consequences of policy, by imagining 'what would happen if . . .' and taking steps to anticipate undesired outcomes. The unintended consequences of policy are often the most important, and sometimes the least desired. This is a form of 'prospective evaluation', which my colleagues and I call 'paper tests'. If they can be done, and data are already available, they are a lot quicker and cheaper than other forms of research. It is a mark of intelligence in policy-making, as in other forms of human endeavour, to learn from experience – and especially smart to learn from others' experience. We can learn from mistakes without making them. As Popper put it, 'we try to let our false theories die in our stead' (quoted in Magee, 1973, p. 64).

Situational logic can be used, too, to understand and explain the outcome of policy. My colleagues and I (Locke *et al.*, 1985) analysed the reorganization of colleges of education in the 1970s and 1980s. Faced with a predicted drop in the numbers of qualified teachers needed, the government invited colleges to find new futures. The research found that there was no specific policy aim, but rather the colleges were placed in a situation and responded to the constraints and opportunities that it presented. As a result, a new sector of colleges of higher education emerged, without planning or specified purpose, but complicating the polytechnic policy. There was now a kind of 'second division' in the public sector of higher education. From the point of view of national policy, it did not appear rational. For individual colleges, it was.

## IMPACT

As a researcher into policy I often feel (though significantly less heroically) like the poet Wilfred Owen: 'all a poet [researcher] can do . . . is warn'. British politicians have not been known for their valuing of policy research, though there are signs now of a fashion for evidence-based policy. However, some of the views and concepts from studies of higher education have entered policy debate. Perhaps the most significant has been the coining, by Tyrrell Burgess, of the term 'academic drift', during our initial study of the polytechnic policy, to describe the historical process of aspiration to university status. The idea became a key issue in discussion, and it may have prompted the polytechnics to redeem in later years some of their early reversals of policy intentions (for example, dropping part-time students). Unfortunately, they were still unable to resist the lure of academic drift in 1992.

Other governments have sometimes been more sympathetic to the lessons of policy research. In the early 1990s I was invited to help with the development of policy to create *Fachhochschulen* (similar to polytechnics) in Austria. A key idea of the policy was to create an accreditation council, the *Fachhochschulrat*, to validate courses in these new colleges, along the lines of the old Council for National Academic Awards (CNAA) in Britain, abolished in the 1992 Further and Higher Education Act. It was a radical departure from the powerful tradition of ministerial control of higher education in Austria, and few people believed that such a council would resist the tradition of party political trading. The analysis of the operation of institutions such as the CNAA convinced me that, if it was properly established, the *Fachhochschulrat* would have a life of its own. So far it appears to have sustained an independent and impartial role. It may be that policy researchers have more impact in countries other than their own.

KEY POINTS

In analysing policy, ask:

- To what problem(s) was this policy a solution?
- To what other problem(s) might it have been a solution?
- What instruments of policy were used to implement it?
- What potential instruments of policy were overlooked?
- What would it look like if it was working?
- What other (unintended) consequences of policy might there be?
- What kinds of evidence are needed to test if it is working or not? And only after this . . .

- What is the best way of collecting that evidence? (Use the easiest, cheapest sources and methods; naturally occurring data are often overlooked.)

## REFERENCES

Bailey, R. (1999) 'The abdication of reason: postmodern attacks upon science and reason', in J. Swann and J. Pratt (eds) *Improving Education: Realist Approaches to Method and Research*, London: Cassell, pp. 30–8.
Barrett, S. and Fudge, C. (1981) 'Examining the policy-action relationship', in S. Barrett and C. Fudge (eds) *Policy and Action: Essays on the Implementation of Public Policy*, London: Methuen.
Burgess, T. (1977) *Education After School*, London: Victor Gollancz.
Burgess, T. and Pratt, J. (1970) *Policy and Practice: The Colleges of Advanced Technology*, London: Allen Lane and The Penguin Press.
Department of Education and Science (1966) *A Plan for Polytechnics and Other Colleges: Higher Education in the Further Education System*, London: Her Majesty's Stationery Office, Cmnd 3006.
Department of Education and Science (1991) *Higher Education: A New Framework*, London: Her Majesty's Stationery Office, Cm 1541.
Farnham, D. and Horton, S. (eds) (1996) *Managing the New Public Services*, Basingstoke, UK: Macmillan (first edition 1993).
Flew, A. (1975) *Thinking about Thinking*, London: Collins Fontana.
Lindblom, C. E. (1959) 'The science of "muddling through"', *Public Administration Review*, 19 (2), pp. 79–88.
Locke, M., Pratt, J. and Burgess, T. (1985) *The Colleges of Higher Education 1972 to 1982: The Central Management of Organic Change*, London: Critical Press.
Lyotard, J.-F. (1984) *The Postmodern Condition: A Report on Knowledge*, trans. G. Bennington and B. Massumi, Manchester, UK: Manchester University Press (first published in French in 1979).
Magee, B. (1973) *Popper*, London: Fontana Press.
Organisation for Economic Co-operation and Development (OECD) (1995) *Educational Research and Development: Trends, Issues and Challenges*, Paris: Organisation for Economic Co-operation and Development.
Ozga, J. (2000) *Policy Research in Educational Settings*, Buckingham, UK: Open University Press.
Popper, K. R. (1966) *The Open Society and its Enemies, Volume 2 – The High Tide of Prophecy: Hegel, Marx, and the Aftermath*, London: Routledge and Kegan Paul (first edition 1945).
Popper, K. R. (1972) *The Logic of Scientific Discovery*, London: Hutchinson (first published in German in 1934) (first English edition 1959).
Popper, K. R. (1979) *Objective Knowledge: An Evolutionary Approach*, Oxford, UK: Oxford University Press (first edition 1972).
Popper, K. R. (1992) *Unended Quest: An Intellectual Autobiography*, London: Routledge. (First published as 'Autobiography of Karl Popper', in P. A. Schilpp (ed.) (1974) *The Philosophy of Karl Popper, Book I*, La Salle, IL: Open Court Publishing.)
Pratt, J. (1997) *The Polytechnic Experiment 1965–1992*, Buckingham, UK: Society for Research into Higher Education and Open University Press.

Pratt, J. (1999) 'Testing policy', in J. Swann and J. Pratt (eds) *Improving Education: Realist Approaches to Method and Research*, London: Cassell, pp. 39–52.

Pratt, J. (2000) 'Sustaining technological universities: the British experience', in L. O. K. Lategan (ed.) *The Making of a University of Technology*, Bloemfontein, South Africa: Technikon Free State, pp. 42–51.

Pratt, J. and Burgess, T. (1974) *Polytechnics: A Report*, London: Sir Isaac Pitman and Sons.

Rustin, M. (2000) 'The university in the network society', in T. Butler (ed.) *Eastern Promise: Education and Social Renewal in London's Docklands*, London: Lawrence and Wishart, pp. 84–108.

Shore, C. and Wright, S. (eds) (1997) *The Anthropology of Public Policy: Critical Perspectives on Governance and Power*, London: Routledge.

Simon, H. A. (1947) *Administrative Behavior: A Study of Decision-Making Processes in Administrative Organizations*, New York: Macmillan.

Swann, J. (1999) 'Making better plans: problem-based versus objectives-based planning', in J. Swann and J. Pratt (eds) *Improving Education: Realist Approaches to Method and Research*, London: Cassell, pp. 53–66.

Swann, J. and Pratt, J. (eds) (1999) *Improving Education: Realist Approaches to Method and Research*, London: Cassell.

# Critical approaches to research in practice

Michael Collins, *University of Saskatchewan, Canada*

> This power it is not as the positive that looks away from the negative – as when we say of something, this is nothing or false, and then, finished with it, turn away from it to something else . . .
>
> (Hegel, 1967[1807], p. 408)

> The dispute about the actuality or non-actuality of thinking that is isolated from practice is a purely *scholastic* question. . . . The philosophers have only *interpreted* the world in various ways; the point is, to *change* it.
>
> (Marx, 1967b[1888], pp. 401–2)

## THE POLITICAL DIMENSION

This chapter is about research in practice informed by critical theory and focusing mainly on education. Its primary concern is with critical theory associated with the 'Frankfurt School', in particular the work of Jürgen Habermas, who is widely viewed as the leading contemporary representative of Frankfurt School critical theory.

Critical theory in this vein abandoned Karl Marx's projection about the historical role of the working class in bringing about revolution, and it distances itself from what it regards as the economic determinism of his later works – *Capital, Volumes I, II, III* (Marx, 1965[1867], 1967a[1885], 1966[1894]) included – and that of orthodox Marxists. Yet it remains significantly connected to the Marxian legacy, largely via the major work of Georg Lukács (1971[1923]).

Thus, critical theory incorporates economic, cultural and ideological analyses in its understanding of why the contradictions of late capitalism, including the everyday oppressions and accompanying widespread sense of alienation, are still sustainable, and to explain the absence of short-term prospects for a breakdown of the system (anticipated by Marx). Such analyses are relevant for a clearer understanding of educational policy formation, curriculum development, the changing structure of educational institutions, teaching and learning processes, and a host of other educational practices.

The fact that neo-conservative, neo-liberal, and now neo-social democratic (New Labour in Britain, for example) governments tend to claim that their policies, and the practices that ensue, are non-ideological (that is, 'pragmatic'), suggests a pressing need for the recovery and legitimation of ideology critique in education. In this regard, we are up against influential versions of an 'end of ideology' discourse represented in the work of Francis Fukuyama (1992), which informs neo-conservative and neo-liberal thinking, and of Anthony Giddens (2001), which provides the intellectual basis for 'Third Way' politics invoked by social democratic parties in transition now seeking to enlarge on their accommodation to the claims of capital. These ideological developments, claimed by their exponents to be non-ideological, present an immediate challenge to a critically oriented research in practice that seeks to illuminate their effects on education.

Critical theory, and its orientation to research in practice, still stands against the claims of late capitalism. A more nuanced, or perhaps academically liberal way of putting it, would be to view critical theory as bringing into question taken-for-granted initiatives, including seemingly progressive educational reforms, that support corporate ideology and the current free-market discourse on globalization. This entails a recognition that critically oriented research in practice is politically engaged. It constitutes a counter-discourse, which aims to disclose the ideological underpinnings, inevitable contradictions, and special interests associated with policy formation, institutional restructuring and other significant developments that emerge alongside the imperatives of late capitalism. In the process, critical theory suggests that there are possibilities for reasonable alternatives to the affirmations determined by these imperatives.

## ON UNIVERSITY RESTRUCTURING: EDUCATION LTD

Most readers of this book have some connection to a university, and will be acutely aware of the increasing trend towards the corporatization of this institution. This has been accompanied by expressions of liberal regret, even from career administrators who have benefited in their corporate business-like roles as chief executive officers of the academy, and understandable lamentation from those concerned about what they perceive to be an erosion of values encompassed by the idea of the university.

From a critical theory perspective, the ascendancy of a corporate business ethos on campus, and increased adoption of market-place values by entrepreneurial academics, are to be understood, and not merely lamented, in the context of the manifestations of capitalist development that are generally defined under the rubric of 'globalization'. Why should we be surprised by the sharp turn taken by the university towards market-place values? Was the academy ever really characterized by the liberal idea of the university, removed from extra-mural interests that are counter to the liberal and, in some instances, deeply conservative values it espoused? Not likely.

These are not intended to be cynical observations on the relevance of liberal aspirations. Critical theory as research in practice is partly about defending genuine liberal concerns and past gains of individual rights, including freedom of speech, educational opportunity, the mitigation of corporate and bureaucratic excess, and so on. And the university is an important institution for illuminating the extent to which these aspirations are under siege, and for identifying, where feasible, counter-strategies in defence of worthwhile educational programmes that are in danger from corporate-style downsizing. At the same time, there is a need to ascertain the ways in which accommodation to corporate ideology has (mis)shaped the goals of academic programmes, teaching, and the learning process. It makes sense for us to investigate in a critical vein developments emerging from the marketization of the (post)modern university.

Practical investigations from a critical theory perspective enable us to identify the contradictions between claims about the 'disinterested' or objective search for knowledge and the erosion of university autonomy that occurs with the hard-right turn to meet market-place interests. A critically oriented research in practice recognizes that research and teaching are not apolitical and, in this light, can investigate how market-place ideologies affect the role of the academic, the way research emphases are determined, how resources are allocated, and how curriculum design, even while it talks of the need for critical thinking skills, tends to suppress serious critique (ridiculed as 'politically correct').

One of the purposes of such critique would be to examine how the distribution of knowledge is steered, via patents, from our publicly supported institutions to private sector interests. On the one hand there is the issue of corporate funding for university programmes (not only in the applied sciences) and its effects on academic integrity, research priorities, and curriculum discourse. On the other there are legitimate concerns to be addressed about the use of scarce publicly funded resources to subsidize business-oriented research and development on university campuses. The full extent of this shift of publicly funded assets to subsidize private sector interests has yet to be documented.

Research of this kind begins with questioning a mainstream educational discourse that places emphasis on developing programmes to meet the needs of employers, along with more intensive enquiry into the conflicts of interests entailed. These conflicts, especially their moral and political implications, are nicely identified by Ibrahim Warde (2001): European business is keenly aware of the value of research, and companies compete to endow new posts and research units; experience in the US, however, suggests that business sponsorship of universities increases conflicts of interest and undermines academics' credibility (p. 13). Clearly, the wider spectrum of education and learning is amenable to critically oriented research in practice into the issue of commercialization. Several contributions to the excellent book *Education Limited* (Education Group II, Department of Cultural Studies, 1991) are still instructive in this regard. John Holford *et al.* (1998) contains chapters pointing to possibilities for further critically oriented research on how the concept of lifelong learning is now accommodated to the requirements of the globalized economy.

## PUTTING OURSELVES INTO PRACTICE

This chapter began with an emphasis on the political dimension because critical theory is concerned with the problem of agency (what ought to be done) and, in regard to research in practice, with the agency of the researcher. In this view, the investigator informed by critical theory and its emancipatory aspirations should have an action-oriented interest in issues of relevance to everyday living. The philosophical underpinnings for a critically informed research in practice are beyond the mandate of this chapter, but they can be discovered, for example, in Richard Bernstein (1971), especially in the chapter on 'Marx and the Hegelian background', where commitment to emancipatory practice and research is shown to be a *normative* process (incorporating moral and political concerns) and, at the same time, a *rational* undertaking.

A concern for the agency of the researcher is not a call for mere activism in response to the contradictions, inequities, and spurious policy initiatives disclosed by critical analysis. Yet this does not preclude critically informed counter-hegemonic initiatives that in some circumstances reasonably entail direct confrontation with non-democratic measures that stifle public debate.

A critically oriented pedagogical strategy to engender reasoned public debate around critical issues is exemplified in the way Habermas took on the attempts by neo-conservative historians to relativize and, thus, diminish Germany's moral responsibility for the Holocaust by claiming that 'Auschwitz grew out of the gulag'. According to John Muller (2001), Habermas is actively concerned with 'ensuring the conditions of rational public debate' (p. 7). This concern for public education regarding key issues of our time accords with Habermas's main theoretical project (1984[1981], 1987[1981]), which incorporates both strategic and communicative action (dialogue) as the *rational* basis for emancipatory praxis. Thus, 'politics, for Habermas, still has a transformative, redemptive quality' (Muller, 2001, p. 7).

Much of significance can be learned about the efficacy of political involvement through critical reflection and dialogue on, as well as participation in, collective action against initiatives by the state and international corporate interests that short-change democratic processes integral to the well-being of civil society. A critical pedagogy that values public education should be attuned, for example, to the emergence of a social movement in the wake of recent demonstrations in Seattle, Vancouver, Quebec City, London, and Gothenburg against closed-door meetings on free trade in the globalized economy.

It appears (for the elite decision-making process is not demonstrably democratic) that the International Monetary Fund (IMF), the World Bank, and the governments involved, favour the public dissemination of only officially sanctioned information. And, in the absence of wider public debate, there is reasonable cause to believe that free trade negotiations are steered more by the interests of international business corporations than by the welfare of ordinary men and women. Within this context of organized protest, where the global dominance of capital and capitalist state institutions is being challenged, the corporatization of our universities, schools, and other public services should now be critically assessed.

While the critique of these tendencies, and their interconnectedness, needs to be deepened, we have learned that even in Western democracies, organized demonstrations demanding genuine public debate about global initiatives in the new economy bring about a massive show of police power. We are now confronted with an absurd situation whereby demonstrations, systematically contained, are allowable so long as they cannot realistically make any difference to a course of events set by the globalization agenda. In any event, the government and government-appointed corporate business representatives of leading economic nations who are negotiating the new world order, with the IMF and the World Bank as facilitators, have many means at their disposal to disqualify reasoned alternatives to their global agenda. Yet the resistance exemplified by the demonstrations, the issues at stake, and the implications for social learning processes and the transformation of public education are relevant for a critically informed research in practice.

## POSITIVISM, INSTRUMENTAL RATIONALITY AND THE CULT OF EFFICIENCY

Typically, any account of critical theory begins with its rejection of positivism, in particular logical positivism, both as a world-view and of the way it is deployed in the social sciences and educational research and practice. Briefly stated (Ingram, 1990, p. 114), 'Positivism maintains that all forms of knowledge, including that proffered by social science, conforms, or ought to conform, to the kind of knowledge proffered by natural science (what Habermas calls *scientism*).' It is not that Habermas, unlike his Frankfurt School predecessors, rejects the method of the natural sciences outright. Rather, he is concerned to show that the methodological approach entailed denies, in its claim for 'objectivity', that it is motivated, just like other forms of enquiry, by practical (that is, subjectively determined) interests.

Positivism – as exemplified in the applied sciences and social science research, which apes the methodology of the natural sciences – disavows the role of reflection (Habermas, 1971a[1968], p. vii). 'Positivism of all kinds was ultimately the abdication of reflection. The result was the absolutizing of "facts" and the reification of the existing order' (Jay, 1973, p. 62). Accordingly, positivism, in this sense, with its pretension of disentangling facts from values, offers a distorted view of reality. A task for a critically oriented research in practice is to uncover the harmful effects of this 'dominant positivist orientation' which makes it 'difficult or impossible to deal with the vital issues of choice and action that we confront all the time' (Bernstein, 1971, p. 307).

For Frankfurt School critical theorists and their successors, positivism's mechanistic 'cause and effect' view manifests itself as an ideological form of late capitalism (including the bureaucratic or state capitalism associated with the command economies and various dictatorships around the world). The positivistic model of research, in this view, plays a significant role in sustaining existing relationships of power. Thus, it is important, when undertaking critical investigations into policy development, institutional arrangements, and research methods, to comprehend the relationship between a positivistic orientation and the larger imperatives of political economy. In this way, policy initiatives, social science and educational research, curriculum development, and institutional regulatory mechanisms, which are guided by a taken-for-granted positivistic orientation that delegitimizes all reflection on normative considerations, can become problematized for public debate.

The non-reflective affirmations of logical positivism and its manifestations in advanced capitalism are reinforced through the enthronement of *instrumental rationality*. For Theodor Adorno and Max Horkheimer, the most eminent founding members of the Frankfurt School, instrumental rationality works against autonomy, the achievements of a just (rational) society, and human happiness:

> The 'critique of instrumental reason' became the principal task of critical theory, for in creating the objective possibility of a truly human society, the progressive mastery of nature through science and technology simultaneously transformed the potential subjects of emancipation. . . . For Horkheimer and Adorno, then, human emancipation could be conceived only as a radical break with merely 'formal' rationality and merely 'instrumental' thought.
>
> (McCarthy, 1987[1978], p. 20)

The implications of this form of critique – which goes against the grain of conventional social science and educational research, curriculum development, and policy formation – are considerable.

Adorno and Horkheimer, in line with Max Weber, ultimately conceded that our destiny is bound by the systematic constraints of an increasingly bureaucratized, overly managed society (as in Weber's metaphor of the 'iron cage', which sets limits to the achievement of individual autonomy and collective practices towards human emancipation). Herbert Marcuse (1964), another early associate of the Frankfurt School, follows in this vein when he deals with the political consequences of technical reason in his critique of advanced capitalism.

Habermas, however, distances himself from the pessimism of his Frankfurt School predecessors about the virtually inescapable repressive effects of positivism and from the narrow Weberian technical view of rationality. He views technical rationality as a preeminent, and not necessarily adverse, influence in modern society, while describing a wider concept of rationality. His concept of rationality encompasses a moral/practical dimension (legitimizing the role of reflection) that incorporates, but is not steered by, technical imperatives. Rather, moral/practical considerations determine, through reflection, how technical rationality (embodied in methodological approaches, techniques, and strategic action) is to be deployed. There are significant implications for learning theory (yet to be carefully mined) of Habermas's work, which provide us with a theoretical basis from which to understand pedagogical practice and policies.

The wider conception of rationality proffered by Habermas points to the emancipatory potential of a *reasoned* (deliberative) discourse that emanates from a fundamental human capacity – language acquisition – for developing *communicative competence*. Thus, Habermas's project, largely defined in the *Theory of Communicative Action* (1984[1981], 1987[1981]), is to show how reason, including its emancipatory potential, is embedded in language and, in particular, dialogue. Rationality presumes communication. Forms of technical rationality – unmediated by relevant practical deliberations, and which interfere with the development of communicative competence in the interactions among individuals and between groups – are irrational.

The critique of technical rationality – as the cult of efficiency that short-changes moral and practical reasoning, careful reflection and dialogue – opens up possibilities to investigate how a narrowly conceived concept of reason (mis)shapes institutional arrangements, policy formation, curriculum design, learning processes, teaching practices, and research and development. The negative effects can also be revealed in how we relate to each other and to ourselves in our workplaces, communities and families. At the same time, Habermas's concept of communicative action provides a rational basis for exploring ways that communicative competence, with its implications for genuine participatory democracy, can be *learned* and sustained. Dialogue itself, in this view, is research in practice and prefigures the possibilities of participatory research addressed below.

In summary, technical rationality, as an unreflective (positivistic) affirmation of the cult of efficiency, is exemplified in the obsession with technique. The concern here is that the fixation on technique disqualifies or, at best, manages to subordinate considerations of practical (including moral and practical) import to its own view of social reality. In such circumstances, critique is important as a way of resisting an over-preoccupation with technique and the way it manifests itself in institutional structures, management practices, professional training, policy formation, pedagogy, forms of enquiry and wide areas of everyday life (Barrett, 1979; Collins, 1991).

## SYSTEM, LIFEWORLD AND CIVIL SOCIETY

There is significant correspondence between, on the one hand, the critique of technical rationality and Habermas's account of system imperatives, and, on the other, the concept of communicative action and the everyday lifeworld. In taking up a theme addressed by many of his predecessors in the Frankfurt School critical theory tradition, as well as by Weber and Marx, Habermas reveals the way in which the values and communicative forms of our everyday lifeworld are being eroded ('colonized') by system imperatives (typically in the form of bureaucratic stipulations) of an 'overly managed' society, and by corporate ideology. Thus, the interaction of lifeworld values and system imperatives, particularly with regard to sustaining a defence of the lifeworld (Welton, 1995) under conditions of advanced capitalism, constitutes a vital context for critical investigations committed to engendering an emancipatory pedagogy. I refer here to pedagogical research for emancipatory strategies favouring public debate on vital issues – research that is not driven by bureaucratic and corporate agendas, and that facilitates reflection and dialogue in the classroom rather than the deployment of pre-packaged standardized curricula.

As well as the emergent counter-hegemonic initiatives from lifeworld contexts, such as the new social movements, there are 'seams' in the system which raise the possibility of protecting and even advancing lifeworld values against the rationalizing tendencies of system-oriented initiatives. A critically informed research in practice, in this view, acknowledges that a concern for lifeworld values is crucial to our well-being, and is still reasonable, even in the face of powerful system imperatives.

There is a clear connection between how the lifeworld is conceived and the current discourse in education on civil society and citizenship training (Collins, 2001). Invoking Habermas, and defining civil society as 'an extension of the lifeworld [which] provides a forum where people may speak freely to one another', Patricia Gouthro (2000) draws our attention to its importance in identifying issues and locations for research in practice: 'Civil society is increasingly being perceived as an alternative focus by which educators and citizens can reassert democratic principles for justice and equity' (p. 60). Gouthro is particularly interested in the 'homeplace' as a vital lifeworld context, and, as an example of research in practice on a topical issue, she refers to a national movement that involves Japanese housewives in environmental activism.

Here is how Habermas (1996[1992], pp. 366–7), defining what is meant by civil society, specifies key locations that would benefit and provide support for critically oriented research in practice: 'its institutional core comprises those nongovernmental and non-economic connections and voluntary associations that anchor the communication structures of the public sphere in the society component of the lifeworld.'

This emphasis on non-governmental agencies and the lifeworld does not entail a rejection of involvement with the system exemplified in Ivan Illich's radical text *Deschooling Society* (1970), which has influenced both progressive and reactionary discourses on alternative education. Rather, Habermas reminds us that we need to take into account, within the purview of civil society as a context for citizens to activate change, the continuing importance of the role of the state in its bureaucratic and political decision-making functions, of the law and duly constituted legal functions, and of prevailing economic functions. Critiques of globalization which take these factors into account can inform public debate on the obstacles to genuine participatory ('deliberative') democracy, and legitimize the concerns of protestors about the influence of international business interests in a global economy. Research in practice around these concerns can perform an educative role, by demonstrating how deliberative politics should engage with the issues of global import now being discussed behind closed doors and pre-packaged for public consumption. In the wake of demonstrations in Seattle and other cities around the world, our schools, universities, workplaces and communities are now ripe for carefully researched counter-hegemonic public education.

## CURRICULUM CONCERNS

The counter-hegemonic potential of investigating curriculum development informed by the critique of positivism and technical rationality is particularly relevant in the context of pervasive neo-liberal policy initiatives in education. It is important to illuminate the ways in which a seemingly progressive curriculum discourse, that emphasizes the merits of measurable objectives and standardized tests, serves bureaucratic needs and the interests of business and industry, and (mis)shapes learning processes and the role of teachers.

This critique needs to be sustained, even though it has been a recurring concern for many educational commentators, including this author (Collins, 1987, 1991, 1998). For while positivistic curriculum design, programme development and policy initiatives in education are often based on the tenets of behavioural psychology (education aping the natural sciences), and are changeable within this framework, the critical concerns remain the same. They need to be reframed to counter the masking effects and ideological intent of what is being officially deployed as a new progressive discourse in education. In recent years we have witnessed curriculum repackaging under new logos: 'competency-based education', 'outcomes-based education', 'human resource development'.

Without a theoretically informed critique, it is difficult to counter the misguided enthusiams of those who promote these recycled curriculum innovations on behalf of educational policy-makers. They are misguided, simply because in practical terms they do not solve the educational problems they purport to address – the competency-based education movement is a case in point (Collins, 1987) – and, more importantly, they short-change those non-instrumental educational values of judgement, aesthetic appreciation and critical thought. Positivistic curriculum initiatives, under any label, are only successful to the extent that they serve the interests of management control.

Critically informed research in practice can offer resistance to positivistic tendencies in curriculum development that are evident in non-reflective and top-down deployment of standardized formats. In this regard, a focus on ways that the reductionism and prescriptiveness of these system-oriented approaches that serve the impulse towards measurement and standardization, can provide telling evidence of the distortion of learning processes and the deskilling of teachers. Critically oriented research in practice can highlight the ways in which, despite the rhetoric about teaching critical thinking skills and the professional involvement of teachers in shaping educational initiatives, a positivistic curriculum reinforces what Jean-Paul Sartre (1977[1975]) has described as *serial thinking*, 'thinking which is not my own thinking but that of the Other' (pp. 201–2).

Other hopeful possibilities for a critical, counter-hegemonic research in practice can be derived from pedagogical strategies envisioned by Martin Heidegger (1968[1954]), who explained how the enthronement of technical rationality, an obsession with technique and the cult of efficiency, undermine learning and the vocation of teaching:

> Teaching is more difficult than learning because what teaching calls for is this: to let learn. . . . The teacher is ahead of his [*sic*] apprentices in this alone, that he has still far more to learn than they – he has to learn to let them learn.
>
> (p. 15)

A reasonable case has to be made for us to engage with the moral and practical implications of this pedagogical insight into learner and teacher autonomy, given that the sense of vocation and the learning principles it represents have been marginalized by a 'pragmatic' discourse on education, plainly inclined towards the interests of business and industry and now exploring the prospects of privatizing public education.

Top-down initiatives in public education, while creating greater stress for teachers and administrators, are couched in terms of reform needed to overcome institutional crisis and malaise. The 'experts', often from the academy, provide a discourse on reform that takes for granted the authenticity of the neo-liberal view of educational change. The emphasis is on how educators should adapt to the 'new reality' and cope with the pressure of change through a performance management framework (Fullan, 1991), which begs the question of how maladroit, ideologically driven policies are increasing job stress among teachers.

Apart from empirical studies on teacher stress (Bernhardt, 2001), which confirm what is obvious to most of us involved in public education, a more urgent need is for ideology critique of allegedly progressive 'expert' discourse that merely legitimizes neo-liberal interpretations of what is needed in education. The task for a critically informed research in practice, in this regard, is to challenge the taken-for-granted (often unstated) assumptions of the legitimizing discourse, illuminate its ideological underpinnings (typically denied), and describe the harmful consequences of educational policies it sustains.

## PARTICIPATORY RESEARCH

Participatory research can be viewed as a relatively pure form of research in practice that privileges the experience and needs of project participants over those of the researcher as 'outside expert'. Relevant variations on the participatory research approach, which can be initiated through organized study circles (Blid, 1989), have considerable potential as a counter-hegemonic and emancipatory pedagogy in our schools, communities and workplaces:

> The basic principles of the approach . . . are based on a recognition that ordinary men and women have the capacity to name their own reality, and to become co-investigators in seeking solutions to the problems that beset them in their everyday lives. The investigative process is viewed as collective, dialogical, educative, and emancipatory. Expertise, whether from within the community or brought in from outside, does not direct procedures, but is incorporated to the project at hand according to collective decision-making.
>
> (Collins, 1998, p. 158)

The approach is consistent with the political, consciousness-raising pedagogy of Paulo Freire (1981), and the communicative ethic that emerges from the critical theory of Habermas (1984[1981], 1987[1981]).

While participatory research fits well with the conception of critically informed research in practice, educational researchers (particularly academics) need to be sensitive to the participatory ethos which insists on the collective ownership of the process and the knowledge generated. In this view, using data from participatory research projects as the basis for an individual academic undertaking, such as a graduate thesis or refereed article, becomes problematic (somewhat like stealing smorgasbord). Nevertheless, educational practitioners, especially adult educators and community-minded academics, are well-qualified to play a significant, though non-privileged, role in furthering social learning, democratic decision-making, and practical initiatives that are developed through participatory research. The special issue of the International Council for Adult Education's journal, *Convergence* (Yarmol-Franko, 1988), is a useful guide to the potential of this approach.

## POSTMODERN/POST-STRUCTURALIST TENDENCIES

Postmodernism and post-structuralism have been widely incorporated into the critical discourse on education and the social sciences, as well as literary criticism. There is considerable overlap between the tendencies invoked by postmodernism and post-structuralism, especially as far as critically oriented research in education and the social sciences is concerned. A useful account of the connections and distinctions between critical theory, post-structuralism and postmodernism is available on the Internet (Agger, 2001).

Along with critical theory, postmodernism and post-structuralism are critiques of positivism, which their authors likewise associate with conditions under late capitalism. Thus, in the sphere of education, they can be relevant to investigations of curriculum development, bureaucratic control, policy formation and professionalizing initiatives. In particular, the 'method' of deconstruction, mainly derived from the work of Jacques Derrida, and the interconnections between knowledge and power, drawing on Michel Foucault's rendering of Nietzschean philosophy, have influenced important feminist critique.

Deconstruction serves to undermine the taken-for-granted authoritative (canonical) perspectives that characterize patriarchy and shape institutional practices and personal relationships. A post-structuralist critique of conventional discourses, exemplified in the critique of written texts (literary criticism), constitutes the model for postmodern critical insights, via deconstruction, of everyday social reality. Thus, a deconstruction of the university as text from a feminist perspective (Schick, 1994) illuminates the way that women are disadvantaged within the patriarchically constituted norms and structures of the institution.

Foucault's work highlights the way in which relationships of power are sustained, and how systems of surveillance and control shape our everyday lives. The political aspirations of those with postmodernist tendencies are to empower the marginalized, and engender critical discourse on the significance of *difference*.

While they share a dominant theme in their rejection of positivism, postmodern analyses also reject critical theory's view that the emancipatory project of modernity (human history in the making) is still in process, and that reasons can be advanced to ground theoretical arguments underlying emancipatory praxis. In short, for postmodernism the quest for a rational society (Habermas, 1971b[1968/1969]) is a futile vanguardist aspiration in the face of an inevitably fragmented contemporary social reality.

From a critical theory standpoint, certainly from one that is identified within Marxian, neo-Marxist, and Frankfurt School legacies, postmodern/post-structuralist sensibilities are seriously flawed – irrational, relativistic, and hopelessly mired in a preoccupation with identity politics (the 'politics of difference') – and fail to understand the need for rationally grounded (that is, theoretically informed) comprehensive emancipatory praxis for our times. A more pressing concern, from a critical theory perspective, is the way that postmodern insights and post-structuralist deconstruction, because of their relativistic purview, can be embraced in support of neo-liberal and neo-fascist agendas.

Contrary to critical arguments advanced against postmodernism (Callinicos, 1990), and claims that its tendencies are dysfunctional for critical pedagogy (Collins, 1998), leading critical theorist Ben Agger (2001) and feminist scholars such as Seyla Benhabib (1996) suggest that there are possibilities for a sensible *rapprochement* between critical theory – as manifested in the work of Habermas, in particular – and postmodern/post-structuralist critique. Though sceptical about how such a *rapprochement* might be expressed in philosophical terms, this author would agree that firmly argued but respectful debates between critical theorists, in the Marxian and neo-Marxist traditions, and postmodern scholars committed to social justice, could now be instructive in identifying emancipatory pedagogical strategies for a critically oriented research in practice.

In the field of education, a critically informed research in practice calls for an interpretation of how social learning processes, institutional practices, and the role of teachers are being shaped according to the imperatives of late capitalism, and for actual engagement in measured but hopeful strategies to counter, most often on a small scale, the deleterious effects brought about by these imperatives.

## REFERENCES

Agger, B. (2001) 'Critical theory, poststructuralism, postmodernism: their socio-logical relevance', *Illuminations*, 5 March: http://www.uta.edu/huma/illuminations/agger2.htm (accessed 7 December 2002).
Barrett, W. (1979) *The Illusion of Technique*, New York: Doubleday.

Benhabib, S. (ed.) (1996) *Democracy and Difference: Contesting the Boundaries of the Political*, Princeton, NJ: Princeton University Press.

Bernhardt, D. (2001) 'Job stress rates soaring for nation's teachers: Canadian Teachers' Federation', *The Star Phoenix*, 14 July, p. A8.

Bernstein, R. J. (1971) *Praxis and Action*, Philadelphia, PA: University of Pennsylvania Press.

Blid, H. (1989) *Education by the People: Study Circles*, Ludvika, Sweden: Brunsvik Folk High School.

Callinicos, A. (1990) *Against Postmodernism: A Marxist Critique*, Cambridge, UK: Polity Press.

Collins, M. (1987) *Competence in Adult Education: A New Perspective*, Lanham, MD: University Press of America.

Collins, M. (1991) *Adult Education as Vocation: A Critical Role for the Adult Educator*, New York: Routledge.

Collins, M. (1998) *Critical Crosscurrents in Education*, Malabar, FL: Krieger.

Collins, M. (2001) 'Critical commentaries on citizenship, civil society, and adult education', *Journal of Adult and Continuing Education*, 4 (X), pp. 41–55.

Education Group II, Department of Cultural Studies (1991) *Education Limited: Schooling, Training and the New Right in England Since 1979*, London: Unwin Hyman.

Freire, P. (1981) *Pedagogy of the Oppressed*, New York: Continuum.

Fukuyama, F. (1992) *The End of History and the Last Man*, New York: Free Press.

Fullan, M. (1991) *The New Meaning of Educational Change*, New York: Teachers College Press.

Giddens, A. (2001) *The Global Third Way Debate*, Malden, MA: Blackwell Publishers.

Gouthro, P. (2000) 'Globalization, civil society, and the homeplace', *Convergence*, XXXIII (1/2), pp. 57–77.

Habermas, J. (1971a) *Knowledge and Human Interests*, trans. J. J. Shapiro, Boston, MA: Beacon Press (first published in German in 1968).

Habermas, J. (1971b) *Toward a Rational Society: Student Protest, Science, and Politics*, trans. J. J. Shapiro, Boston, MA: Beacon Press (first published in German in 1968/1969).

Habermas, J. (1984, 1987) *Theory of Communicative Action, Volumes 1 and 2*, trans. T. McCarthy, Boston, MA: Beacon (first published in German in 1981).

Habermas, J. (1996) *Between Facts and Norms: Contributions to a Discourse Theory of Law and Democracy*, trans. W. Rehg, Cambridge, MA: The Massachusetts Institute of Technology Press (first published in German in 1992).

Hegel, G. W. F. (1967) 'The Preface to The Phenomenology of Mind', in W. Kaufmann, *Hegel: Reinterpretation, Texts, and Comments*, trans. W. Kaufmann, New York: Doubleday, pp. 363–459 (first published in German in 1807).

Heidegger, M. (1968) *What Is Called Thinking?*, trans. J. Glenn Gray and F. Wieck, New York: Harper and Row (first published in German in 1954).

Holford, J., Jarvis, P. and Griffin, C. (eds) (1998) *International Perspectives on Lifelong Learning*, London: Kogan Page.

Illich, I. (1970) *Deschooling Society*, New York: Harper and Row.

Ingram, D. (1990) *Critical Theory and Philosophy*, New York: Paragon House.

Jay, M. (1973) *The Dialectical Imagination: A History of the Frankfurt School and the Institute of Social Research, 1923–1950* , Boston, MA: Little, Brown and Co.

Lukács, G. (1971) *History and Class Consciousness*, trans. R. Livingston, Cambridge, MA: MIT Press (first published in Hungarian in 1923).

McCarthy, T. (1987) *The Critical Theory of Jürgen Habermas*, Cambridge, MA: MIT Press (first edition 1978).

Marcuse, H. (1964) *One Dimensional Man: Studies in the Ideology of Advanced Industrial Society*, Boston, MA: Beacon Press.

Marx, K. (1965) *Capital: A Critical Analysis of Capitalist Production, Volume I*, ed. F. Engels and trans. S. Moore and E. Aveling, Moscow: Progress Publishers (first published in German in 1867).

Marx, K. (1966) *Capital: A Critique of Political Economy, Volume III: Book III, The Process of Capitalist Production as a Whole*, ed. F. Engels, Moscow: Progress Publishers (first published in 1894).

Marx, K. (1967a) *Capital: A Critique of Political Economy, Volume II: Book II, The Process of Circulation of Capital*, ed. F. Engels and trans. I. Lasker, Moscow: Progress Publishers (first published in German in 1885).

Marx, K. (1967b) 'Theses on Feuerbach', in L. D. Easton and K. H. Guddat (eds) *Writings of the Young Marx on Philosophy and Society*, trans. L. D. Easton and K. H. Guddat, New York: Doubleday, pp. 400–2 (written in 1845 and first published in German in 1888).

Muller, J. (2001) 'Portrait: Jürgen Habermas', *Prospect*, March 1: http://www.prospect-magazine.co.uk/highlights/portrait_muller_mar01/index.html, pp. 1–7.

Sartre, J.-P. (1977) *Life/Situations: Essays Written and Spoken*, trans. P. Auster and L. Davies, New York: Pantheon (first published in French in 1975).

Schick, C. (1994) *The University as Text: Women and the University Context*, Halifax, Canada: Fernwood Press.

Warde, I. (2001) 'For sale: US academic integrity', *Le Monde Diplomatique*, March, p. 13.

Welton, M. (ed.) (1995) *In Defense of the Lifeworld: Critical Perspectives on Adult Learning*, Albany, NY: SUNY Press.

Yarmol-Franko, K. (1988) 'Editorial introduction', *Convergence*, XXI (2/3), pp. 3–4.

# Science in educational research

William E. Tunmer, Jane E. Prochnow and
James W. Chapman, *Massey University, New Zealand*

## INTRODUCTION

We wish to indicate from the outset that, in arguing for the role of science in educational research, we do not espouse methodological monism, the idea that only quantitative or only qualitative methods can be used in carrying out research. As Mayer (2000, p. 39) stated, 'science involves arguing from methodologically sound data, but science is agnostic on the issue of whether the data need to be quantitative or qualitative'. Educational researchers can use either qualitative or quantitative data in scientific ways.

## THE PURPOSE OF EDUCATIONAL RESEARCH

We agree with Eisner (1993) that the major aim of educational research is to improve educational practice so that the lives of those who teach and learn are themselves enhanced. 'We do research to understand', Eisner suggested, and 'we try to understand in order to make our schools better places for both the children and adults who share their lives there' (ibid., p. 10).

One of our major areas of interest is reading intervention research, which focuses on helping children who are experiencing, or are at risk of experiencing, difficulties in learning to read. Because learning to read is basic to success in school, much of our research has concentrated on finding the most effective intervention strategies for preventing or overcoming early reading difficulties and, in so doing, minimizing the potentially serious negative consequences of beginning reading problems.

Relatively small differences in reading ability and reading-related knowledge and skills at the beginning of school often develop into very large generalized differences in school-related skills and academic achievement. Struggling beginning readers not only receive less practice in reading, but soon begin to confront materials that are too difficult for them. As Stanovich (1986, p. 394) pointed out:

Reading becomes less and less pleasurable as the poor reader spends an increasing amount of time in materials beyond his or her capability. He or she avoids reading, and the resultant lack of practice relative to his or her peers widens achievement deficits.

Poor readers are thus prevented from taking advantage of the reciprocally facilitating relationship between reading achievement and other aspects of development such as vocabulary growth, ability to comprehend syntactically complex sentences, and development of richer and more elaborated knowledge bases, all of which facilitate further growth in reading achievement by enabling readers to cope with more difficult materials. As a result of repeated learning failures, many struggling readers also develop negative self-perceptions of ability, and do not try as hard as other children because of their low expectations of success. What begins as a relatively small difference in reading ability can then soon develop into a downward spiral of achievement deficits and negative motivational spin-offs, referred to as 'negative Matthew effects' (Stanovich, 1986). The longer this situation is allowed to continue, the more generalized the deficits become, affecting an increasing number of areas of cognition, self-confidence, motivation and behaviour. Spear-Swerling and Sternberg (1994, p. 101) provided a graphic description of this process: 'Once children become mired in the swamp of negative expectations, lowered motivation, and lowered levels of practice, it becomes increasingly difficult for them to get back to the road to proficient reading.'

Lyon (1993, p. 3) has suggested that the challenge researchers face, in addressing the problem of how to prevent or remedy early reading problems and consequential negative Matthew effects, can be expressed in the form of a question:

Which instructional reading approach or method, or combination of approaches or methods, provided in which setting or combination of settings, under which student-teacher ratio conditions and teacher-student interactions, provided for what period of time and by which type of teacher, have the greatest impact on well-defined elements of reading behaviour and reading-related behaviours, for which children, for how long, and for what reasons?

Our claim is that an overall scientific approach is required to answer this question, an approach that involves both qualitative and quantitative research methods.

## HOW WE CHARACTERIZE OUR RESEARCH AND OURSELVES AS RESEARCHERS

Each of us was trained in either educational psychology or experimental psychology. The defining feature of psychology is that it is the data-based scientific study of human behaviour. Science deals with solvable, or specifiable, problems that are answerable with currently available empirical techniques. It involves making systematic observations to test different hypotheses, explanations or theories that are amenable to being falsified by the observations. The aim of science is to yield generalizable findings that are publicly verifiable and cumulative.

To illustrate the way in which we have used a scientific approach to answer questions relating to educational practice, we provide two examples from our own research, both of which involved collaboration with students and other colleagues. The first example concerns Reading Recovery, a widely used early intervention programme designed by Clay (1993) to help children who are having trouble learning to read after a year of formal reading instruction. We began by asking the following general question: 'Holding the basic parameters of the Reading Recovery programme constant, namely that it involves one-to-one instruction for 30 to 40 minutes per day for 12 to 20 weeks by a specially trained teacher, and that it supplements regular classroom reading instruction, are the specific procedures and instructional strategies of Reading Recovery more effective than any other one-to-one tutoring programme for struggling readers?' In short, is the programme optimal? We then identified what we believed to be a major shortcoming of the instructional philosophy of Reading Recovery, which is that it stresses the importance of using information from many sources in identifying unfamiliar words in text, without recognizing that skills and strategies involving phonological information are of primary importance in beginning literacy development.

Using an alternative theory of how children acquire literacy skills, and why some children experience unusual difficulties in learning to read (Gough and Tunmer, 1986; Tunmer and Hoover, 1992, 1993), we hypothesized that the effectiveness of Reading Recovery could be improved considerably by incorporating into the programme more explicit and systematic training in phonological awareness (the awareness of the sound components of spoken words) and the use of letter-sound patterns in identifying unfamiliar words. A major assumption of the theoretical framework from which our hypothesis was derived is that knowledge and use of phonologically based word identification strategies provide the basic mechanism for acquiring fast, accurate word recognition ability (Ehri, 1997).

Our hypothesis, that the effectiveness of Reading Recovery could be greatly improved by changing the instructional focus of the programme, was confirmed in a carefully designed study that used appropriate empirical techniques (Iversen and Tunmer, 1993). These included the creation of operational definitions of constructs and ways of measuring them, the use of comparison groups along with treatment groups, the unbiased assignment of participants to treatment and comparison groups, and the manipulation of one variable (instructional strategy) while holding other variables constant. The most important finding of the study was that explicit instruction in alphabetic coding skills was much more effective than standard Reading Recovery instruction in which word analysis activities arose incidentally from the child's responses during text reading or writing activities. The conclusions drawn from this initial study were confirmed and extended in a longitudinal study (Chapman *et al.*, 2001). Results indicated that children selected by their schools for Reading Recovery experienced severe difficulties in detecting sound sequences in words (phonological awareness) and in relating letters to sounds during the year prior to admission to the programme. Participation in Reading Recovery did not appreciably reduce these deficiencies, and the failure to remedy these problems severely limited the immediate and long-term effectiveness of the programme. The few children who received some benefit from Reading Recovery were more advanced in phonological processing skills at the beginning of the programme than children who derived little or no benefit from it, and progress in learning to read following participation in Reading Recovery was strongly related to phonological processing skills at discontinuation from the programme.

A second example of research we have conducted using a scientific approach concerns gender differences in academic achievement (Prochnow *et al.*, 2001). On the basis of findings that boys consistently achieve lower than girls on School Certificate results, the (New Zealand) Education Review Office (ERO, 1999) concluded that boys and girls learn and respond in different ways, with boys tending towards surface learning managed with memorization and speed rather than deeper, more sustained learning, which is thought to be typical of girls. The ERO report made the general recommendation that teachers become more knowledgeable about the preferred learning styles of boys and girls, and develop teaching strategies to accommodate these differences.

In considering this issue, we first noted that 'learning styles' is an ill-defined notion. Although there is little disagreement with the idea that teachers should adjust their teaching to accommodate student differences in cultural/family background, prior knowledge and experience, academic ability, personality, motivation, and preferred ways of doing things, the term 'learning style' is narrower in meaning, referring to a more biologically determined, relatively fixed style of perceiving, interacting and responding to the learning environment. A major difficulty with the ERO recommendation is that the available research on learning style as a fixed and readily measurable characteristic of students provides little, if any, support for the idea that assessing children's learning styles and matching to instructional methods significantly influences their learning (Stahl, 1999).

Because learning styles are considered to be fairly stable characteristics of learners, a prediction that follows from the ERO report is that boys should achieve less well than girls from the outset of schooling. An alternative explanation, however, for the finding of later achievement differences between boys and girls, is that there are initially no gender differences in academic achievement, especially in literacy acquisition. Instead, later differences in achievement gradually emerge as a consequence of the tendency of boys to engage more frequently in classroom behaviours that impede their learning (Fergusson and Horwood, 1997). Relatedly, boys may respond more negatively than girls when confronted with difficulties in learning to read, which is the most important learning task confronting young learners in school. Behavioural differences between boys and girls may also provide an explanation for the finding that boys tend to be identified three to four times more frequently than girls as having early learning difficulties, especially reading difficulties (Spear-Swerling and Sternberg, 1996). Recent research reported in the US suggests that school-based identification for placement in remedial programmes is biased in favour of boys because of their tendency to display inappropriate classroom behaviours (Shaywitz *et al.*, 1990).

Data from a longitudinal study of beginning literacy development (Tunmer *et al.*, 1998) were analysed to test four hypotheses arising from these considerations. First, if achievement differences emerge as a consequence (that is, as a *secondary* effect) of classroom behaviour differences and/or differential responses to learning difficulties, then gender differences in academic achievement should not occur until somewhat later in schooling. Second, if the identification of students for remedial programmes in New Zealand is similarly biased by classroom behaviour as in the US, then a significantly greater proportion of boys than girls from our sample should be selected by their schools for Reading Recovery. Third, if the unequal sex ratio in identification of struggling beginning readers results from a referral bias based on classroom behaviour, then there should be no significant differences between boys and girls placed in Reading Recovery on the Observation Survey tests (Clay, 1993) used by schools (in conjunction with teacher judgements) to select children for participation in the Reading Recovery programme. Fourth, if school-based identification of problem readers is biased in favour of boys because of their tendency to display inappropriate classroom behaviours, which may be exacerbated by learning difficulties, then boys identified as poor readers should be rated by their teachers as exhibiting significantly more inappropriate classroom behaviours than girls identified as poor readers.

Analyses of the longitudinal data indicated that all four hypotheses were confirmed. On the basis of these findings, we concluded that rather than attempting to cater for questionable individual 'learning styles', as suggested by ERO (1999), more effective and valid assessment practices should be encouraged to prevent the under-selection of girls for remedial instruction. Additionally, instructional practices for boys should focus on efficient learning strategies, motivation, and strategies for reducing disruptive classroom behaviours.

## METHODOLOGICAL ISSUES THAT CONCERN US MOST

We are especially concerned with the anti-science attitude that is becoming pervasive in the social sciences generally, and in education in particular. As Mayer (2000, p. 38) recently noted, 'our field is actually considering whether or not science is a good idea for educational research'. The following examples from New Zealand literacy research illustrate this attitude:

> New Zealand teachers assume that learning to read is best when it is informal, natural, spontaneous, continuous and enjoyable. So the experimentalists' findings are inevitably difficult to relate to New Zealand classroom programmes. Some of us read and note their elegantly designed studies with interest, but we do not use their findings to undermine a tried philosophy that works well for most children.
>
> (Smith and Elley, 1996, p. 89)

> a classical study involving large numbers of subjects and sophisticated statistical analyses [is] only one form of evidence. This evidence [has] to be weighed against the anecdotal evidence of practising teachers, together with a substantial body of qualitative research that supports the use of context as the primary cue to be used by beginning readers. . . . A narrow experimental research paradigm may not assist classroom practices. What is published in referenced international journals, while satisfying stringent criteria from university-based researchers, may be of little help in the complex world of the classroom.
>
> (Smith, 2000, pp. 141–2)

One manifestation of the rejection of science in educational research is the claim that quantitative and qualitative research methods are fundamentally incompatible, a position referred to as the *incompatibility thesis*. According to this view, quantitative methods fall within the domain of scientific research, whereas qualitative methods are associated with non-scientific research (Mayer, 2000). The central claim of the incompatibility thesis is that quantitative and qualitative methodologies reflect underlying epistemological paradigms that are of necessity mutually exclusive and antagonistic (Smith, 1983; Smith and Heshusius, 1986). The interpretivist paradigm is claimed to support qualitative methods, and the positivist paradigm is claimed to support quantitative methods.

According to the interpretivist paradigm, the scientific study of the social world is impossible because all human activities, including learning and teaching, involve beliefs, values, intentions, and goals that give the activities meaning. But to understand the meanings assigned to activities requires that the meanings be placed within a social context; that is, *interpretations* of human actions are contextually bound. Literacy experiences, for example, are seen as firmly embedded in social contexts that uniquely give meaning to the uses of literacy (Street, 1993). As Taylor (1999, p. 223) argues:

> In positivistic research there is a total lack of recognition that literacy . . . is embedded in everyday activities, or that the use of complex symbolic systems is an everyday phenomenon constitutive of and grounded in the everyday lives of young children and their families.

Because social contexts uniquely give meaning to actions, educational researchers can only provide findings that are bound to particular settings, according to the incompatibility thesis. Smith (1983, p. 12) maintained that 'the essence of understanding is to put oneself in the place of the other – something which is possible if one possesses a degree of empathy with the other or has the disposition to recreate the experiences'. This conceptualization gave rise to the view that educational research should focus on 'the construction and reconstruction of personal and social stories; teachers and learners are storytellers and characters in their own and other's [sic] stories' (Connelly and Clandinin, 1990, p. 2). As Smith and Heshusius (1986, p. 11) put it, perhaps educational research 'is nothing more or less than another voice in the conversation – one that stands alongside those of parents, teachers, and others'.

Sokal and Bricmont (1998, p. 209) draw attention to an immediate difficulty with the interpretivist paradigm:

> If all discourses are merely 'stories' or 'narrations', and none is more objective or truthful than another, then one must concede that the worst sexist or racist prejudices and the most reactionary socio-economic theories are 'equally valid', at least as descriptions or analyses of the real world (assuming that one admits the existence of a real world). Clearly, relativism is an extremely weak foundation on which to build a criticism of the existing social order.

In response to the claim that developing and fluent readers/ writers cannot be (scientifically) studied separately from the society that gives meaning to their uses of literacy, Gough (1995, p. 81) asks, why not?

> When I watch a Wimbledon tennis match, I separate those players from the society which gives meaning to their uses of their racquets; I am interested in the players and their game, not that society. Why can't I do the same with readers?

According to Gough's view, then, literacy is an autonomous set of cognitive and linguistic skills that enable individuals in different cultures to do different things in response to cultural demands. If literacy is defined solely in terms of its uses in social contexts, then there would be as many definitions of literacy as there are social groups (Tunmer *et al.*, 1999).

Another major shortcoming of the thesis is that it incorrectly links objective-quantitative research to positivism, an epistemological position that was rejected decades ago as an accurate portrayal of the scientific method. Positivism defined truth as a correspondence between language and an independently existing reality. The structures of elementary propositions were thought to correspond in some way with the structures of objects in the state of affairs in the world that make the propositions true. The core tenet of positivism was the verifiability principle, the idea that statements are meaningful if and only if they can be verified empirically. The verifiability principle, and positivism more generally, have been thoroughly repudiated. As Howe and Eisenhart (1990, p. 3) pointed out:

> the picture of empirical science envisioned by positivism, in which observation could be strictly separated from and remain untainted by the purposes that animate the conduct and evaluation of scientific investigation, has been replaced by the notion that all scientific investigation is inherently theory-laden. Consequently, because all scientific investigation is inherently laden with theory, inherently an outgrowth of human purposes and theoretical constructions, it is, broadly speaking, inherently interpretive.

In recent years, support for the incompatibility thesis has fallen, as there are currently no strong pragmatic or epistemological reasons for viewing quantitative and qualitative approaches as mutually exclusive. As Mayer (2000, p. 39) argues, 'Scientific research can involve either quantitative or qualitative data; what characterizes research as scientific is the way that data are used to support arguments.' Quantitative and qualitative approaches are not only compatible, but often mutually supportive (Gage, 1989). In principle then, a thoroughgoing integration of qualitative and quantitative methods is not only possible, but highly desirable.

But suppose these arguments are rejected, and the interpretivist claim is accepted that educational research can only provide findings that are firmly embedded in social contexts, in which case researchers would be restricted to using qualitative methods like narrative enquiry, or storytelling. Where would this leave us? Nowhere, we believe. To paraphrase Cizek (1995, p. 27), if research doesn't relate to anything we currently know (that is, if it isn't theory-driven), if it doesn't address a question of interest posed by the researcher (that is, if it isn't hypothesis-testing), or if it doesn't produce knowledge that others can use because it is *bound* to a particular setting (that is, if it isn't generalizable), then how can it even be called research? Even critical theorists who engage in discourse analysis are guided by hypotheses that are generalizable, such as that the ultimate aim of recent government policy in New Zealand was to privatize education. This hypothesis can in turn be placed within a broader socio-economic theory of the distribution of power and wealth in the country.

In short, the incompatibility thesis is simply wrong. Educational research is more than just telling stories. As Mayer (2000, p. 39) warns:

it would be a grave mistake for educational researchers to turn their backs on science. It is both misleading and unwise to link the call for qualitative research methods to the movement to diminish the role of science in educational research. While the former reflects a potentially valuable contribution to our field, the latter reflects a fatal leap into the abyss of relativism.

Another major area of concern we have about educational research is the tendency for many published articles to be saturated with semi-meaningless jargon, especially those that adopt a radical postmodernist perspective in which the rationalist tradition is rejected and replaced by cognitive and cultural relativism. As the philosophers Quine and Ullian (1970, p. 79) argue:

We must be wary ... of explanations couched in fancy language. It is a basic maxim for serious thought that whatever there is to be said can, through perseverance, be said clearly. Something that persistently resists clear expression, far from meriting reverence for its profundity, merits suspicion. Pressing the question 'What does this really say?' can reveal that the fancy language masked a featureless face.

Sokal and Bricmont (1998) argue along similar lines in their discussion of those aspects of postmodernism that have had a negative impact on the humanities and social sciences. These include:

a fascination with obscure discourses; an epistemic relativism linked to a generalized skepticism toward modern science; an excessive interest in subjective beliefs independently of their truth or falsity; and an emphasis on discourse and language as opposed to the facts to which those discourses refer (or, worse, the rejection of the very idea that facts exist or that one may refer to them).

(p. 183)

Sokal and Bricmont maintain that 'There is a huge difference between discourses that are difficult because of the inherent nature of their subject and those whose vacuity or banality is carefully hidden behind deliberately obscure prose' (ibid., p. 186).

Sokal (1996a) demonstrated the reality of 'fashionable nonsense' by submitting an article for publication that parodied the language of a leading postmodernist cultural studies journal. The title of his article, which was intended to be a joke, was 'Transgressing the boundaries: toward a transformative hermeneutics of quantum gravity'. Amazingly, the article was reviewed, accepted, and published by *Social Text* in 1996. Sokal (1996b) justified his hoax as an attempt to expose postmodernists' misguided views about science; namely, that scientific theories are nothing more than 'myths', 'narratives', or 'social constructions'. Science has its limits, but its positive features and remarkable achievements cannot be denied.

## ASPECTS OF DOING RESEARCH THAT WE FIND MOST DIFFICULT

Finding sufficient time to carry out quality research is becoming increasingly difficult, as steadily shrinking resources have resulted in heavier teaching loads and greater administrative responsibilities than in the past. Most areas of psychology relevant to education are continuing to develop rapidly, which sometimes makes it difficult to keep up with the latest research findings and theoretical advances. Also, some recently developed theoretical tools (for example, parallel distributed processing models, neural net theory) and data analysis procedures (for example, structural equation modelling) require the development of high levels of technical competence.

## IMPACT OF OUR RESEARCH ON EDUCATIONAL POLICY AND PRACTICE

The research we have reported contributed significantly to two unanimously agreed recommendations of the (New Zealand) Literacy Experts Group (Ministry of Education, 1999a) to the Literacy

Taskforce (Ministry of Education, 1999b). These are listed below:

Literacy Experts Group Recommendation 1:

We do not support the view that beginning reading instruction should focus on teaching children to rely on sentence context cues as the primary strategy for identifying unfamiliar words in text. Rather, greater attention needs to be focussed on the development of word-level skills and strategies in beginning reading instruction, including the development of phonological awareness.

(Ministry Education, 1999a, p. 6)

Literacy Experts Group Recommendation 9:

We recommend that Reading Recovery places greater emphasis on explicit instruction in phonological awareness and the use of spelling-to-sound patterns in recognising unfamiliar words in text.

(Ibid.)

Our research on beginning literacy development has also been cited in reviews of research on best practice in teaching literacy, commissioned by various government agencies, such as the United States Congress. More recently, two of us were invited to speak to the (New Zealand) Parliamentary Select Committee on Science and Education Inquiry into the Teaching of Reading. With regard to the future, we are hopeful that the work described earlier (Prochnow *et al.*, 2001) on gender differences in academic achievement will result in the Education Review Office withdrawing its unsupported recommendation that teachers should develop instructional strategies to accommodate 'learning style' differences between boys and girls.

## KEY POINTS WE WISH TO CONVEY TO NEW RESEARCHERS

1. Develop a solid understanding of critical meta-theoretical issues in the philosophy of science.
2. Do not adopt a radical postmodernist view of science.
3. Reject the incompatibility thesis.
4. Understand that scientific research can involve either quantitative or qualitative data (or both).
5. Learn how to develop a clearly defined research question that stems from a well-developed theoretical framework.
6. Always let the research question dictate the research methodology, not the other way round.

7. Follow Quine and Ullian's dictum that 'whatever there is to be said can, through perseverance, be said clearly' (1970, p. 79).
8. Avoid naïve, retrograde empiricism (that is, hypotheses without theory).
9. Learn the basics of research design and statistics, even if only to understand the published research of others.
10. Realize that educational research is more than just telling stories or analysing discourses.

## REFERENCES

Chapman, J. W., Tunmer, W. E. and Prochnow, J. E. (2001) 'Does success in the Reading Recovery program depend on developing proficiency in phonological processing skills? A longitudinal study in a whole language instructional context', *Scientific Studies of Reading*, 5 (2), pp. 141–76.

Cizek, G. (1995) 'Crunchy granola and the hegemony of the narrative', *Educational Researcher*, 24 (2), pp. 26–8.

Clay, M. M. (1993) *Reading Recovery*, Auckland, New Zealand: Heinemann.

Connelly, F. M. and Clandinin, D. J. (1990) 'Stories of experience and narrative inquiry', *Educational Researcher*, 19 (5), pp. 2–14.

Education Review Office (ERO) (1999) *The Achievement of Boys*, Wellington, New Zealand: Education Review Office.

Ehri, L. C. (1997) 'Sight word learning in normal readers and dyslexics', in B. Blachman (ed.) *Foundations of Reading Acquisition and Dyslexia: Implications for Early Intervention*, Mahwah, NJ: Lawrence Erlbaum Associates, pp. 163–89.

Eisner, E. W. (1993) 'Forms of understanding and the future of educational research', *Educational Researcher*, 22 (7), pp. 5–11.

Fergusson, D. M. and Horwood, L. J. (1997) 'Gender differences in educational achievement in a New Zealand birth cohort', *New Zealand Journal of Educational Studies*, 32 (1), pp. 3–96.

Gage, N. L. (1989) 'The paradigm wars and their aftermath: a "historical" sketch of research on teaching since 1989', *Educational Researcher*, 18 (7), pp. 4–10.

Gough, P. B. (1995) 'The new literacy: caveat emptor', *Journal of Research in Reading*, 18 (2), pp. 79–86.

Gough, P. B. and Tunmer, W. E. (1986) 'Decoding, reading and reading disability', *Remedial and Special Education*, 7 (2), pp. 6–10.

Howe, K. and Eisenhart, M. (1990) 'Standards for qualitative (and quantitative) research: a prolegomenon', *Educational Researcher*, 19 (4), pp. 2–9.

Iversen, A. and Tunmer, W. (1993) 'Phonological processing skills and the Reading Recovery program', *Journal of Educational Psychology*, 85 (1), pp. 112–26.

Lyon, G. R. (1993) *Treatment Effectiveness for the Learning Disabled*, Bethesda, MD: National Institute of Child Health and Human Development.

Mayer, R. E. (2000) 'What is the place of science in educational research?', *Educational Researcher*, 29 (6), pp. 38–9.

Ministry of Education (1999a) *Literacy Experts Group Report to the Secretary for Education*, Wellington, New Zealand: Ministry of Education.

Ministry of Education (1999b) *Report on the Literacy Taskforce: a report prepared for the Minister of Education*, Wellington, New Zealand: Ministry of Education.

Prochnow, J. E., Tunmer, W. E., Chapman, J. W. and Greaney, K. T. (2001) 'A longitudinal study of early literacy achievement and gender', *New Zealand Journal of Educational Studies*, 36 (2), pp. 221–36.

Quine, W. V. and Ullian, J. S. (1970) *The Web of Belief*, New York: Random House.

Shaywitz, S. E., Shaywitz, B. A., Fletcher, J. M. and Escobar, M. (1990) 'Prevalence of reading disability in boys and girls', *Journal of the American Medical Association*, 264 (8), pp. 998–1002.

Smith, J. (2000) 'The Literacy Taskforce in context', in J. Soler and J. Smith (eds) *Literacy in New Zealand: Practices, Politics and Policy since 1900*, Auckland, New Zealand: Pearson Education, pp. 134–43.

Smith, J. K. (1983) 'Quantitative versus qualitative research: an attempt to clarify the issue', *Educational Researcher*, 12 (2), pp. 6–13.

Smith, J. K. and Heshusius, L. (1986) 'Closing down the conversation: the end of the quantitative-qualitative debate among educational inquirers', *Educational Researcher*, 15 (1), pp. 4–12.

Smith, J. W. A. and Elley, W. B. (1996) 'Making sense out of nonsense', *New Zealand Journal of Educational Studies*, 31 (1), pp. 85–9.

Sokal, A. (1996a) 'Transgressing the boundaries: toward a transformative hermeneutics of quantum gravity', *Social Text*, 46/47 (Spring/Summer), pp. 217–52.

Sokal, A. (1996b) 'A physicist experiments with cultural studies', *Lingua Franca*, May/June, pp. 62–4.

Sokal, A. and Bricmont, J. (1998) *Fashionable Nonsense: Postmodern Intellectuals' Abuse of Science*, New York: Picador.

Spear-Swerling, L. and Sternberg, R. J. (1994) 'The road not taken: an integrative theoretical model of reading disability', *Journal of Learning Disabilities*, 27 (2), pp. 91–103, 122.

Spear-Swerling, L. and Sternberg, R. J. (1996) *Off track: when poor readers become 'learning disabled'*, Boulder, CO: Westview Press.

Stahl, S. (1999) 'Different strokes for different folks?: a critique of learning styles', *American Educator*, 23 (Fall), pp. 27–31.

Stanovich, K. E. (1986) 'Matthew effects in reading: some consequences of individual differences in the acquisition of literacy', *Reading Research Quarterly*, 21 (4), pp. 360–406.

Street, B. V. (1993) 'The new literacy studies: guest editorial', *Journal of Research in Reading*, 16 (2), pp. 81–97.

Taylor, D. (1999) 'Beginning to read and the spin doctors of science: an excerpt', *Language Arts*, 76 (3), pp. 217–31.

Tunmer, W. E., Chapman, J. W., Ryan, H. and Prochnow, J. E. (1998) 'The importance of providing beginning readers with explicit training in phonological processing skills', *Australian Journal of Learning Disabilities*, 3 (2), pp. 4–14.

Tunmer, W. E. and Hoover, W. (1992) 'Cognitive and linguistics factors in learning to read', in P. Gough, L. Ehri and R. Treiman (eds) *Reading Acquisition*, Hillsdale, NJ: Lawrence Erlbaum, pp. 175–214.

Tunmer, W. and Hoover, W. (1993) 'Components of variance models of language-related factors in reading disability: a conceptual overview', in M. Joshi and C. K. Leong (eds) *Reading Disabilities: Diagnosis and Component Processes*, Dordrecht, The Netherlands: Kluwer Academic Publishers, pp. 135–73.

Tunmer, W. E., Prochnow, J. E. and Chapman, J. W. (1999) 'Science can inform educational practice: the case of literacy', *New Zealand Annual Review of Education*, 9, pp. 133–56.

# —7

# Research in a bicultural context: the case of Aotearoa/New Zealand

Patricia Maringi G. Johnston, *Te Whare Wananga o Awanuiarangi, New Zealand*

## METHODOLOGICAL, CULTURAL AND ETHICAL ISSUES THAT CONCERN ME MOST

Ideas about research, and what counts as research in Aotearoa/New Zealand, have historically been founded on unchallenged and unquestioned Western frameworks and norms. These have represented scientific rationality as 'pure', 'objective' and 'neutral', unbiased (yet unspoken) and equally applicable to all (Waitere-Ang and Johnston, 1999, p. 5). Furthermore, the act and the outcomes of research have reinforced the 'pure', objective scientific rationality, while presenting the methodologies and methods of indigenous groups as inferior.

Western frameworks, however, are as biased as those they claim to surpass, because they operate as a universalizing blueprint that names every world according to their interpretations of how those worlds exist. The contribution offered by 'others' to the research fraternity is often bound by the Western framework; it may be dismissed, dismantled, consumed or regurgitated in a typically Western way. For example, research outcomes are presented as 'findings' that often name us, claim us and gain ownership over our knowledge, our images and our representations:

> for such is the power of research – the power to lay claim to our knowledge and position it as inferior; the power to know us and to name us in specific ways; the power to represent us as 'problems', deficits, deprived and disadvantaged.
>
> (Waitere-Ang and Johnston, 1999, p. 4)

Colonial centrism has influenced how groups around the globe have been perceived by their imperial colonizers. Theoretical beliefs about Maori[1] have been based on 'research' about races, and the assumption that Maori are a primitive race, operating from an inferior cultural and linguistic base (Johnston, 1999). Within Aotearoa, Maori were positioned in opposition to, and as *different* from, Pakeha[2] (Johnston, 1998). Thus, accounts of research are the result of a colonizing gaze (hooks, 1992) that centres on us as the problem, that explains us in terms of how we deviate from a particular norm-reference point (Johnston, 1999). These accounts are often 'clinical', and the research findings are presented as neutral; but they are dangerous because they represent us in ways that do not accord with how we see ourselves, and are actually representations of Pakeha bias. Linda Smith, following Patricia Grace (1985), has argued that representations of Maori in books:

(1) . . . do not reinforce our values, actions, customs, culture and identity; (2) when they tell us only about others they are saying that we do not exist; (3) they may be writing about us but are writing things which are untrue; and (4) they are writing about us but saying negative and insensitive things which tell us that we are not good.

(Smith, 1999, p. 35)

While Smith points out that Grace was referring to school texts and journals, her comments about the ways that Maori are represented are just as applicable to academic writing. They are also relevant to research. The outcomes of research – the projects, data and publications – have created problems for Maori because they have reinforced prejudice, stereotypes, and 'common-sense' explanations of who we are. In many instances, this type of research has misrepresented and distorted our lives; it has been used to describe us, label us and explain our appalling circumstances of unemployment, jail-occupancy and educational under-achievement.

Because of these colonial frameworks, Maori knowledge and practices were (and continue to be) construed as inferior, as having little worth (or contribution to make) to New Zealand society – except to add 'spice' to an otherwise flavourless smorgasbord. The repercussions of this viewpoint have had a devastating impact on Maori in terms of how our knowledge and world-views are presented, and misrepresented, through research projects/discussions and negotiations. Research in New Zealand is shaped by a number of issues, including: what counts as research, how research is conducted, who can talk about the researched. These factors are controlled by and supportive of the dominant Pakeha culture because 'Most research is carried out by Pakeha people; the whole definition of Research has been prescripted by Pakeha people; various gate-keeping sanctions are available to maintain Pakeha control over "what is counted as valid research"' (Smith, 1986, p. 1).

Moving away from entrenched research practices and traditional ideas about research has not been easy. Basic ideas about research have to be challenged at a number of levels. For example, Pakeha research, according to Smith (ibid., p. 3), has largely been about satisfying the need to know – extending the boundaries of knowledge – research for the sake of research. Research of this type has mostly served the interests of those undertaking the work – academics, researchers, and students seeking a degree.

Historically, our experiences of being 'the researched' have been neither pleasant nor beneficial. As Ranginui Walker (1980, p. 231) has so aptly stated, what has happened in terms of research and Maori is that

> Maori education [has] become the happy hunting ground of academics as neophytes cut their research teeth on the hapless Maori. It has the advantage that Maoris are in the subordinate position, with little or no social power to keep out prying Pakehas. Furthermore, being marginal to the social mainstream, Maoris are not in a position to challenge the findings of published research, let alone the esoteric findings of academic elites.

As a Maori researcher and university-based educationist, issues about research impact on my every waking moment. Research has contributed to how members of the dominant Pakeha group might engage/disengage with me, react to/ignore me, think about/not think about me. Research has reinforced prejudicial beliefs and practices with regard to who I am as Maori and, therefore, what I might believe and be capable of doing. Academics, researchers and other educationists can (and often do) consider my contributions to be invalid, or substandard, because I am located at the 'business-end' of research discussions and debates. Even so, Maori do not disengage from debate and discussion. As an indigenous researcher – or, to use Gramsci's terminology, as an 'organic intellectual' – I'm involved in 'disrupting hegemonic spaces' as a way of challenging and contesting the taken-for-granted assumptions that members of the dominant group hold about Maori, about research, and about Maori research in general (Johnston and McLeod, 2001).

Consider, for example, a question posed by Smith (1999, p. 183): 'What happens to research when the researched become the researchers?' In Aotearoa/New Zealand this question is being answered; those (like myself) who were once research subjects are now entering the academy as students, academics and researchers. Our involvement in research challenges theoretical explanations of narrow problem-solving approaches (Cox, 1981) to issues such as educational under-achievement, unemployment and poor health; it also presents solutions that are Maori in perspective, which take into account Maori knowledge, language and tikanga (culture).

The practices and methods/methodology associated with research are also persistently being challenged and contested by those Maori who, to all intents and purposes, have historically been defined as the research subjects, the studied, the illustrated, the 'judged' (Said, 1985). Smith (1999) has argued that the ownership of research – as an archive, as a Western framework, as a methodology with specific research methods – can no longer be considered to be neutral, objective and pure, with unspoken, unbiased objectives. Supplanting those 'scientific rationalities', and views of objectivity, are research practices that incorporate the 'researched' into the equation – as able participants who can engage/disengage and contribute in ways that research has historically been unwilling to countenance because of ideas about the contamination of data and the 'need for objectivity'.

Increasingly, for example, Maori communities are declining to participate in research that does not allow them meaningful input or control over research design, methods and the dissemination of results. Ownership of the information, and even the contributions that Maori make in terms of what happens to our tissue samples, experiences and knowledge, are now being carefully negotiated. Research focusing on Maori as 'the problem' is effectively being closed down, and researchers who try to operate with this assumption are being shut out.

## THE PURPOSE OF EDUCATIONAL RESEARCH

As an indigenous educator in a bicultural context, I see research as an educative process with a number of key objectives. The first objective is to explore and discover potential solutions to educational problems for groups like Maori. This includes expanding, challenging and contributing to debate, and developing the field of research knowledge and practices to include Maori frameworks.

The second objective is to contest the relations of dominance. This involves challenging the ways in which research has described us, humiliated us, and enforced our subordination. Challenges to relations of power and authority, and to assumptions about whose interests are served by research, are integral to what I do as a researcher. Significantly, most of the research in which I engage is related to, or specifically focused on, Maori. As a Maori researcher, I think about the ways in which research serves (or does not serve) to inform Maori, and to affect Maori life-chances and choice. In particular, I think about how research advantages or disadvantages Maori, and why. I also consider the politics associated with the research, and how complementary or opposing knowledge systems relate to each other, and in what context one takes precedence over the other, and why. I engage in a process of informing, while also challenging and contesting taken-for-granted assumptions within which specific research contexts, methodologies and methods may be operating.

As a means to this end, I also seek to provide answers for those who are disadvantaged by the 'business-end' activities associated with research, and as such one of my roles is to engage in consciousness-raising for both Maori and Pakeha. This involves providing Maori with information about the research process, engaging Maori as research advisers and consultants, and considering (and incorporating) ideas and methods of operation which derive from those involved in the research as participants and recipients. Such processes utilize what is referred to as a Kaupapa Maori methodology, a total philosophical, theoretical and practical research paradigm that is premised on a world-view that is distinctly Maori, drawing on Maori knowledge, experiences, tikanga (culture) and language. Kaupapa Maori approaches are distinctive because they are generated by the context and the people involved, and will thus differ from context to context in recognition of different experiences, cultural practices and knowledge bases.

Kaupapa Maori methodology clearly features principles of accountability and responsibility for the researchers and the researched – principles that are not necessarily a part of conventional research methodology. Smith (1999, p. 120) has identified some of these:

1. Aroha ki te tangata (a respect for people).
2. Kanohi kitea (the seen face – that is, present yourself to people face to face).
3. Titiro, whakarongo . . . korero (look, listen . . . speak).
4. Manaaki ki te tangata (share and host people, be generous).

5. Kia tupato (be cautious [in terms of confidentiality and protection of both researcher and researched]).
6. Kaua e takahia te mana o te tangata (do not trample on the *mana* [authority] of people).
7. Kaua e mahaki (do not flaunt your knowledge [as academic institutions encourage you to do]).

Teorongonui Keelan (2001, p. 53) argues that these features are part of a set of cultural imperatives about how one should conduct oneself in the research process, and how the collection of data should be carried out. They are underpinned by protocol (including reciprocity, accountability and responsibility) that moves well beyond the parameters within which research is often located. They also move well beyond the experiences of Pakeha researchers, as such protocols are based on insider knowledge and experiences related to tikanga.

For Pakeha, my consciousness-raising role is one that includes challenging their perceptions in order to shift the parameters of how they might think both about research and about how Maori might engage with it/them. For example, there has been a major shift in the practices of research agencies (in response to challenges laid down by Maori about the inequities of research practices), and Maori are now involved in the research process in ways that are more appropriate. Such research aims to sensitize environments/ individuals/groups towards matters Maori, based on cultural/ personal recognition of Maori cultural differences. Thus, we see the inclusion of ethnically diverse researchers, the acceptance of verbal (rather than written) consent as a culturally sensitive way to access groups, and perhaps the leaving of koha.[3]

Such forms of inclusion are, however, recognized by Maori researchers as only the first step in a developing framework, because such inclusion is still symptomatic of the tendency of Pakeha to treat Maori as marginal to decision-making, and as addenda to processes and frameworks that have already been established. These processes include the research methodologies which define issues such as how Maori should be represented, who is involved, and how the research findings will be disseminated. Many of these are already in place before Maori are invited to participate, so our participation has already been thought about in specific ways without consultation and without our permission.

I have argued elsewhere (Johnston, 1998) that historically, theory, praxis and research have not been empowering for Maori. Our inclusion within research has not created changes to educational under-achievement, poverty or high incidences of suicide or incarceration. We are often invited to participate in policy reform processes, teaching and research, but the positions to which we are assigned do not permit full cultural representation of Maori viewpoints and norms. Nor does our inclusion shape the research agenda.

A question that Waitere-Ang and I have asked is, 'If *all* inclusion means is the addition of researchers that look different, have you really included me at all?' (Waitere-Ang and Johnston, 1999). Such questions serve to challenge those in positions of power to consider the levels at which Maori will be involved, when consultation should occur, and what is meant by consultation and participation.

My research is located within a philosophy of empowerment. Research should not be merely a 'happy hunting ground' for academics (Walker, 1980); rather, it should empower those groups who have previously been marginalized, oppressed and disempowered by research. Patti Lather refers to this as the 'politics of empowerment', which she describes as

> the development of research approaches which empower those involved to change as well as understand the world. My usage of empowerment opposes the reduction of the term as it is used in the current fashion of individual self-assertion, upward mobility and the psychological experience of feeling powerful. . . . I use empowerment to mean analyzing ideas about the causes of powerlessness, recognizing systemic oppressive forces, and acting both individually and collectively to change the conditions of our lives.
>
> (Lather, 1991, pp. 3–4)

I believe strongly that research should enable those whom the research is about/for to take control of their own circumstances, to create understanding and possibilities for optimism and change – ultimately to take greater control of their destinies. Such research will generate practices designed to transform social relations, to overcome domination and subordination. In effect, I engage in a revolutionary practice that seeks to change research frameworks and ideas about what counts as research – a pedagogical and politically transformative process for both Maori and Pakeha. I believe that researchers should be accountable to those who are researched, which means that researchers may have to disseminate their research in ways that more accurately reflect the cultural perspectives (and sensitivities) of their research communities. Often, however, what happens in a research context is that the researcher is positioned as the all-knowing, all-seeing expert, and her or his subjects as unknowing and naïve. Consequently, while researchers may gain recognition and prestige from their activities, the researched communities – particularly those who are Maori – remain powerless, uninformed, and unable to facilitate change.

## HOW I CHARACTERIZE MYSELF AS A RESEARCHER

As a researcher, I draw on a theoretical (and practical) position which incorporates a critical theory approach that is political in context. As Cox (1981, p. 129) has stated, critical theory is

> critical in the sense that it stands apart from the prevailing order of the world and asks how that order came about. Critical theory . . . does not take institutions and social and power relations for granted but calls them into question by concerning itself with their origins and how and whether they might be in the process of changing. It is directed towards an appraisal of the very framework for action, or problematic, which problem-solving theory accepts as its parameters. Critical theory is directed to the social and political complex as a whole rather than to the separate parts. As a matter of practice, critical theory, like problem-solving theory, takes as its starting point some aspect or particular sphere of human activity. . . . the critical approach leads towards the construction of a larger picture of the whole of which the initially contemplated part is just one component, and seeks to understand the processes of change in which both parts and whole are involved.

My stance is thus one of activism, contestation, resistance and protest, which challenges what counts as research. This is also underpinned by Kaupapa Maori theory and practice (outlined earlier), which places Maori at the centre. It recognizes structural and cultural dynamics, and regards them as pivotal to how Maori issues are addressed within research. More importantly, a Kaupapa Maori approach is underpinned by a philosophy which aims to redress the unequal power relations between Maori and Pakeha – by incorporating appropriate decision-making forums for Maori.

## ASPECTS OF DOING RESEARCH THAT I FIND MOST DIFFICULT

One of the most challenging and difficult aspects of doing research is working with non-Maori/Pakeha in a Maori context. This is challenging for a number of reasons. First, even though the intention may be to work *with* Maori communities, the research may already have been developed from an *on* Maori perspective (that is, Maori as the subjects to be studied), which is a difficult focus to change.

Second, my participation as a researcher may have been sought merely to confer credibility on a Pakeha project involving Maori as the target group. I have learned to avoid situations of this sort, not least because the research is likely to have been developed within a Western framework, and my participation is likely to be marginal from the outset.

Third, my role can end up being that of 'cultural educator' rather than researcher. I might be required to educate colleagues/researchers about Maori culture, practices, experiences, knowledge and so on. This can become frustrating, as I may be asked to justify practices and beliefs that I take for granted and consider to be normal.

## WORKING WITH STUDENT RESEARCHERS AND ACADEMIC COLLEAGUES

Increasingly, as an educator, my work has been designed to encourage students and colleagues to consider the moral and ethical issues associated with bicultural or inter-cultural/cross-cultural research. For example, I currently lecture on a research methods paper that is compulsory for all masters students, and I contribute to an education doctorate programme. The masters paper in particular is taken by students with diverse backgrounds, in terms of their undergraduate degrees, ethnicity, research experience, and understanding of research methods, methodologies and practices. As part of their assessment, students are required to submit a research proposal which, in principle, will be developed into the major research component (project/dissertation or thesis) for their degree.

I present students with a range of questions developed from the writings and ideas of a number of Maori researchers with whom I have worked. These questions are designed to encourage students to think about the nature of research, what type of research they might undertake, with whom they might wish to engage and why. More specifically, I encourage them to consider whether the research should be conducted at all, and, if so, on what terms they will interact with the research participants.

These questions include:

1. *What are the basic assumptions about the research and yourself as the researcher?* In addressing this question, I outline four approaches that researchers can adopt about the research context, and of which I am highly critical. They are: (i) 'observing the scene' – whereby the researcher thinks of herself as invisible and not implicated in, or having an influence on, the research setting; (ii) 'I'm not involved' – the researcher accepts no responsibility for the research, and is not accountable to the research participants; (iii) 'I'm the boss' – the all-knowing, all-seeing researcher (which I also refer to as the 'academic arrogance' approach); and (iv) 'rape research' (self-explanatory).

2. *How is the research conducted?* For example, what is the relationship between the researcher and the researched? How was participation initiated, interpreted and enacted? Have you consulted with Maori?

3. *Who has designed the research methods?* Are they culturally appropriate? How do you know?

4. *Whose methodologies drive the research?* Are they culturally appropriate? How do you know? Can you do this research?

5. *Who designed the questions?* Are they culturally appropriate? How do you know? Have you consulted with Maori?

6. *Whose interests are served by the research?* Will the community benefit from your work? Does it enable participants to move forward? Who is driving the research? Why are you doing the research? Is your heart clear? Do you have ulterior motives? (Smith, 1999)

7. *Who owns the research?* To whom does the information belong?

8. *Who benefits from the research?* Will the research make a difference?

9. *Who will carry out the research?* Are you familiar with the culture and context in which you are engaging? Will you create havoc or damage? Are you the right person to do the research?

10. *Who will write up the research?* Have you misinterpreted something? Who will check your work?

11. *How will the results be disseminated?* Will the research merely sit on a shelf somewhere? How will you feed the information back to the participants?

12. *What is your role, and what responsibility do you have to the research and research participants?* How will you thank them? Will there be a need for 'damage control'? If you 'stuff it up', how will you address that situation? Who will you ask? Have you thought this through carefully? If not, start again.

These questions always provoke much discussion, and students always pick up the point that challenges to the traditional view of research have been levelled at researchers who show little or no accountability and responsibility to the groups they research. Accountability and responsibility to the research subjects is increasingly required, as part of the research design, by groups such as Maori. They wish to secure greater control over the information and how it is disseminated, greater control over how participation will occur, and greater accountability to those who are the target and focus of the research.

## CONCLUDING COMMENTS

At a seminar that Waitere-Ang and I led at the University of Bath (Waitere-Ang and Johnston, 1999), we discussed research in terms of accountability and responsibility to research participants. Our views were challenged by academics who supported traditional research relationships. This tradition upholds

- the position of the researcher as expert, and all-powerful;
- the tendency for research to be done by white middle-class men, studying and creating a literate (as opposed to an oral) account for a myriad of less powerful 'others' – that is, research driven by the interests and values of the already powerful; and
- the assumption that objectivity is achievable and desirable.

The reasons given in opposition to our arguments centred on contamination of data, and being objective and neutral. However, we understood the nature of the argument to be about power and control. Our struggle was (and is) to contest dominant ways of knowing and representing the world (Smith, 1999), to show that the academic terrain is negotiable, that there are legitimate methodologies, pedagogies and knowledge other than those which currently dominate academia. We were, in effect, questioning deep-seated ideas about the 'right' of academics to do research.

We were also challenged about what counts as inclusion for Maori researchers. We explained our position, and emphasized that Maori are no longer passive in the face of research that is being conducted *on* them, that the shift is towards research conducted *with* Maori communities, groups and individuals. We acknowledged that non-Maori continue to undertake research on Maori communities, groups and individuals, but what has changed is that researchers are increasingly being expected to devise research that involves Maori in decision-making roles.

Research in New Zealand is being shaped by ideas that challenge the subordinate position of Maori. Issues of power and authority, and whose interests are being served by research, are more widely recognized as components of research ethics. As, too, is the idea that Maori should be involved in research at decision-making levels. There is, however, still a long way to go. The value and beliefs systems that underpin what counts as research are still firmly embedded in Western frameworks and scientific rationality. The principal challenge for researchers and educators like myself is to address the politics of research by continually asking questions, like 'Whose interests are being served?' Only when the political (as opposed to neutral/normal) nature of the whole research activity is addressed – right down to the fundamental practices and beliefs that underpin such activity – can we hope to see research that equates to empowerment, choices and life-chances for Maori.

## NOTES

1. Indigenous people of Aotearoa/New Zealand.
2. A name that referred originally to British settlers and colonists, but is used more contemporarily to refer to those who are not Maori.
3. The term 'koha' is loosely defined as a 'gift' (not necessarily tangible), often given as a token of appreciation for something someone has done. Culturally, it is also part of a reciprocity process that acknowledges the occurrence of an exchange. For example, when interviewing participants for research purposes, koha is an acknowledgement that information has been gifted to the researcher. Koha is also the reciprocal acknowledgement of that process.

## REFERENCES

Cox, R. W. (1981) 'Social forces, states and world orders: beyond international relations theory', *Millennium: Journal of International Studies*, 10 (2), pp. 126–55.

Grace, P. (1985) 'Books are dangerous', paper presented at the Fourth Early Childhood Convention, Wellington, New Zealand.

hooks, b. (1992) *Black Looks: Race and Representation*, Boston, MA: South End Press.

Johnston, P. (1998) 'He ao rereke: education policy and Maori educational under-achievement – mechanisms of power and difference', unpublished PhD thesis in education, University of Auckland, New Zealand.

Johnston, P. (1999) 'Our identity is not of our own making: de-constructing conceptions of identity and difference', paper presented at the conference on 'Nationalism, Identity, Minority Rights', University of Bristol, UK, 16–19 September.

Johnston, P. and McLeod, J. (2001) 'Disrupting hegemonic spaces: challenging teachers to think indigenized', paper presented at the conference of the Canadian Indian Native Studies Association, University of Saskatchewan, Canada, 30 May to 1 June.

Keelan, T. (2001) 'E tipu e rea: the examination of the process used to design a taiohi Maori development framework', unpublished MA thesis in development studies, University of Auckland, New Zealand.

Lather, P. (1991) *Getting Smart: Feminist Research and Pedagogy With/In the Postmodern*, New York: Routledge.

Said, E. (1985) *Orientalism: Western Concepts of the Orient*, Auckland, New Zealand: Penguin Books.

Smith, L. (1986) 'Te rapunga I te ao marama: the search for the world of light', in G. Smith (compiler) *Nga Kete Wananga, Te Kete Tuarua*, Auckland, New Zealand: Maori Studies Department, Auckland College of Education.

Smith, L. (1999) *Decolonizing Methodologies: Research and Indigenous Peoples*, London: Zed Books.

Waitere-Ang, H. and Johnston, P. (1999) 'If *all* inclusion in research means is the addition of researchers that look different, have you really included me at all?', paper presented at the Australian Association for Research in Education and the New Zealand Association for Research in Education conference on 'Global Issues and Local Effects: The Challenge for Educational Research', Melbourne, 27 November to 2 December.

Walker, R. (1980) 'Educational replanning for a multicultural society', in G. Robinson and B. O'Rourke (eds) *Schools in New Zealand Society*, Auckland, New Zealand: Paul Longman, pp. 227–41.

# Case study research

Michael Bassey, *Nottingham Trent University, UK*

## THE PURPOSE OF EDUCATIONAL RESEARCH

I have a well-trodden answer to the question, 'What is the purpose of educational research?' My answer is this: educational research is critical and systematic enquiry aimed at informing educational judgements and decisions in order to improve educational action. The focus is on what happens in learning situations –that is, educational action –and on a value-orientation towards improvement of that action. I make a distinction between this and disciplinary research in education, which I see as critical and systematic enquiry aimed at informing understandings of phenomena (in educational settings) which are pertinent to the discipline. Thus sociologists study sociological phenomena, psychologists psychological phenomena, economists economic phenomena, etc. Both educational research and disciplinary research in education are concerned with theory, but, to me, educational research is concerned more with improving action through theoretical understanding; discipline research with increasing theoretical knowledge of the discipline. The boundary is often, though not always, clear-cut.

## WHY I ENGAGE IN RESEARCH

I believe that research, in the long run, is the most effective way of coming to know what is happening in the world, and of responding to the social problems that arise. In this sense, my concept of research embraces not only asking questions and observing actions, but also reading what others have written about the issue in hand. In each case it is a matter of trying to make sense of something that seems problematic, which ultimately means trying to relate ideas within some form of theoretical understanding. But whatever research approach is used, fundamentally it must be critical. The researcher must keep asking questions like: 'Does this mean what it appears to mean?', 'Am I observing what I think I'm looking at?', 'Does my question have the same meaning to the person that I'm interviewing as it has to me, and if so, am I getting his or her version of the truth?' There are, of course, quicker ways of finding out what is going on. Working uncritically – taking everything at face value – is quicker. Relying on professional experience to solve a problem will certainly be much quicker than setting out to gather evidence and look for theoretical understanding – and often it may be at least as reliable. But sometimes there are deeper issues which deserve exploration through painstaking and challenging enquiry.

## HOW I CHARACTERIZE MY RESEARCH AND MYSELF AS A RESEARCHER

I tackle a research topic because it excites or concerns me, because I have 'fire in my belly' about it, and because I think the outcome will be worth publishing for an appropriate audience.

A study I made in the early days of performance-related pay for teachers in England arose from my anger at what I perceived the government to be doing (Bassey, 1999b). It led me to research into unfamiliar literature (of industrial experiences of performance-related pay), and then write a very short case study of the collegial management practice of one primary school into which I had considerable insight. This is worth reproducing here to illustrate my meaning.

One primary school that I know well, can serve for speculation on the consequences of implementing the Government's plans. There are nine class teachers (one is also deputy head) and a head. The class teachers are all at the present maximum of their pay scales, five have additional salary points for particular responsibilities. The children achieve high at both key stage assessments. The recent OFSTED (Office for Standards in Education) report was very positive. The school is popular with parents and has many out-of-catchment area children.

The head is undoubtedly educational leader of the school and senior manager, but she ensures that all the teachers have a share in the decision-making and in the exercise of duties. Each teacher is subject co-ordinator for at least one subject – with responsibilities for policy, scheme of work, resources and monitoring progress. A limited amount of non-contact time is available for this, according to need. This year's development plan has 29 items for action – which have been shared among the staff (including a substantial number allocated to the head): each item is monitored by the responsible person with the head checking that it happens. Regular staff meetings discuss new developments and the progress of the school. There is plenty of contact with parents and with the local community. As each new Government initiative has arrived, the staff have changed the school to accommodate it. But they also have school initiatives that benefit the children, such as youth hostel visits to new environments. The staff are all competent teachers firmly committed to providing the best for the children.

The head informally monitors and, when she judges necessary, challenges what is happening in the school and gives support where appropriate. She knows what is happening by making regular daily classroom visits, by taking some lessons to free individual teachers for other tasks, by some playground duty, by talking with parents, by seeing teaching plans, by reading half-termly evaluations, by analysing assessments – and by being in the staff room at breaks.

The staff room is the centre of the school for staff. At breaktimes coffee and laughter flow, with serious snippets of conversation and urgent messages. The staff know each other well, they trust each other – and the head, in the staff room, is 'one of the crowd'. They share their successes, problems, joys, and disappointments; they support each other professionally and emotionally and in this reflect the school's mission statement in encouraging 'attitudes of mutual respect, care, sensitivity, compassion, and co-operation towards others in our school'.

(Ibid., pp. 22–3)

That was written on the basis of what I knew about the school, and my claim to its trustworthiness was based on the head agreeing that I had described the practice accurately. Of course, I could have interviewed some of the teachers to check on points and, say, the local education authority inspector, but in the event I considered this unnecessary, particularly since I felt the need to get the whole paper into print quickly if it was to have any political impact. (Later, when the published paper was put on the staffroom noticeboard, nobody challenged the veracity of this account – and I am sure some teachers would have done so if they had disagreed with what I had said.)

Having described the situation in these terms (a 'picture-drawing' case study in my typology – see below) I went on to argue that the new government initiative is likely to damage this collegial process:

> The introduction of Pay and Performance Management, as described in the Technical Green Paper, is likely to change this. Appraisal, currently conducted by fellow members of staff and controlled by the appraisee as a form of staff development, will become a managerial operation ('based on the teacher's job description and at least three objectives' according to the Technical Green Paper paragraph 13). The outcome of this appraisal will be that the head should 'make a recommendation to the governing body about the teachers' pay' (idem paragraph 18). Where teachers are at the top of the existing scale it will only be significant if they apply to cross the threshold. In this case (and conceivably all of these teachers might do so) the teacher will prepare a portfolio of evidence and the head will make 'a judgement whether the applicant meets the threshold standards' (idem paragraph 25). An external assessor will read the head's written recommendation and decide whether further lesson observations and interviews are needed.
>
> The collegial management system will collapse because linking pay to performance will cut the headteacher off from the rest of the staff. Staff and head will be wary of each other. Each classroom visit, each question asked, each request made, may be interpreted as something which could affect a judgement about pay. The head will feel constrained about entering the staff room. The flow of informal information between head and staff will dry up. Jealousies may arise among staff in terms of who is successful and who is turned down. Staff may expect those who have been promoted to take the hitherto shared duties. Bureaucratic management will ensue. In bureaucratic management, decisions are made on high, the staff are told what to do and a sense of alienation can develop. The school will suffer. Standards may drop.
>
> (Ibid., pp. 23–4)

Methodologically I believe that rational argument, based on empirical evidence, is an important part of the research process. I ended my article with a polemical paragraph:

> The Government should know that whilst teachers look for a fair salary, their real reward is in the success of their pupils in any personal, social or curricula achievement. Teachers

work hard because of their professional commitment to children, not for small differential salary bonuses. In a successful school with a collegial system all salaries should be raised, not just some – because everyone is working together to contribute to educational advance.

(Ibid., p. 24)

Again, I am a firm believer, when the circumstances warrant it, in researchers putting their conclusions in polemical form – provided that there is a clear-cut separation of evidence, argument, and polemic, such that the reader is left in no doubt as to the relative status of each form of writing. I would claim that doing this is exercising the social responsibility of a researcher by seeking to ensure that policy is informed by research. In the above instance, the main thrust of my article was to seek pilot testing with thorough evaluation before the government introduced its system of performance-related pay. This plea was ignored; however, two years later an officer from the Department for Education and Skills requested a copy of this paper. Perhaps the issue is still being debated!

## WHAT IS CASE STUDY AND WHERE CAN ONE FIND OUT ABOUT IT?

For readers who are looking for a generalized account of case study, I will draw attention to some recent writings.

Gomm *et al.* (2000) is a compilation of ten articles written in the last half of the twentieth century on different aspects of case study. The editors recognize that the term 'case study' is ill-defined; they see it not as experiment, not as survey, but essentially as investigation in considerable depth into one or a few cases in naturally occurring social situations. They focus on the problem of generalizability, causal or narrative analysis, the nature of theory in case study, and issues of authenticity and authority.

Within the book, Stake argues that case studies can have general relevance by providing vicarious experience leading to what he calls 'naturalistic generalization': this requires full description in order to capture the unique features of a case. Lincoln and Guba suggest that there are ways of expressing the conclusions of one context that might hold in another, and this entails 'thick descriptions' of cases. Donmoyer takes this further and argues that not only similarities but also differences between contexts may be illuminating. Schofield's contribution distinguishes between generalizing to what is, to what may be, and to what could be. Further articles in this collection focus on the capacity of case study research to produce theoretical conclusions.

At a more practical level, Stake's (1995) *The Art of Case Study Research*, and Yin's (1994) *Case Study Research: Design and Methods*, are valuable, as is Stake's article on case studies in Denzin and Lincoln's (2000) *Handbook of Qualitative Research*. More recently, Gillham's (2000) *Case Study Research Methods* gives useful suggestions to newcomers about this kind of research.

Finally, I would draw attention to my own *Case Study Research in Educational Settings* (Bassey, 1999a). In this book I reviewed earlier work in the context of educational research, and produced a 'reconstruction' of the concept of case study. This is central to the discussion of this chapter, and so is reproduced in full in Box 8.1 (reproduced from ibid., p. 58). In my book each of the terms used in this conceptualizing is carefully justified.

## THE CHARACTERISTICS OF GOOD EDUCATIONAL RESEARCH IN TERMS OF CASE STUDY

First, the outcomes must be trustworthy. In case study I prefer this term to validity and reliability. I have written about this elsewhere (ibid., pp. 74–7), and, drawing on the work of Lincoln and Guba (1985), I identified eight tests for trustworthiness. These are set out in Box 8.2.

Second, the conduct of the enquiry and its report must be ethical, particularly in terms of respect for persons. Box 8.3 gives four tests that I have written about elsewhere (Bassey, 1999a, pp. 77–9), again drawing on the work of Lincoln and Guba (1985).

Third, an outcome of the research must be that it says something significant to someone (teacher, manager, policy-maker, parent, learner, etc.), thereby informing her or his work and potentially helping to improve it.

Fourth, the research must be reported in forms which are mean-ingful and readable to the various audiences who may read them. It is worth referring to the British Educational Research Association's (2000) booklet *Good Practice in Educational Research Writing*. This identifies at least four forms of writing about research. For case study they might look like this:

● *Case record*: the agreed interview transcripts or reports and obser-vation reports, the final versions of analytical statements, the

**Box 8.1:** A conceptual reconstruction of educational case study

An educational case study is an empirical enquiry that is conducted:

- within a localized boundary of space and time (i.e. a singularity);
- into *interesting* aspects of an educational activity, or programme, or institution, or system;
- mainly in its natural context and within an ethic of respect for persons;
- in order to inform the judgements and decisions of practitioners or policy-makers, or of theoreticians who are working to these ends;
- in such a way that sufficient data are collected for the researcher to be able to:

   (a) explore *significant* features of the case;
   (b) create *plausible* interpretations of what is found;
   (c) test for the trustworthiness of these interpretations;
   (d) construct a *worthwhile* argument or story;
   (e) relate the argument or story to any relevant research in the literature;
   (f) convey *convincingly* to an audience this argument or story; and
   (g) provide an audit trail by which other researchers may validate or challenge the findings, or construct alternative arguments.

(Inevitably the terms 'interesting', 'significant', 'plausible', 'worthwhile' and 'convincingly' entail value judgements being made by the researcher.)

At least three types of educational case study can be conceived:

- *Theory-seeking and theory-testing case studies*: particular studies of general issues – aiming to lead to fuzzy propositions (more tentative) or fuzzy generalizations (less tentative) and conveying these, their context and the evidence leading to them to interested audiences.
- *Storytelling and picture-drawing case studies*: narrative stories and descriptive accounts of educational events, projects, programmes, institutions or systems, which deserve to be told to interested audiences, after careful analysis.
- *Evaluative case studies*: enquiries into educational programmes, systems, projects or events to determine their worthwhileness, as judged by analysis by researchers, and to convey this to interested audiences.

interpretative writings, the final draft of conceptual background statements, the day-by-day journal of the research, etc. This compilation of working records, edited to be suitable for public access, shows in detail how the researcher has collected data, analysed it, interpreted it, tested findings and so on. There may be only one copy of this document, kept by the researcher.

- *Case report*: the end-point of the research into the case, which may serve the purpose of positing a theoretical position, or telling an educational story, or sketching an educational picture, or

**Box 8.2:** Tests of trustworthiness of case studies

---

1. Has there been prolonged engagement with data sources?
2. Has there been persistent observation of emerging issues?
3. Have raw data been adequately checked with their sources?
4. Has there been sufficient triangulation of raw data leading to analytical statements?
5. Has the working hypothesis, or evaluation, or emerging story been systematically tested against the analytical statements?
6. Has a critical friend thoroughly tried to challenge the findings?
7. Is the account of the research sufficiently detailed to give the reader confidence in the findings?
8. Does the case record provide an adequate audit trail?

---

**Box 8.3:** Tests of the respect for persons of a case study

---

1. Has permission been given to conduct the research in terms of the identification of an issue, problem, or hypothesis, in this particular setting?
2. Have arrangements been agreed for transferring the ownership of the record of utterances and activities to the researcher, thus enabling the researcher to use these in compiling the case record?
3. Have arrangements been agreed for either identifying or concealing the contributing individuals and the particular setting of the research in the case report?
4. Have arrangements been agreed for negotiating permission to publish the case report?

---

evaluating some educational event or institution, etc. This is the academic paper which in principle should be subject to peer scrutiny by academic referees to vouch for its trustworthiness and probity. Hopefully, it will be published in an academic journal.

- *Professional report*: there may be several of these arising from the case report, tailored to the interests and needs of particular professional audiences. Professional reports are the main form of message from the research to potential users. They may be published in professional journals or on websites.
- *News report*: because case studies tend to be long it can be valuable to draw attention to the professional reports by writing brief 'news reports', which may feature in, say, *The Times Educational Supplement*, or on appropriate websites.

## METHODOLOGICAL ISSUES OF CASE STUDY THAT CONCERN ME MOST

Over the years I have worried about the issue of generalizability. In the 1980s I argued that there are no generalizations of any use to teachers (Bassey, 1981, 1983). I advocated that case studies, for example, should be written in such a way that teachers or policy-makers could try to relate their own context to that of the research. To the extent that they could find similarities, I argued that they could learn something from another situation. From this position, I then argued for the proliferation of case studies of what teachers considered to be good practice.

More recently (Bassey, 2001), I have changed my mind – or, rather, changed the definition of generalization! In place of the scientific generalization, which states what *is*, I have introduced the idea of a fuzzy generalization, which states what *may be*. With this perspective it is possible to generalize (in fuzzy terms) from a single case. But, of course, the statement that something *may be true* embraces the idea that it *may not be true*. This has led me to the idea of a BET, that is, a best estimate of trustworthiness – which is a professional judgement, based on experience in the absence of research data. This issue features in Chapter 12, so I will say no more about it here.

## OTHER METHODOLOGICAL ISSUES THAT CONCERN ME

Like many of my colleagues, I am concerned about the quality of educational research. When virtually all research publication was in refereed journals or books from reputable publishers, there was occasional concern about standards of refereeing; but, by and large, we knew that poor research would not surface. But now, with the Internet, a lot of research, including case study work, gets into circulation without prior careful scrutiny. This is known as the 'grey literature'. I have argued for a system of critical friend audit, so that someone who has completed a case study, for example, persuades a colleague to spend time going through it and issuing, as a professional document, a statement similar to that made by a financial auditor. For example, it could be something like this: 'I certify that as far as I am aware this research is trustworthy and has been conducted according to accepted ethical standards.'

## WHAT ABOUT CONTRACT RESEARCH? DO I STILL HAVE 'FIRE IN MY BELLY'?

I have been fortunate in that I haven't needed to take on any research which has not excited me. Let me give an instance from an evaluation that I carried out in 1987 for Nottinghamshire Local Education Authority of its Staff Development Project for teachers across the county. It is described in the form of what I call a 'storytelling' case study (see Box 8.1, and Bassey, 1999a, pp. 95–115). On the basis of transcripts of interviews, and open-ended discussions and documents, I began to realize that a strong ideology underpinned the project.

This is a good example of how, in case study research, a constant sifting of the incoming data and a search for patterns can lead to unexpected findings. I formulated my concept of this ideology, tested it on 19 of the participants in the project, modified it in the light of their comments, and then put it in my first report to the sponsors. This is what it looked like:

- All teachers are professional equals – irrespective of seniority.
- All teachers can improve their classroom performance.
- All teachers should have an intrinsic desire to improve their classroom performance.
- The hierarchic structure of a school is not the instrument to direct the professional development of individual teachers, in terms of improving classroom performance.
- Professional development, in terms of striving to improve classroom performance, should be under the control of the individual teacher.
- Staff engaged in promoting professional development should only work with individual teachers on the basis of freely made contracts about the ownership of data that arises in any appraisal of the teacher's professional needs.

I found some of these points quite significant and, if the project had not been killed off when central government reduced the funding, I think they would have made quite an impact on professional development nationally as well as locally.

As reported elsewhere (ibid., p. 110), the sponsors were not happy with my use of the word ideology because this implied the need to socialize new teachers into it, whereas they saw the project as a grass-roots movement. Since it is relevant to the nature of case study, I shall repeat here what Helen Simon (who was a consultant to my evaluation) said to me: 'If your report is any good you can't expect the sponsors to love you for it.'

Researchers need to recognize that the findings of research enquiries, however trustworthy they may be, may not be welcomed by those who currently operate the practices or policies under study. Research can be painful.

## THE IMPACT OF MY RESEARCH ON EDUCATIONAL POLICY AND PRACTICE

What impact has my research had on educational policy and practice, and/or what impact might it have in future? The honest answer to the question is 'probably none' – and it will remain so unless our policy-makers begin to take seriously the research that challenges their preconceptions! But that is to be flippant. In actuality, one can never know. Every teacher in every class is using research results that have long since moved across the horizon of memory and become assimilated into professional craft knowledge. Likewise, every policy-maker is drawing on long-forgotten original work in formulating new policies.

I would like to end this chapter with a concept map I have used in several places (for example: Bassey, 1998, p. 41; 1999a, p. 50); it suggests how educational research (including, of course, case study) impinges on the craft knowledge of classroom practice and educational policy-making (see Figure 8.1). I believe it is the best answer to the above question. It can be 'read' by going from one box to another using the following interpretations of the arrows.

A     Educational research uses and contributes to methodologies of the other social sciences.

B     Reports of educational research contribute to professional discourse and vice versa.

C     Reports of professional experience contribute to professional discourse.

D     Professional discourse provides ideas that add to craft knowledge.

E     Professional experience provides knowledge of what has worked.

F     Subject knowledge is transmuted through craft knowledge into a teachable form.

G     Craft knowledge of teaching determines the practice of teaching.

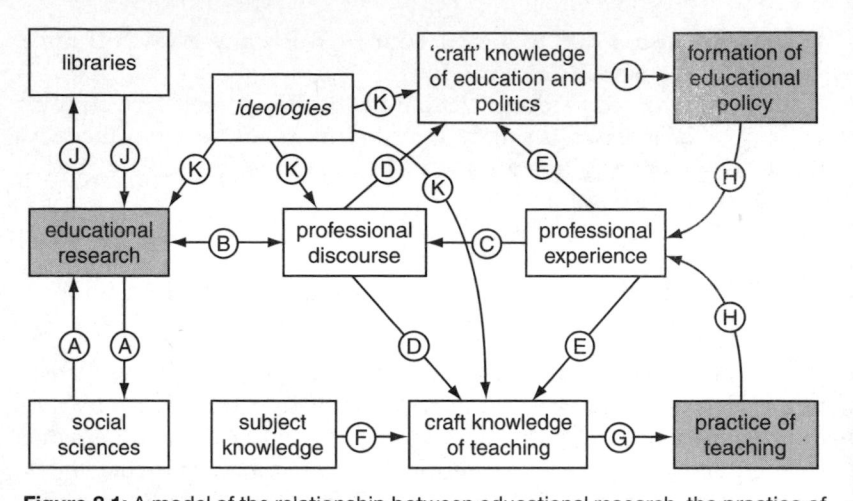

**Figure 8.1:** A model of the relationship between educational research, the practice of teaching and the making of educational policy

H    Memories of practice and of policy formation are stored as professional experience.

I    'Craft' knowledge of management and politics determines policy formation.

J    Libraries store and inform educational research.

K    Usually unrecognized, ideologies impact on knowledge, discourse and research.

## REFERENCES

Bassey, M. (1981) 'Pedagogic research: on the relative merits of search for generalisation and study of single events', *Oxford Review of Education*, 7 (1), pp. 73–94.

Bassey, M. (1983) 'Pedagogic research into singularities: case studies, probes and curriculum innovations', *Oxford Review of Education*, 9 (2), pp. 109–21.

Bassey, M. (1998) 'Enhancing teaching through research', *Professional Development Today*, 1 (2), pp. 39–46.

Bassey, M. (1999a) *Case Study Research in Educational Settings*, Buckingham, UK: Open University Press.

Bassey, M. (1999b) 'Performance related pay for teachers: research is needed', *Professional Development Today*, 2 (3), pp. 15–28.

Bassey, M. (2001) 'A solution to the problem of generalisation in educational research: fuzzy prediction', *Oxford Review of Education*, 27 (1), pp. 5–22.

British Educational Research Association (2000) *Good Practice in Educational Research Writing*, Southwell, Nottinghamshire, UK: British Educational Research Association.

Denzin, N. K. and Lincoln, Y. S. (2000) *Handbook of Qualitative Research*, London: Sage.

Gillham, B. (2000) *Case Study Research Methods*, London: Continuum.

Gomm, R., Hammersley, M. and Foster, P. (eds) (2000) *Case Study Method*, London: Sage.

Lincoln, Y. S., and Guba, E. G. (1985) *Naturalistic Inquiry*. Newbury Park, CA: Sage.

Stake, R. E. (1995) *The Art of Case Study Research*. London: Sage.

Yin, R. K. (1994) *Case Study Research: Design and Methods*, London: Sage.

# Part III

Dialogues from a
Research Community

---

# Decision-making in the real world: postmodernism versus fallibilist realism

Elizabeth Atkinson, *University of Sunderland, UK*
Joanna Swann, *King's College London, UK*

*JS:*     Elizabeth, I think it would be useful to clarify some of the issues about which you and I agree as, respectively, adherents to postmodernism and fallibilist realism. With reference to your lucid account of postmodernism's characteristic features (Chapter 3), I agree that certainty is a chimera, life is complex, and we need to acknowledge the subjective world of human experience. I also think that one of our principal tasks as learners, teachers and researchers is to challenge assumptions and expectations. And I'm certainly not averse to irony. With regard to specific educational policies, I too have strong reservations about the value of England's national curriculum for initial teacher training, and the national literacy and numeracy strategies.

Where we begin to part company is over the relationship between expectations and reality. I hold the view that we inhabit a shared reality, a world of physical objects and processes, of social practices and institutions, and of ideas that have been produced by human thought but which exist independently of the people who created them and/or who continue to believe in them. I acknowledge that significant elements of this reality are socially and culturally constructed, and that each of us experiences the shared external reality in a unique way. But, by and large, our individual and collective judgements about the nature of the world are not arbitrary. If they were, we, as individuals and as a species, would be unable to function successfully; we would not be able to survive.

We act, and when we do we make decisions (which can be unconscious or conscious) about whether to do one thing rather than another (Burgess, 1999). We can, of course, act on whim (indeed, we often do), but, as humans, we also have the potential to act rationally. We can develop reasoned preferences. For example, we can argue against hitting children when they make a mistake, on the grounds that it is both cruel to do so and inconsistent with encouraging them to learn. We can argue (as I have done in Swann, 1983, 1988, 1998, 1999c, 2002; also, see Chapter 2) in favour of the development of student-initiated curricula, on the grounds that such an approach to learning and teaching acknowledges and develops learner autonomy – in itself (we may wish to argue) a good thing – and that it promotes learning more effectively than other approaches (an assertion that can, to some degree, be subjected to empirical testing). In essence, there are reasons for doing one thing rather than another, and these reasons are imbued with assumptions of value and expectations of fact.

By assumptions of value, I mean ideas about what is good and worthwhile. By expectations of fact, I mean ideas about what is and what is not so. My main interest as an educational researcher is in assumptions and expectations which relate to the organization and conduct of education. As someone who engages in empirical research, my particular concern is with developing better expectations of what is so and why about learning and teaching. For example, if we want students to learn how to learn, we need to identify practices and forms of organization that discourage such learning – with a view to eliminating them. We also need to develop ideas about how learning how to learn can be encouraged. Not that we can achieve certain or even secure knowledge about these matters. But logical reasoning, common sense and argument suggest that some practices may be better than others, and we can develop programmes of empirical research – specifically, a science of education (Swann, 2003) – which challenge existing expectations (including common sense) about what works and why, and produce new theories which conjecturally are better.

The pursuit of truth (which I distinguish from certainty – see Swann, 1999a) and the pursuit of practical improvement are not unproblematic. But the latter is inextricably linked with the former. If we desire practical improvement, we must search for and eliminate false expectations about what is the case in the world, and, on this basis, create new expectations. The fact that truth is elusive and practice is messy does not relieve us from the responsibility of striving to eliminate error and to achieve better states of affairs, not unless we are content to live in a world where human experience is marred by disease, illness, despair, poverty, squalor, ignorance, incapacity and oppression.

I recognize that your postmodern agenda is not disassociated from social change, and I fully acknowledge that social inequality and injustice are among your principal concerns. However, as you point out, 'A postmodern research perspective is more likely to raise questions ... than to provide answers' (Chapter 3, p. 47). In response, I suggest that the postmodern programme doesn't go far enough. Is it sufficient merely to disrupt and deconstruct? Surely, what we need in any field of social endeavour is criticism that relates directly to practice and empowers us to do things differently; specifically, to do things better. Given that learners, teachers and educational researchers need to act, why should they choose one course of action rather than another? And how, in your view, should they evaluate the consequences of their actions?

*EA:*    Let me begin by taking up your first points. Yes, we're both keen to challenge foundationalist assumptions about 'truth'; we refuse to accept what is taken for granted; and we want to challenge the complacency and the perceived injustice of contemporary educational and social situations, including those created by current educational and social policy in Britain and elsewhere. Yet the differences between our views are so great that we will never agree on *how* to go about this, unless one of us crosses the boundary and enters the other camp. Perhaps this doesn't matter; in a diverse world there's a lot to be said for diverse approaches. And as I've pointed out to Mike Cole, who has argued against my views from a Marxist perspective (Cole, 2001), 'perhaps one of the benefits of living in our flawed democracy is that we are free to continue to disagree' (Atkinson, 2001, p. 93). However, it's clear that you and I (and others) care enough about our respective approaches to argue – at times fairly evangelically – in their defence.

So what is it that divides us so strongly? To me, the fundamental difference between us lies not so much in our understanding of the relationship between expectations and 'reality' as in the ways we negotiate, make use of, or challenge the 'shared understandings of reality' which direct our actions in the physical and social world. In my view, too much harm has been done – within societies and between societies – in the name of 'shared understandings of reality' simply to dismiss – or accept – these understandings as 'not arbitrary' (as you describe them). Too many ways of thinking, acting and being in the social and physical world have been suppressed, marginalized or eliminated because they do not share the 'non-arbitrary' perceptions of 'reality' held by those who have certain sorts of power – whether political, military, economic, social or sexual. This view is not unique to postmodernism, of course: it is expressed by feminists, Marxists, postcolonialists, queer theorists, and others, as I have pointed out elsewhere (Atkinson, 2000a). Postmodernism does not claim 'owner rights' to the unpacking of these dominant discourses, but it has a way of diffracting and refracting them which invites us to step out of our ethno/anglo/egocentric perspectives – if only partially and in a way which is necessarily contingent upon multiple and complex factors – and to see 'reality' with new eyes.

*JS:*    I need to interrupt you here, Elizabeth. First, the phrase, 'shared understandings of reality' is not one I would use. As I see it, although there is only one external reality, which we share, our perceptions of it are likely to differ. Indeed, the variety of understandings which exist at the individual subjective level is vast. What we deal with are the ideas that people make public, the things they do, make, say and write – things which, to use a Popperian idea, become part of the world of objective knowledge (Popper, 1979[1972]). 'Knowledge' is used here as a generic term for all kinds of expectations (conscious or unconscious, inborn or acquired through development and/or learning), assumptions (explicit or implicit), and theoretical constructs (valid or invalid, true or false). An idea is a part of the world of objective knowledge insofar as it is in the public domain where it can be criticized, modified and developed by anyone who has access to it. (See Chapter 2, p. 15.)

Second, I agree entirely that many ideas and ways of doing things are wrongly 'suppressed, marginalized or eliminated' because they conflict with the values and perceptions of those who hold power. And, although many people wish for consensus with regard to our accounts of what is 'out there' in the external reality, this aspiration is misconceived. A degree of consensus is, of course, necessary in order for people to work together. But the pursuit of consensus can impede learning and the growth of knowledge – because it can result in the suppression of criticism and the marginalization of alternative viewpoints. (See the second epigraph on p. v – from Popper, 1994, p. 34.)

As a Popperian philosopher of education, I know what it is like to have the theories one espouses marginalized. Popperian ideas are frequently misunderstood because they confound expectations. They are often rejected because they represent a radical challenge to many commonly held assumptions about knowledge, learning and method.

*EA:*      OK, we agree on certain points about marginalization and criticism, but what I like about postmodern thinking is that it brings together the voices of marginalized Others to ask, 'Ideas about what is good and worthwhile for *whom*? Who owns the knowledge? Who owns the values? Who decides?' In light of these questions, the value judgements to which you refer with such confidence lose a great deal of their assumed moral superiority, and become much more provisional – and even 'arbitrary' – than a fallibilist realist might wish to admit.

You go on to say that 'logical reasoning, common sense and argument suggest that some practices may be better than others', and suggest that we can develop a 'science of education . . . which challenge[s] existing expectations (including common sense) about what works and why'. I am relieved that you do, at least, want to challenge 'common sense' (in my view, one of the greatest enemies of critical thinking), but I still want to demand, '*Whose* logical reasoning? *Whose* common sense? *Whose* argument? On whose ground do "we" stand when we operate this "science of education"?' You are taking for granted that 'we' all share the same values, ideas and ways of thinking about what is 'best' for everyone. Postmodernism simply cannot accept this, although it offers useful conceptual tools (broadly described as 'deconstruction') for unpacking the discourses which create, perpetuate and give credence to the disease, illness, despair, poverty, squalor, ignorance, incapacity and oppression which you – and I – so abhor. These discourses – of capitalization, globalization, colonialism, racism, sexism and others – shape the ways in which 'we' construct the very 'good' to which you refer. Yes, we all have reasons for doing one thing rather than another, but we are often trapped in those reasons – and their associated logic – in ways which are so embedded, so implicit in our thinking, that we never take time to question them. This questioning is what I value so much about postmodern thinking. If this makes you think I am permanently trapped in the inaction of indecision, you are wrong: stepping outside my own values, if only partially and momentarily, makes me think and act in ways which significantly alter my relationship to those around me – both in my immediate environment and in the wider world.

*JS:*    When you speak of 'value judgements to which [I] refer with such confidence', I don't know what you mean. We all make value judgements, but I am far from confident that many of our judgements are valid. I certainly don't assume that we all share the same values, ideas and ways of thinking about what is best for everyone. I also believe, and have tried to make clear in my publications and papers, that there is nothing that should not be questioned; though in practice we can't question everything. I also agree with you that it is important to question who benefits from the application of particular ideas, and who decides what will be done.

But I am perplexed by your questions, 'Who owns the knowledge? Who owns the values?' My answer is, 'No-one does'. Individuals and groups can restrict access to knowledge and manipulate it (tell lies and wilfully distort facts, for example), but they don't *own* knowledge. As I mentioned earlier in this dialogue, once an idea enters the public domain it exists independently of the person or persons who produced it. By implying that there can be no universal ownership of public knowledge, you risk ceding ground to those who wish to perpetuate the notion that some individuals and groups should be denied access to what everyone should have the right to know. Rather than promoting a discourse of empowerment, inadvertently your questions may have the opposite effect.

There are times when we need to consider whether we are being manipulated, or are ourselves acting as manipulators. But one of the safeguards against manipulation is to evaluate what we are told (or tell others) in terms of, 'Is it true? Is some important information missing, distorted or withheld? Is the argument valid?' The question, 'What motivates the proponent of this idea?' can be useful, but, unless we are engaged in psychoanalysis, only rarely is it the most important question to ask. Questioning the motivation of the perpetrator of the national literacy strategy is of lesser importance than questioning whether the strategy does indeed promote literacy, and whether the reasoning used to support it is valid.

Of course, I acknowledge that science is socially constructed (as is any activity or artefact involving language), and the acceptance of scientific knowledge depends on the values of those in power. But I wish to argue that the question 'Who decides?' is fundamentally different in emphasis from 'What is the underlying logic to learning and the growth in knowledge?' (see Chapter 2) and from 'Does this decision fly in the face of fact and valid argument?' When presented with a statement about the world (that is, about reality), it is generally more appropriate to ask 'Does this correspond to the facts?'

rather than 'How many people believe this?' (a question posed by those who see truth as consensus) or 'Who believes this, and why?' (a question that is integral to postmodernism).

As an illustration: with regard to the facts about the teaching of reading, research of the kind discussed by Bill Tunmer *et al.* in Chapter 6 is relevant and potentially useful to teachers of reading, particularly within the New Zealand education system where the Reading Recovery early intervention programme is widely recommended and used. Their research supports the idea that it is better for teachers to adapt the Reading Recovery programme, by incorporating into it more explicit and systematic training in phonological awareness, rather than use the programme as it was originally conceived. In short, the outcomes of their research challenge many teachers' expectations – including expectations of fact – about Reading Recovery. In so doing, their research helps to create new expectations of fact, which similarly may come to be challenged and replaced.

I'm not saying that the research of Tunmer *et al. proves* anything. With no disrespect to Bill and his colleagues, it is conceivable in principle that they have misconceived, misconstrued or misreported some aspect(s) of their research. I'm not implying that this is the case, but we have no way of telling for sure that it is not. When evaluating the outcomes of empirical research, one has to make judgements about the quality of the design and conduct of the research, how it compares with other research on the same topic, and about the extent to which the 'findings' relate to one's own situation. If one decides that a particular set of research findings is relevant to one's own practice, and that it challenges assumptions on which one's current practice is based, one reaches this conclusion on the basis of argument. That is, one handles the evidence within a framework of critical discussion.

When one acts in the light of evidence and argument, one should nonetheless adopt a critical attitude to the outcomes of one's endeavours. If one is committed to learning and to practical improvement, one has to adopt a 'try it and see' approach. The 'and see' bit is crucial, because (as I know we agree) things often don't turn out as we expect and hope. (In Swann, 1999b, I have set out a methodology for pursuing the improvement of practice, based on a Popperian theory of learning; see also Chapter 2, pp. 30–1.)

As practitioners, whether or not we are engaged in systematic research or development, we are best advised to adopt practices that are consistent with what appear to be the best arguments, and which are not based on theories that have been shown to be false. The method by which we increase our (conjectural) knowledge of the relevant facts – the method of pursuing the development of true theories about reality – is that of trial and error. This can take the form of thought experiments, involving critical discussion in which various ideas (such as those of Tunmer *et al.*) and their implications are reviewed, and, in some cases, rejected. However, if we are intent on exploring the best ways of doing things – that is, ways which enable us to achieve whatever it is we wish to achieve – we must commit ourselves to the practical investigation of the proposed method that survives each thought experiment, such as the method by which we attempt to help every child in our class to become a confident reader.

I'm not saying there are practices which will be effective in all conceivable situations. But I do wish to argue that there are principles, deriving from an analysis of learning and the growth of knowledge, that appear to be promising for the pursuit of learning and the growth of knowledge. In particular, searching for error is an approach which has particular promise. However, searching for error is insufficient. In order for learning to take place, one must be able to respond creatively to error (as discussed in Chapter 2, pp. 19–21).

I need to make a point about values. I've discussed elsewhere (Swann, 2003) the idea that we can formulate problems not only about the facts of reading but also about their value. Our solutions to the latter will relate to the ways in which we construe the primary purpose of an education service and the schools which operate within it. Possible answers to the question, 'What value is there in teaching children to read?' include: 'To enable them eventually to become effective members of the workforce', 'To enable them to become critical autonomous learners', 'So that their lives may be enriched by the pleasures of reading'. Although these answers are not incompatible, each implies a different set of values.

Thus, I acknowledge that there is no single shared idea of what it means to be a reader, rather there are overlapping sets of assumptions and expectations, including assumptions of value. I also acknowledge that the choice of questions (problems) we pose as the basis for our research into reading will be influenced by what we consider to be of value. Nevertheless, whatever value-laden reason(s) we give for wanting to promote reading, there are still facts to be investigated, such as, 'Is it true that teaching children to read enables them to become critical autonomous learners?' and 'Which practices and strategies should I adopt in my classroom in order to promote reading?' (By the way, my answer to the first of these questions is 'Not necessarily'.)

With regard to your questions, 'Whose logical reasoning?' and 'Whose argument?', I think, quite simply, that there are rules of logic which help us to pursue truth. Note that, as a Popperian, I talk about pursuing truth rather than attaining truth. Truth is a regulative ideal, a standard at which to aim. There is no method that will provide a criterion for determining whether truth has been attained (Popper, 1979[1972], Chapter 8). Similarly, although we may (wisely) evaluate a practice or strategy in terms of whether, or to what extent, it solved the problem it was intended to solve, we cannot know for sure that the practice or strategy could not have been bettered. We must assume that important aspects of the situation are likely to be elusive and may remain unknown.

*EA:*    I need to take you up on several points here. You argue (on p. 132 of this chapter) as though 'knowledge' is out there waiting for anyone who desires it . . .

*JS:*    I don't think I do, but please continue.

*EA:*    But 'knowledge' doesn't just float around in the ether: it is conveyed primarily through language; and language is, above all, open to manipulation, control and suppression (as you concede on p. 130 of this chapter). You argue as though the 'world . . . of ideas that has been produced by human thought' (p. 127) is an open book. But your ideal (p. 132) of 'what everyone should have the right to know' is the book *within* the book: a book which states that we are striving for the truth, and this is as close as we can currently get to it. The clarification and purification – in your terms, the 'improvement' – of this knowledge comes about through 'the elimination of error' (Chapter 2). But postmodernism is about opening up, not closing off: 'elimination of error' cannot be on the postmodern agenda. Postmodernism does not prevent a discourse of empowerment; it opens up new discourses which accept that all knowledge is always and necessarily contingent, provisional, dependent for its meaning upon some previous understanding, which may not be shared by all who encounter it. So, for example, knowledge of whether a particular approach does indeed 'promote literacy' is necessarily contingent upon 'what counts' as literacy – as you yourself imply on p. 134. And the recognition of this contingency is inescapably bound up with the question, 'Who believes this, and why?' While, for you, this question is of secondary importance in comparison with questions about 'what works', to me it is impossible even to begin to ask the latter (whatever their validity) without reference to the former. While your concerns, in relation to the validity of a specific research project, are about design, conduct, comparability and reporting, mine are about the fundamental assumptions underlying both the research question and the paradigm within which the research is conducted.

*JS:*     Elizabeth, I'm sorry, I must interrupt you again. My *principal* concerns when evaluating a research project are not as you suggest. Rather, they are: 'Did the research formulate or address an important problem? Has it produced one or more potentially valuable solutions? Has it produced ideas which challenge commonplace or otherwise significant assumptions? Is there reason to suppose that these ideas are not true? Was the research conducted ethically?'

*EA:*     But your position regarding how to make a difference in educational and social contexts seems to require a reductionist view which, for all its acknowledgement of unexpected outcomes, still relies on the possibility of finding 'an answer' that can be used as a key to success – and as a recommendation that others should do the same. You are prepared to reduce the complexities of learning in, for example, English or mathematics to something which either 'works' or 'doesn't work': a view reminiscent of that expressed by David Hargreaves in his much-criticized Teacher Training Agency lecture on evidence-based practice (Hargreaves, 1996; Atkinson, 2000b). While you may be no happier than I am about the introduction of the national literacy and numeracy strategies into schools in England, your argument suggests that, although the government has got it wrong at the moment (because, in your view, the current objectives-based model is misguided), it would be possible to introduce national literacy and numeracy strategies which *would* be in the best interests of all pupils. From a postmodern perspective, this unitary view of teaching and learning is untenable, not only because it does not acknowledge other ways of understanding the learning process, but because it implies that once you have found out the 'best way' to do something, the only new possibility is for another 'best way' to replace it – rather than acknowledging a multiplicity of ways of approaching human situations which are inevitably both complex and unpredictable.

*JS:*     No, I'm not 'prepared to reduce the complexities of learning in, for example, English or mathematics to something which either "works" or "doesn't work"'. What I'm saying is that questions of what works and why are important, though my preference is for evaluative questions which conceptualize the situation in terms of problems and trial solutions (as mentioned above, and see Chapters 2 and 4). For example, if a government asserts that the promotion of learning is one of its highest priorities, and if there is evidence and/ or argument which suggests that what it does fails to promote learning, I think both the government and the electorate should be informed that the policies are failing – that is, not working. And the evidence should be made publicly available, so that all parties can subject it to critical scrutiny. In an ideal world, a government would be interested in evidence and argument which suggested that its policies needed revision. But politicians are primarily interested in retaining power. The promotion of learning – be it their own, or that of children and the electorate – is of lesser importance to them.

*EA:*     It is this very fact which points to the relevance (and not only to psychoanalysis, p. 132) of the question, 'What motivates the proponent of this idea?' Exploring textual silences helps researchers to identify the terrain within which learners, teachers and educational researchers need to act. But you ask (p. 129), 'Why should they choose one course of action rather than another? And how, in your view, should they evaluate the consequences of their actions?' My answer is this: learners, teachers and educational researchers are often constrained – in a whole range of ways – by the dominant discourses which operate in their particular contexts. These discourses are often so powerful (constituting what Foucault describes as 'regimes of truth' – see Atkinson, 2000a) that it can be all but impossible to 'step out of the box' and to think about their actions in new and different ways. (A simple current example is provided in virtually every primary school in England, where to think about teaching literacy in ways not defined by the processes, procedures and terminology of the national literacy strategy almost constitutes a sort of heresy.) For this reason, my suggestion, from a postmodern perspective, is that when we as learners, teachers and educational researchers act, we would do well to ask ourselves whose discourse we are enacting; whose 'truth' we are both reflecting and perpetuating. And when we evaluate the consequences of those actions, we would do well to ask ourselves whether the resulting changes and 'improvements' have contributed to the strengthening of discourses which marginalize diversity and difference, or whether they make possible ways of learning, teaching and researching which are polyvocal, multiple and radically ready to open up new ways of thinking.

You feel that, if I want to change the world, I should get out there and do good, by conducting some practical research which will demonstrate that one thing works better than another. To you, postmodernism is an intellectual indulgence which will make not one jot of difference to the social world. You ask (p. 129), 'Is it sufficient merely to disrupt and deconstruct?', but the assumption that 'deconstruction' is the same as 'destruction' is one which has been challenged already (Atkinson, 2002): deconstruction is not about destroying, but about rethinking – and raising questions is, in itself, a way of creating new answers. This is what Elizabeth St Pierre (1997, p. 175) describes as 'producing different knowledge and producing knowledge differently', and it is something that postmodernism does *par excellence*.

*JS:*    Two further points of clarification: first, although I can conceive that a government might have a benign national policy with regard to funding books and equipment, I am fervently against interventions which deny teachers and students responsibility for, and control over, curriculum organization and content. The national literacy and numeracy strategies are extensions of the national curriculum. These initiatives prevent the development of student-initiated curricula in state schools. (For a summary of my arguments against national curricula, see Swann, 2000.) Note that my commitment to student-initiated curricula goes hand in hand with a commitment to diversity – the diversity that results when students are encouraged to initiate and develop their own learning programmes (Swann, 1983, 1988, 1998, 1999c, 2002).

Second, I don't equate deconstruction with destruction, and I did not imply that empirical research is the only research worth doing. I'm certainly not criticizing you for being a philosopher! My concern is with the sort of philosophy that interests you. I welcome postmodernism's successful challenge to orthodoxy, achieved in part by the deconstruction of discourses of power, and I acknowledge the value that postmodern thinking attaches to diversity and difference. But I'm still wondering by what criteria might you judge an idea or action, other than (a) it doesn't strengthen the marginalization of diversity and difference, and (b) it opens up new ways of thinking? And by what means would you evaluate whether a policy or action has had the effect you desire?

*EA:*    Isn't this enough? Isn't the recognition of diversity – including diversity in ways of thinking about and understanding the world – so powerful, so empowering, that it revolutionizes educa-tion? You seek 'criticism that relates directly to practice and empowers us to do things differently' (p. 129). What I have found, in the possibilities for thinking otherwise that postmodernism opens up, is just such a criticism.

*JS:*     Elizabeth, this discussion could continue almost indefinitely, but I'm obliged to bring it to a close. I'd like to make two brief points.

First, if I'm told something that's false, which doesn't correspond to the facts, it matters – and it matters whatever the speaker's motiv-ation, and irrespective of whether she or he is politically empowered or disempowered. Analysis of the political and social context of arguments and statements about reality, and of the practices (or policies) associated with them, may be useful, but we still need to judge the arguments, statements and practices in terms of 'Is this argument logically valid?', 'Is this idea true?', 'Does this practice solve the problem it is intended to solve? Does it have undesirable consequences? Are there (potentially) better solutions?'

Second, my answer to your final questions is, 'No, acknowledge-ment of diversity is not enough'. Diversity and difference increase our potential to create better solutions to problems, but we still need to be able to decide between one solution (idea or practice) and another. There is, quite simply, no escape from this requirement – not if we are to continue to prosper as a species. In this regard, fallibilist realism is, as I have tried to show in our dialogue, more fruitful than postmodernism. The fallibilist realism I espouse acknowledges the importance of creativity and the potential value of diversity; it has also produced principles for the improvement of our practices as learners. In particular, while acknowledging that our knowledge is conjectural, we can pursue the truth about the nature of the reality we all inhabit by adopting the principle of searching for, and trying to eliminate, error.

## REFERENCES

Atkinson, E. (2000a) 'The promise of uncertainty: education, postmodernism and the politics of possibility', *International Studies in Sociology of Education*, 10 (1), pp. 81–99.

Atkinson, E. (2000b) 'In defence of ideas, or why "what works" is not enough', *British Journal of Sociology of Education*, 21 (3), pp. 317–30.

Atkinson, E. (2001) 'A response to Mike Cole's "Educational postmodernism, social justice and societal change: an incompatible ménage-à-trois"', *The*

*School Field: International Journal of Theory and Research in Education*, 12 (1/2), pp. 87–94.

Atkinson, E. (2002) 'The responsible anarchist: postmodernism and social change', *British Journal of Sociology of Education*, 23 (1), pp. 73–87.

Burgess, T. (1999) 'Why do one thing rather than another?: rescuing postmodernism from vacuity', paper presented at the annual conference of the Scottish Educational Research Association, University of Dundee, 30 September to 2 October.

Cole M. (2001) 'Educational postmodernism, social justice and societal change: an incompatible ménage-à-trois', *The School Field: International Journal of Theory and Research in Education*, 12 (1/2), pp. 69–85.

Hargreaves, D. H. (1996) 'Teaching as a research-based profession: possibilities and prospects', Teacher Training Agency Annual Lecture 1996, London: Teacher Training Agency.

Popper, K. R. (1979) *Objective Knowledge: An Evolutionary Approach*, Oxford, UK: Oxford University Press (first edition 1972).

Popper, K. R. (1994) *The Myth of the Framework: In Defence of Science and Rationality*, ed. by M. A. Notturno, London: Routledge.

St Pierre, E. A. (1997) 'Methodology in the fold and the irruption of transgressive data', *International Journal of Qualitative Studies in Education*, 10 (2), pp. 175–89.

Swann, J. (1983) 'Teaching and the logic of learning', *Higher Education Review*, 15 (2), pp. 31–57.

Swann, J. (1988) 'How can classroom practice be improved?: an investigation of the logic of learning in classroom practice', unpublished PhD thesis, London: Council for National Academic Awards.

Swann, J. (1998) 'What doesn't happen in teaching and learning?', *Oxford Review of Education*, 24 (2), pp. 211–23.

Swann, J. (1999a) 'Pursuing truth: a science of education', in J. Swann and J. Pratt (eds) *Improving Education: Realist Approaches to Method and Research*, London: Cassell, pp. 15–29.

Swann, J. (1999b) 'Making better plans: problem-based versus objectives-based planning', in J. Swann and J. Pratt (eds) *Improving Education: Realist Approaches to Method and Research*, London: Cassell, pp. 53–66.

Swann, J. (1999c) 'The logic-of-learning approach to teaching: a testable theory', in J. Swann and J. Pratt (eds) *Improving Education: Realist Approaches to Method and Research*, London: Cassell, pp. 109–20.

Swann, J. (2000) 'Be prepared: a check list of arguments against a national curriculum', *Education Now*, 27, p. 2.

Swann, J. (2002) 'How to avoid giving unwanted answers to unasked questions: realising Karl Popper's educational dream', paper presented at the Karl Popper 2002 Centenary Congress, University of Vienna, 3–7 July.

Swann, J. (2003) 'How science can contribute to the improvement of educational practice', *Oxford Review of Education*, 29 (2) (in press).

# Research and social improvement: critical theory and the politics of change

Michael Collins, *University of Saskatchewan, Canada*
Joanna Swann, *King's College London, UK*

---

**JS:**     Michael, in your chapter you present the reader with a succinct, closely argued account of the nature of critical theory (specifically that of the Frankfurt School) and its philosophical basis, and you contrast it with other approaches to research – positivist, post-structuralist and postmodern. In light of the questions you were asked to address (Box 1.1 in Chapter 1), I'd be grateful if you would illustrate your account by making reference to your own research. I was also wondering what a researcher who is interested in critical theory might be advised to do, apart from (a) study critical theory, (b) analyse and discuss public social policy on the basis of critical theory, and (c) adopt a particular ethical approach to field-work, in which emphasis is placed on conducting research with, rather than on, other people.

I realize you might respond to this by saying that (a), (b) and (c) are what it takes to be a good researcher. Adopted together, these activities might be thought to address the point raised by Marx in the quotation heading your chapter. However, I'm not clear how engaging in (b) will effect significant institutional change. You discuss the notion of dialogue, but dialogue is a two-way process. What can be done when the people with whom one wishes to communicate are reluctant or refuse to participate? To my mind, only (c) is concerned with direct action, and that too is somewhat vague. I can see what research participants might talk about, but what else are they going to do apart from engage in rational discourse? Clearly, talk that leads one to be better informed is important, but that's only a part of social empowerment. Perhaps your response to this will hinge on what you have in mind when calling for 'engagement in measured but hopeful strategies to counter, most often on a small scale, the deleterious effects brought about by [the] imperatives [of late capitalism]' (p. 81)?

More importantly, I wish to ask: 'How, in your opinion, will the adoption of critical theory as an approach to the development of understanding lead to practical improvement?', and 'How might a researcher who adopts a critical theorist viewpoint evaluate the consequences of her or his research?' In short, my concern is not with the content of your political/social analysis, but with the relationship between critical theory and the improvement of educational practice.

*MC:*    My initial response to your thoughtful comments on my chapter is that if it prompts novice researchers in education to follow in a systematic fashion the implications you have drawn in (a), (b), and (c), we have not done a bad job. However, if in what follows there still remains a need for us to address (a), (b) and (c), we should do that.

Clearly, we are thinking of social improvement, and its relationship to educational practice and research, in quite different terms to that envisaged and substantially deployed over the past two decades under Reagan/Thatcherite neo-conservatism and subsequent neo-liberal policies.

*JS:*    I agree.

*MC:*    The critically oriented view of social improvement envisaged in my chapter is oppositional to 'significant institutional change' brought about through the imposition of standardized curriculum formats, the erosion of teacher autonomy, clawbacks in support for publicly funded education and the enthronement of a business corporate ethos.

Investigations informed by critical theory, particularly in the form of critical pedagogy, illuminate possibilities for more genuinely democratic participation (bottom-up rather than top-down) in decision-making among teachers, parents, students and other members of the community. For example, well-researched (that is, providing the evidence) critical commentaries of Ofsted's (Office for Standards in Education) initiatives in England and Wales, linking them to their ideological underpinnings and to their contributions to the current crisis in schools, would be useful to teacher unions, teachers in schools, and other significant stakeholders who have an interest in countering the deleterious effects of top-down mandatory education policies. It would be instructive to trace how Ofsted now attempts to co-opt the discourse on participation to mask the practical short-comings of its large-scale top-down management directives for changing schools and teaching practices.

I hope this conveys a sense of how research in practice can connect to social improvement – that is, somewhat in accordance with what Canadian sociologist Raymond A. Morrow (1994) had in mind when he emphasized that critical theory is concerned with social trans-formation. That said, I think that much of our pedagogical work informed by critical theory has been on the defensive since the early 1980s in the face of the neo-conservative ascendancy and its neo-liberal legacy. So the challenge has been to bring a concern for agency, of putting ourselves into practice, in defence of lifeworld values within an educational context.

*JS:* Could you provide an illustration of how these ideas trans-late into research practice?

*MC:* In the mid-1990s, in a book of readings (Welton, 1995), a group of five critically concerned educators, myself included, wrote about our own (individual) pedagogical research and practice. The importance of the project (in which each of us responded to the initial chapters written by the other contributors) was that it enabled us to reflect critically on pedagogical commitments and strategies – consistent with a concern for sustaining lifeworld values – that can sensibly be undertaken in the face of institutionalized system imperatives. I am referring here to the potential of a critical dis-course, dialogical in intent, that induces us to reflect on our roles as educators (Collins, 1991) in search of an emancipatory pedagogy. This calls for a sustained challenge to the irrationality at the heart of constraining system imperatives (the obsession with standardized curriculum formats and testing, increasing bureaucratic demands, the consequent deskilling of educators, and the elevation of man-agement concerns over those which focus our attention on the aims of education and learning), along with the identification and description of pedagogical practices which favour dialogue and genuinely democratic involvement.

In *Critical Crosscurrents in Education* (Collins, 1998) I have attempted to show what such work entails, in chapters on the dimensions of critical pedagogy, schooling, lifelong learning, and internationalist pedagogy. My concern is with critical reflection in

various contexts, and how it connects to the identification of carefully weighed, contextually relevant, counter-hegemonic pedagogical strategies. In this regard, the quotations from Hegel and
Marx, which open my chapter for this book, obtain for educational
research in practice informed by critical theory. However, it does not
make sense to talk about changing the world through social
improvement if first of all we do not understand it better. Here's
what David Ingram has to say about this matter: 'Every successful
understanding applies new meaning to the current situation –
thereby revealing new possibilities for action' (Ingram, 1987, p. 9).

Critically informed investigations do not describe 'the current
situation' from a merely positivistic, taken-for-granted standpoint.
From the outset, the situation at hand is investigated in a critical
way, not cynically, but from the standpoint of a 'hermeneutics of
suspicion' (ibid.). Thus, the hermeneutical task of interpretation is
approached with an expectation that a sound understanding of the
situation being investigated will likely be obscured by systemic dis-
tortions. Institutional norms, bureaucratic regulations or various
consensus formation strategies typically get in the way of our potential for genuine democratic (communicative) decision-making. An
initial challenge facing critically informed research for social improvement is to identify these systemic barriers to understanding and
their harmful (real and potential) effects. With this in mind, a critically informed research in practice can still effectively incorporate
empirical, 'qualitative', case study, and narrative methods.

From a critical perspective, I am much more concerned about the
identification of an interesting problem for research before getting
into a consideration about the deployment of method. A practical
concern about the relevance of the problem at hand comes before
method. What I mean here is that we should be critical of the overly
positivistic discourse about 'putting theory [or method] into practice', as though we carry theories and research techniques around in
a methods toolbox while looking for a relevant problem to address.
(Of course, as we become inclined towards, and more informed
about, critical theory, the kinds of problems that emerge for us to
address, and the form in which we address them, are influenced by a
critical perspective.)

*JS:*    I agree that positivism is discredited. Indeed, the view of
research which John Pratt and I take in this book is emphatically not
positivist (see Chapter 1). The adoption of a multiplicity of approaches to research is consistent with our fallibilist epistemology.

We argue that the principal purpose of doing research is not to try to confirm existing theory, nor to create ideas for others to adopt uncritically; it is to challenge existing assumptions and expectations, and to develop new ideas and better ways of doing things.

*MC:*   For that to happen, I would suggest that educational research should begin with the identification and clarification of a meaningful topic. This might at first seem a facile suggestion. During my early days as a professor of education at a US university, anxious students who had successfully completed their course work with other tutors would come to me with research methods to hand but at a loss to identify a topic that interested them enough for a thesis or dissertation. Other professors had told them to wait until they had mastered the research techniques. In my view, this pedagogical approach is a clear example of 'methodolatory', and it is dysfunctional.

Accordingly, my approach is always to guide initial conversations about research away from a narrow preoccupation with adopting the right method, towards getting students to talk about what problems, issues and/or trends in education are of particular relevance to them. Even now, however, 20 years on, and after wider acceptance of 'qualitative' research, I still encounter graduate students (from such areas as educational psychology, where tests and measurements are still revered, and those health profession colleges which find 'scientific' legitimation exclusively in statistical methods) who initially find it difficult to identify the practical problem for research that accords with their interests.

So, from this perspective, I first ask the student researcher, 'What issue in education most interests you?', 'Why is it important to you?', 'In what ways do you think it is relevant to the institution, learning processes, or educational research?'

Given the influence in recent years of what I, along with other critical theorists, regard as the evasive relativizing influence of postmodern sensibilities (Collins, 1998), I try to achieve a nuanced approach when posing these foundational questions.

*JS:*   Again, we seem to agree. In Chapter 13, John Pratt and I also discourage researchers from deciding on a method prior to formulating a research problem. We also argue that student researchers should be encouraged to recognize that good research begins with the identification of a consequential mismatch between expectation and experience (actual or anticipated) (p. 179). However, such mismatches have to be turned into problems. The idea of an issue is too vague. We encourage the formulation of problems – that is, as questions – on the grounds that it sharpens thinking and clarifies the nature of the research.

*MC:*   I still prefer to talk about the identification of contradictions, opening the way for ideology critique of allegedly progressive discourse which may really be serving status quo hegemonic interests. One of my part-time graduate students (a full-time teacher) recently began his research by investigating the contemporary discourse on managing educational change. Though this topic is widely viewed as progressive and draws much favourable attention from educational decision-makers in a number of countries, he began to pose questions to himself concerning the ideological assumptions ('Whose notion of educational change and the management thereof?') underlying management of educational change discourse, its connections to business management literature, and the way it is adaptable to educational policy development under neo-conservative and neo-liberal jurisdictions. In short, he began to problematize a currently fashionable discourse on adapting to educational change that has otherwise been widely embraced in a taken-for-granted way as 'progressive' development.

Along with a careful reading of the current literature on managing educational change, he is studying critical theory – good advice, and the way to go in accordance with what you noted in item (a) (p. 141) – with a view to providing a well-grounded critical analysis – item (b) – and to exploring the feasibility of a more participatory approach prefigured in the Habermasian concept of a 'communicative ethic'. This ethical stance is consistent with what you note in item (c). Without exaggerating its potential effects, this research should introduce into the public debate on education a hitherto significantly absent critique of an already legitimated discourse on educational change.

Regarding your reference to the major role of dialogue for a critically informed practice and research in education, I would add that we should aspire to much more than a 'two-way process', especially where the power relations between the parties concerned are unequal. In a dialogic approach we are learning and teaching democracy together.

*JS:*   Michael, I'm not sure what you mean. Who is the 'we' in your last sentence? Also, what particular value is there in analysing discourse rather than practice?

*MC:* I am using 'we' broadly, in a generic sense. In pedagogical settings, 'we' could refer to students and teachers working together, researchers and respondents, or to a professional or community group gathered around shared interests, where relationships of power are more evenly distributed. The last of these might well be exemplified in the participatory research and study circle approaches I alluded to in my chapter. 'Discourse' for me refers both to the way we talk about situations, trends or issues, and the practices they entail. See my analysis of deskilling educators and competency-based education (for example, Collins, 1998).

While critical theory as immanent critique does not in itself 'effect institutional change' (this can also be said of other forms of research, including theoretical investigations and political economy studies most closely in line with the Marxian legacy), it does inform pedagogies of resistance and of hope that make problematic the claims on education of contemporary capitalism. Thus, a critical theory perspective acknowledges that transformative social and institutional change will be driven more by forces outside the institution (the university, for example) than within. In this regard, it is incumbent on those of us who draw on critical theory for research, which we have noted entails political engagement, also to involve ourselves in relevant political initiatives that emerge outside of the institution. (Take, for example, the well-reasoned engagement undertaken by Habermas with an influential new generation of far-right intellectuals who set out, through a relativizing postmodern discourse, to diminish within the German history curriculum the reality of the concentration camps.) Involvement in social improvement in this sense is expressed through the conjunction of critical analysis and political practice.

*JS:* You seem to be saying that your student's research will impact on practice because it will lead people to think differently about the context in which they are engaged in action. This idea makes sense to me, but I still wonder how the outcomes of your student's research should be evaluated. By what criteria would the student evaluate the impact of his analysis? How will people assess the validity of his analysis?

*MC:* In the first instance, of course, his research in the form of a masters thesis will be evaluated conventionally by committee members and an external examiner for relevance, cogency, theoretical support, methodology, presentation of evidence (examples), and so on. However, as research in progress, his critical investigations are already affording him greater clarity about his role as schoolteacher and community educator. Given a reasoned understanding of what prevailing circumstances will allow, he can assess how effectively his critical understanding of the way that even seemingly progressive discourse excludes significant pedagogical concerns can form the basis of public debate.

As for immediate relevance: in the current context (that is, in the immediate aftermath of the events of 11 September 2001), his ideology critique provides rational support for an educational project to engender debate about how mainstream discourses on the war against Afghanistan and about terrorism are being framed and assimilated. No doubt we will see evidence of this kind of reasoned analysis, and its implications for educators, in the months ahead.

Already, we can recognize the potential of critical investigations which illuminate the costly 'mismatch' between a seemingly progressive discourse on managing educational change and what is happening in our schools and within the teaching profession despite, or partly as a result of, management-oriented educational policy.

In summary, a critically oriented research project which successfully demonstrates the ideological underpinnings of a mainstream authoritative discourse on how to manage educational change will have done its job. It will reveal in part what progressively minded educators are up against, and where they can most effectively locate their efforts, in the quest for a transformative pedagogy that connects relevantly to meaningful social change.

*JS:*    Thank you, Michael – you've made your position clear. Is there anything in my chapter you would like to comment on?

*MC:*    I agree with you that the feelings of individuals and groups about the current state of affairs have an impact on which research ideas are taken up. But how would you, as a researcher interested in the application of research, respond to a critical concern that certain individuals and interest groups are more influential in determining what research is undertaken and how it is applied? For example, we might reasonably be concerned about how a humanistic conception of learning how to learn can readily be co-opted to a mechanistic (behaviouristic, outcomes-based, competency-based) model which provides measurable effects but distorts the humanistic intent of your research agenda. Am I wrong to suggest, then, that the researcher needs to take into account how she or he is positioned within the politics of education?

*JS:*    I agree that a researcher needs to 'take into account how she or he is positioned within the politics of education'. Indeed, where you (a critical theorist), Elizabeth Atkinson (a postmodernist), Trish Johnston (an indigenous researcher) and I seem to agree is that 'Who makes the decision? And in whose interest is it made?' are questions that may lead to answers which illuminate our understanding of society and our place within it. And, on this basis, we might help ourselves to work towards educational and/or social improvement (however this is conceived).

Thus, I recognize that it would be naïve to believe that all decisions affecting the conduct and organization of education and educational research are made purely on the basis of evidence and argument, (a) without being influenced by power struggles between different educational factions, and (b) regardless of gender, class and race. I also recognize that many decisions associated with education and educational research are taken largely out of self-interest. A degree of self-interest is justified, but there is, I believe, little hope for a society in which self-interest becomes the overriding consideration, and in which the ideal of pursuing improvement for all is sidelined or abandoned.

However, it is one thing to be aware of political considerations, another to formulate practical problems of a political nature, and yet another to pursue successful solutions. Political competence is something one demonstrates in action – it is not merely an abstract process. Political action necessarily entails individual agency, and for it to be effective it requires collaboration and negotiation. The political principles most widely discussed within education, such as those derived from Marxian analyses, best address macro- rather than micro-politics. Although they provide some illumination, they are of limited use when an individual or group questions what to do to effect change in a specific context. Dealing with political concerns in the field, so to speak, requires the kind of know-how that comes from an understanding of social psychology. This know-how must also be accompanied by the development of psychological characteristics which enable one to deal effectively with issues of power.

The type of know-how one needs will vary according to whether one is born into privilege and, in the Western world, whether one is white and male (characteristics which generally confer advantage). Other relevant factors over which one has limited control include physical attributes and early experiences within the home and family; these will also influence the kind of knowledge (explicit or implicit) needed in order to become politically effective in adult life.

It is important that critical discussion and systematic study do not focus solely on political concerns. I suggest that in practice one must strive to achieve a balance between, on the one hand, developing one's arguments with regard to questions of fact and value (which may involve empirical research), and, on the other, developing one's political competency, so that one's arguments are not only intellectually convincing, but can also breach the barriers they will encounter if they challenge existing power relationships.

For much of my academic career I've concentrated on trying to develop arguments which are logically coherent and consistent with the facts. I haven't needed to persuade people of the value of learning, because most people value it, at least in principle. So my work has developed in accordance with the idea that if you value learning then you should also support, among other things, student-initiated curricula. I have attempted to demonstrate the connection between student-initiated curricula and greater learning. Of course, in practice, people don't always value learning unequivocally. The idea of student-initiated curricula, and the theory of the logic of learning which supports it, are not only difficult to understand because they confound expectations, they also challenge existing power relationships. I have recently come to realize that I need to devote more time to the practical politics of change (with a view to improvement).

Nevertheless, I wish to emphasize that some things are more worthy of being defended and promoted than others, and some methods of pursuing social improvement (including the pursuit of politics) will be more promising than others. I don't want my work to be noticed merely because I am associated with a particular interest group; I want it to be acknowledged if, and only if, it is creative in terms of the characteristics of good research I set out in Chapter 2 (p. 12).

With regard to your implied question about 'how a humanistic conception of learning how to learn can readily be co-opted to a mechanistic (behaviouristic, outcomes-based, competency-based) model which provides measurable effects but distorts the humanistic intent of [my] research agenda', my answer is, 'I'm working on it!'

*MC:*    In the course of writing my chapter and in our dialogue here, I have been struck by how much the concept of research *in* practice (as praxis or as 'putting ourselves into practice' rather than putting theory into practice) corresponds with the aims of critical theory.

Your observation that political competence is something one demonstrates in action makes sense to me. I would say that such competence is properly developed through systematic planning and on-going critical assessment that distinguishes thoughtful from mindless activism. At the same time, investigations into what is learned by individuals and groups participating in political action would be relevant to a critically informed research in practice.

I would like to take you up on your characterization of Marxian analyses (p. 149), but unfortunately we don't have the space. Suffice to say, Marxists do make reasoned connections between their political practice, including very specific strategies for 'practical problems', and Marxian analyses.

It is reasonable, in my view, to ask educators whose work is informed by critical theory what they do, in terms of political action, that is sensibly consistent with their critical perspectives on education under contemporary (postmodern?) capitalism. In this regard, I am obliged to reflect on the appropriateness of my own political activism within the university, the wider community, and with teachers. At this time, I would argue that a critically informed research in practice can make a meaningful contribution by illuminating, in their interconnectedness, and then confronting the further corporatization of universities, the marketization of knowledge, the privatization of public education, the loss of teacher autonomy to managerialist innovation and a misplaced preoccupation with the cult of efficiency around curriculum development and school organization. In revealing the depth and extent of the damage that has been inflicted on educators' work since the early 1980s, a critically informed research in practice is in a position to identify those practices that are more democratic, more educative, and more alert to a political agenda for progressive social change.

## REFERENCES

Collins, M. (1991) *Adult Education as Vocation: A Critical Role for the Adult Educator*, New York: Routledge.

Collins, M. (1998) *Critical Crosscurrents in Education*, Malabar, FL: Krieger.

Ingram, D. (1987) *Habermas and the Dialectic of Reason*, New Haven, CT: Yale University Press.

Morrow, R. A. (1994) *Critical Theory and Methodology*, London: Sage.

Welton, M. (ed.) (1995) *In Defense of the Lifeworld: Critical Perspectives on Adult Learning*, Albany, NY: SUNY Press.

# Culture, race and discourse

Patricia Maringi G. Johnston, *Te Whare Wananga o Awanuiarangi, New Zealand*
John Pratt, *University of East London, UK*

*JP:* You present a strong argument in your chapter (Chapter 7) about the way in which much research – based on what you characterize as 'Western frameworks' – has contributed to (or perhaps even helped to create) a view of one section of New Zealand society as a 'problem' or 'inferior'. I am not familiar with the detail of educational research in New Zealand, but I do not doubt that there is truth in what you say. Indeed, there is a substantial literature from across the world which makes a similar case, and offers supporting evidence for the general proposition that all investigation, and hence knowledge, is situated and context-bound. In the UK, for example, such accusations have been made about research into deprivation (which has often viewed the 'poor' as the 'problem'), ethnicity, sexism, etc. I share your distaste, if not your experience, of (so-called?) research which discriminates, denigrates or dismisses in this way.

*PJ:* Here in Aotearoa/New Zealand, the trouble is not only with research which treats the victims as the problem, but also with the adoption of research methods/methodologies – drawn from a specific cultural context that is not Maori – which reinforce problems of this kind. It's not enough to ask why round pegs will not fit into square holes. We need to go one step further and ask why specific types of research persistently lead to 'findings' in which Maori are characterized as under-achievers.

Because of the colonial experience, and the impact of racial beliefs, there is a deeply entrenched view that Maori cannot contribute to research methodologies/methods, because our culture is too simplistic, cannot cope with the complexities of scientific rigour, is practical (as opposed to theoretical and abstract), and so on.

Everyone assumes this is the case. Our engagement with research has thus largely been as the research focus, 'something one judges (as in a court of law), something one studies and depicts (as in a curriculum), something one disciplines (as in a school or prison), something one illustrates (as in a zoological manual)' (Said, 1985, p. 40). I continually try to persuade researchers to abandon that particular racist colonial framework. This is a difficult task, because it involves challenging dominant ways of knowing, as well as those who support and endorse such frameworks.

*JP:* Yes, you go on to argue that research should challenge the dominance of these 'Western frameworks'. One way this should be done is by treating the people upon whom the research is focused – in this case Maori – with respect, and involving them in the research endeavour. Again, this approach is familiar elsewhere (for example, Reason and Rowan, 1981), and I would have thought that it is generally accepted as good practice even among 'Western framework' researchers. I would be very happy to offer (and almost certainly will!) your list of questions for researchers to any of my students embarking on any research.

*PJ:* The problem is that not all researchers engage in these types of practice. As Maori, our contribution to the academic archives is only fairly recent. Until the early 1990s there were relatively few Maori with postgraduate qualifications employed in universities or undertaking research. As a result of that situation, we have been the receivers of research rather than the suppliers. Our early engagements with research were also predominantly anthropological. Not only did researchers see us as the 'exotic other', but until *c.* 1960s Maori who were initially trained in anthropological circles unwittingly contributed to and reinforced those anthropological views. It has been (and still is) difficult to shift some of those views. However, as more and more Maori become qualified and employed in universities as researchers, etc., we are increasingly able to mount a challenge against racial stereotypes and the status quo.

*JP:* OK. But you go further, I think. Certainly, in your discussion about the involvement of Maori researchers, some of the authors you quote say more than this. You assert that Maori researchers bring to research something that non-Maori cannot. That seems unexceptional, since, as I said above, all research is context-bound. I do not doubt the value of investigating a variety of hypotheses, and of employing a variety of approaches and methods, including those generated within a particular community. Indeed, this is central to my (and Joanna's) understanding of how knowledge advances. But whether members of one group can claim exclusivity – that *only* they can bring a particular point of view to the research and/or investigate it – is, I think, questionable. As a non-Maori, I can consider ideas generated by Maori, even though I did not myself generate them.

Nor do I doubt the value of a researcher understanding a community or culture. But I think we need to be careful about going down a path which concludes that the only valid knowledge about a culture, community or group is that generated by its members. I consider this to be logically false as well as politically and socially dangerous. It is a commonplace of daily life that looking at things from a different perspective can be useful. So too in research. It is possible that I could hold views about Maori that, because of my 'otherness', are illuminating – even for Maori. In terms of research, what matters is how well-founded those views are, which means they must have been subject to a critical process.

It seems to me you are in danger of claiming a value for social customs and cultural beliefs beyond their context. By positing an antithesis between 'Maori knowledge and practices' and the research generated by 'Western frameworks', you are, I think, not opposing like with like. The kind of knowledge and social habit that is generated and valued by any community is not the same kind of knowledge that is sought by research. (If it was, there would be no point in either Maori or Pakeha doing research.) The former has developed over aeons, and while it has been subject (to some extent or other, though rarely – if ever – formally) to a process of trial and error, it consists as much of beliefs as tested propositions. Its function is largely to preserve the identity of the community, and for this reason it is generally hard to challenge.

*PJ:*    These are interesting challenges, and ones with which I'm familiar. Indeed, feminists have grappled with some of these same issues. Their challenges, in terms of the 'politics of gender', focus on the feasibility of men researching and writing about women's experiences, experiences which men do not and cannot have (although a Hollywood film I saw recently, about men taking hormonal medication and giving birth, tends to suggest otherwise).

I think the arguments raised by feminists are valid in terms of our discussion here. Some ideas from Carol Gilligan (1995) put it in a nutshell for me. She stated that study (or research) was like 'seeing a picture without seeing the frame, and the picture of the human world had become so large and all-encompassing that it looked like reality or a mirror of reality, rather than a representation' (ibid., p. 120). Thus the argument about men researching women's issues becomes, at one level, associated with the former being able to see the picture but being blind to the frame (or, in this case, framework). This framework is actually based on an unspoken and taken-for-granted male norm. The framework is challenged by feminists because it 'frames' what the picture will look like – the shape of it, the content and, indeed, even the composition.

At a second level, the representation of women by men results in the former being framed by the latter's views of what women are. Women are not only the other (in terms of power relationships) but *his* other – 'caught in the endless and enduring circle of *his* representation' (Feral, 1980, p. 89). This begs the question: 'How can one research, describe and represent experiences one has never had?' There is a vast difference between reading and writing about childbirth and the actual experience of it. This question and the issues it raises are not new, and they will continue to be debated.

However, the politics associated with the framework are integral to these discussions, because they shape both the picture and its frame. The issues, then, are not only about who does the research, but how it is represented – 'Who gets to speak about whom?', 'Is the researched framed within an indigenous world-view or that of the colonizer?' – some of the very questions I raised in my chapter. Research is not neutral. We bring to a research situation our own cultural baggage that influences the ways in which we engage in research, and our reporting of it. Clearly, there will be differences between the findings and interpretations of research, depending on whether the researcher is a member of the dominant group (Pakeha) or that of a subordinate group (Maori), and whether Maori researchers have been 'hegemonized'. The history of research in New Zealand clearly demonstrates (with some exceptions) that this has been the case.

Research, after all, is also highly political. It is only recently that research on Maori has started to focus on 'what works' as opposed to 'our supposed failings'. That shift has resulted from our engagement in research.

In terms of Maori and research, there are two clear polarized positions. First, there are those who argue that only Maori should do research with Maori communities/groups/individuals. This position irritates a great many individuals, particularly those whose careers have been made by researching Maori, and who would like that situation to continue. Maori communities have not necessarily benefited from this research and, as I noted previously, the research tended to reinforce stereotypes, prejudices and deficit views about Maori. Much of that research was also based on taken-for-granted racist colonial frameworks, which treated us as objects. Add a smattering of paternalism and we ended up being told what we should do, and that researchers knew what was best for us. The point raised by Maori about these sorts of issues is that Pakeha researchers have had unprecedented exclusive licence to conduct research on Maori, and it hasn't changed our situation (unemployment, educational under-achievement, etc.) at all. One can safely assume that such researchers have been consistently getting it wrong; deliberately so, a conspiracy theorist might argue.

This position is one that Maori debate rigorously. After all, we are not a homogenous group, and much of the rigour and debate about research occurs intra-culturally (between ourselves as Maori researchers) as well as inter-culturally with Pakeha.

Second, while non-Maori continue to undertake research on Maori communities, groups and individuals, what has changed is that research (which was traditionally premised on Maori participating as token researchers, or as research subjects) is also increasingly being challenged. This challenge involves Maori in decision-making roles, while also encouraging non-Maori researchers to consider how they might become more 'culturally aware and appropriate researchers'. Maori communities have become increasingly disinclined to participate in research that does not provide them with meaningful input or control over the design of the research, its methods or the dissemination of findings. Ownership of information, and how Maori experiences, knowledge and even tissue samples are treated, are now subject to careful negotiation within research contexts.

Our participation may thus require different forms of accountability from those individuals who choose to do research with us, or for us. Accountability may come through reporting findings back to our own people in ways that are more appropriate – in hui (meetings) and workshops as well as in more academic forums, such as conferences and theses. Accountability may also relate to who gains access to what knowledge, and how that information is to be shared – the politics of representation.

Research *on* Maori is effectively being 'closed down', and researchers who attempt to operate from that position are increasingly being 'shut out'. Maori communities are now more guarded about researchers and research because of the damage that has been done. As Ranginui Walker (1980, p. 231) so aptly stated:

> Maori education [has] become the happy hunting ground of academics as neophytes cut their research teeth on the hapless Maori. It has the advantage that Maoris are in the subordinate position with little or no social power to keep out the prying Pakehas. Furthermore, being marginal to the social mainstream, Maoris are not in a position to challenge the findings of published research, let alone the esoteric findings of academic elites.

The 'stomping ground' created by researchers has effectively resulted in Maori communities closing their doors to research communities. Negotiation for entrance has become a long and arduous process, but one that gives Maori more control over the research process, for research, as Walker stated, should not be merely a 'happy hunting ground' for academics, but rather a process of empowerment for those groups who have been marginalized, oppressed and disempowered by research.

There are numerous reasons for closure, the most common of which relate to: damage within communities caused by researchers who have no idea what they are doing; cultural inappropriateness; deficit-model approaches which define Maori as the 'problem to be dealt with'; and research findings that have enabled some researchers to further their careers but have in no way benefited Maori communities. As a result, Maori shut out researchers, and this has led to a drastic rethink about the ways in which research is conducted, and about how Maori may participate within it.

It is easier to deal with cultural contexts if one is socialized into them. Some non-Maori have endeavoured to do this, and have commanded great respect from Maori communities because they gained fluency in Maori language and cultural norms, and considered the needs and interests of the communities with which they worked. Some even gained endorsement from these communities. Unfortunately, their own colleagues have accused them of 'going native'.

Crossing cultural barriers for non-Maori means putting aside their own cultural norms (that is, the researcher as 'god-like', controlling, etc.) and operating without a cultural safety net. For example, educational research in contexts in which the language medium is Maori requires the researchers to be fluent in Maori language. They will also need to know Maori protocols, which vary considerably not only from context to context, but also within individual contexts. These protocols are difficult to navigate, because it means being able to 'read' the situation-disagreements, even wars, have been occasioned by situations being misread. Previously, the expectation was that Maori language contexts would change to suit the language and cultural limitations of the researchers (that is, Maori participants would speak English). This is no longer the case.

Now, the context does not change to suit the limitations of the researcher – rather the researcher has to change to suit the cultural context. The problem is getting researchers to 'shift'. Not an easy task when a colonial history has denigrated Maori culture and society – our own ways of 'knowing'.

*JP:*    You raise a number of issues here. One is about the singularity of experience. I think there's some danger of our talking at cross-purposes, or, at least, about slightly different things. You talk of the problem of one group writing about, experiencing or researching the experiences of another. Clearly, no-one can write of or understand another's experience in the same way as that other person. I think the argument about the singularity of experience can be over-extended. To take one of your examples just a stage further: a tragic hazard of childbirth is the death of the mother. Only those who die have the experience, but no-one, I imagine, would argue that we are all precluded from research into this as a result.

Research, however, is about something different from understanding experience or writing about it. It produces public and tested 'knowledge' – the other kind of knowledge I refer to above, sought by 'Western framework' research. This seems to me to be different from the kind of community-valued knowledge you have mentioned. And, moreover, different from the way I think you characterize it. As Joanna and I argue in our chapters, what distinguishes this sort of (so-called 'Western') knowledge is the process of critically testing hypotheses against evidence. It is not knowledge in the sense that I think you mean when you write of 'pure', 'objective' scientific rationality. Scientific rationality is always conjectural and subject to revision. What makes it 'research' is the process of subjecting it to scrutiny.

In this context, the problem of singular experience is not, I think, quite as significant as you argue. It is possible for anyone to postulate hypotheses about the experience of others, and these can be subject to test, including by those others who have the experience. I can make guesses about your experiences, feelings, etc., as a Maori or as a female researcher, or even about women's experience of childbirth. My guesses would be uninformed and probably unperceptive, but they would be available for you (or anyone else) to subject to criticism and improvement. True, the argument about the 'frame' implies that I might never be able to guess what the experience is like, because I'm trapped in my own perceptions and prejudices, but I fear that there are too many (even though exceptional) instances of people who do break out of the frame to claim total determinism in this regard. You yourself refer to exceptions to the history of research in New Zealand, which support my point here. True, too, if the views or prejudices of one group dominate, then the choice of research topic will be skewed; however, that seems to me to argue for a multiplicity of viewpoints, as do you, and is more a political than a methodological issue.

Nonetheless, I have to say, I'm surprised by the myopia of the researchers you describe, and of their colleagues who see them as 'going native' – particularly in the context of the widespread research literature on (and recognition of the value of) 'new paradigm' and other sympathetic/empathetic approaches in social research. I do not doubt the practical and political difficulty of securing a shift in the focus of and approaches used in research.

You raise also the issue of 'neutrality'. Again we may need to distinguish between different things. Research, in my view, is 'neutral' in the sense that it permits the generation and testing of any hypothesis – even offensive racist ones. Researchers, however, are not. Even those who seek to be neutral cannot, in the nature of things, achieve this. But research offers a form of objectivity – in that hypotheses are subject to test. My personal preference is not to posit, for example, racist hypotheses, and to hope that those which are put forward will fail to stand up to the test, though I have to be open to the unpleasant possibility that they may not.

To go back to my point about different kinds of knowledge, one of the tasks that 'Western framework' research can undertake is the scrutiny of beliefs of particular cultures, and this can include those characterized as colonizing as well as the colonized. I do not think there are different methodologies for the two kinds of societies. Is the key issue not about distinctive methodologies for different groups, but about developing a methodology which produces knowledge we can *all* consider, criticize and use to good purpose?

*PJ:*    The last few points you've made are important, but I'm aware that methodologies are themselves cultural – research has a culture – culture is not limited to ethnic groups like Maori alone.

*JP:*    Yes, but then everything in a sense is cultural! The issue for me here is that this approach (whatever its origins) means that ideas, beliefs, thoughts, etc., generated in any context and with whatever cultural meaning, value or validity, can be scrutinized – not only by people from that culture, but by others.

*PJ:*    I agree, and this is something to hope for, but we're a long way off that stage. I think we also need to consider what the purpose of research is. You've said that research is context-bound, and I agree with you. Sometimes, however, the context is the very framework which needs challenging. In the context of a university situation, for example, Pakeha research has predominantly been about satisfying the need to know – extending the boundaries of knowledge, the rigour, the critique, the discussion – an academic exercise (Smith, 1986). But what does this exercise do for Maori communities, individuals and groups? Absolutely nothing, because at the end of the day the majority of Maori do not have access to those contexts; and contributing to those contexts is merely a matter of informing others of what we already know. We'd be kidding ourselves if we thought that engaging in those forums would change our situation in terms of under-achievement. It won't, because the purpose of doing that sort of research is not at all about changing our conditions. This, as I mentioned in my chapter, is the politics of disempowerment.

Our purpose as academics is a different one: to challenge the frameworks and ideas about 'what counts as research', to educate Pakeha researchers. I undertake research not because it has an academic purpose, but because there are issues that need to be addressed. Research enables us to seek answers; it is not an exercise which merely contributes to knowledge archives. Its purpose is to contribute to our own well-being, to improve our conditions and our own lives. I welcome those non-Maori who take up these challenges and are themselves prepared to be challenged and to operate outside of their own comfort zones.

However, the relatively new entrance of Maori into a research culture means that we are operating in areas where the ground rules are well-established. We do know that our participation is changing those rules. The nature of how research is conceptualized, undertaken and disseminated here in Aotearoa/New Zealand has had to change – it is difficult to undertake research when one party won't participate until conditions change. This is an area of development and negotiation in which there is constant challenge and refinement. Waitere-Ang and I (Waitere-Ang and Johnston, 1999) talked about these developments in terms of 'four frontiers' (depicted in Figure 11.1).

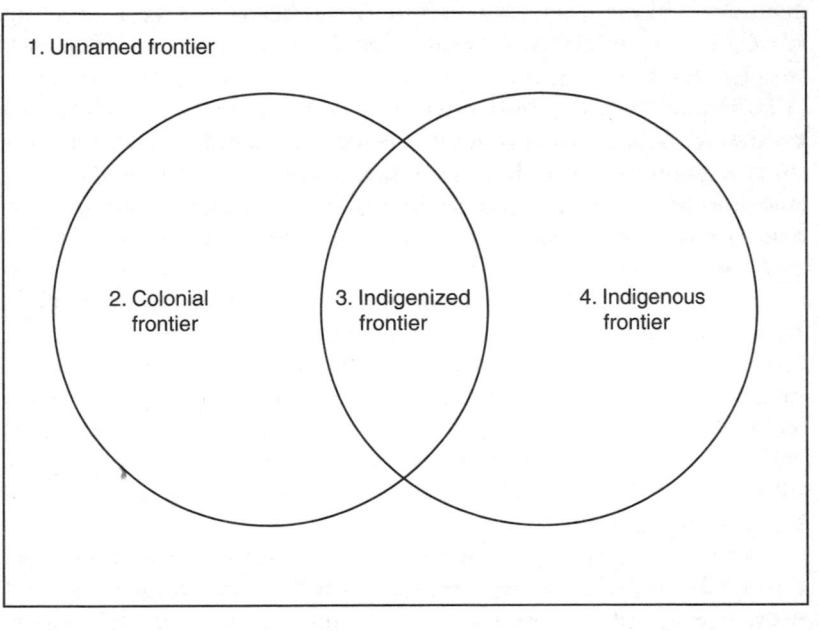

**Figure 11.1:** Four research frontiers

The unnamed frontier is a universalized neutral frame that sought to order the world, defining and claiming it for the imperial centre. It is this frontier that influences and impacts upon what is considered to count as research. Scientific rationality defined who was research material and who was researcher. We were defined by a pre-existing, theoretical, abstract blueprint which merely required our 'discovery' during imperial conditions, so that it could be applied.

The colonial frontier (the identified frame) provided the points of demarcation from which the antipodes were to be named and claimed for the imperial centre. Maori were positioned as the subject, the 'other'. Inclusion in this frame meant the named discovery of our kind, our genre, our class; the imperial and colonial filters through which each indigenous group passed in the process of our placement within racial hierarchies – thus marking our named/identified physical presence upon the imperial blueprint.

The indigenized frontier (the cultural additive frame) acknowledged problems with the colonial centre's position of naming and claiming Maori as research subjects. Moves towards including Maori as research participants resulted in cultural additives without challenging the power structures of the colonial centre. Inclusion in this frame meant that our physical presence and cultural adornments adhered to the unchanging philosophies, methods and practices of science.

In Figure 11.1, the indigenized frontier is where negotiation is occurring, where world-views, differences/similarities in beliefs and perceptions about research meet. This is the frontier where negotiation, challenges and contestation are occurring, where ideas (like those in this chapter) are outlined, considered and put on the table to be debated over.

The indigenous frontier (cultural and structural frame) talked back to the other three frontiers while also moving forward in both a constructive and positive manner. Inclusion of Maori was premised on a centre that recognized both cultural and structural components as integrated parts of the same whole. Inclusion in this frame meant structural and cultural existence in research, and a recognition of the diversity of epistemological, axiological and ontological positions that inform our lives.

As these four frontiers demonstrate, the framework has clearly created the picture, so has influenced how research *on* Maori has been carried out. The problem is that all of these research frontiers exist simultaneously in the New Zealand context. Some researchers sit on their 'science is pure, superior and neutral' backsides, just as they sit on their absolute racist ones. What we require is the opportunity to 'create space' for Maori within research archives, frameworks, methods and methodologies, as a means by which challenges may be mounted while also trying to stay 'safe'.

At times we have been accused of being 'precious' or exclusionary, of employing separatist methods and processes that 'shut out' those who are not 'insiders' and who wish to engage. That space is, however, one that affords us a 'breathing space' – one in which to recover from the onslaught of the colonial exploitation of our resources, our bodies, our language, cultural knowledge, and our minds. The continual haranguing about our ways of life, our stories, our culture and our people, which all indigenous people have received through colonization, has left devastating results in terms of unemployment, social inadequacies and educational under-achievement. The healing process afforded by 'breathing space' enables us to regroup, to reread, rethink and reconnect to places, people and life-ways that colonization has disrupted.

The exclusionary forces of scientific and Western methodologies, of academics, research archives and the right of Western forms of knowledge to describe, label and categorize us, has only very recently been put on the table for discussion. That discussion will continue to be wined and dined over for some time to come.

*JP:*    Although I think your argument about the 'imperial centre' is overstated – because it is contradicted by the (better) statements of the conjectural and socially constructed nature of knowledge – I certainly look forward to the wining and dining!

## REFERENCES

Feral, J. (1980) 'The powers of difference', in H. Eisenstein and A. Jardine (eds) *The Future of Difference*, New York: Barnard College Women's Centre, pp. 88–94.

Gilligan, C. (1995) 'Hearing the difference: theorizing connection', *Hypatia*, 10 (2), pp. 120–7.

Reason, P. and Rowan, J. (1981) 'Afterword', in J. Rowan and P. Reason (eds) *Human Inquiry: A Sourcebook of New Paradigm Research*, Chichester: Wiley, pp. 489–92.

Said, E. (1985) *Orientalism: Western Concepts of the Orient*, Auckland, New Zealand: Penguin Books.

Smith, L. (1986) 'Te rapunga I te ao marama: the search for the world of light', in G. Smith (compiler) *Nga Kete Wananga, Te Kete Tuarua*, Auckland, New Zealand: Maori Studies Department, Auckland College of Education.

Waitere-Ang, H. and Johnston, P. (1999) 'If *all* inclusion in research means is the addition of researchers that look different, have you really included me at all?', paper presented at the Australian Association for Research in Education and the New Zealand Association for Research in Education conference on 'Global Issues and Local Effects: The Challenge for Educational Research', Melbourne, 27 November to 2 December.

Walker, R. (1980) 'Educational replanning for a multicultural society', in G. Robinson and B. O'Rourke (eds) *Schools in New Zealand Society*, Auckland, New Zealand: Paul Longman, pp. 227–41.

# How general are generalizations?

Michael Bassey, *Nottingham Trent University, UK*
John Pratt, *University of East London, UK*

*JP:* I enjoyed your account of the use of case study. It is clear, concise and convincing – though, of course, I have a few points that I'd like to raise. In particular I am looking for a more specific and, pardon the presumption, more logically robust justification of case studies than the one you offer.

*MB:* OK. Can you focus your critique for me?

*JP:* I'll try. There is, as you note, some controversy about the value of and epistemological basis for case study. I think, and I guess you do too, that much of this is misconceived. The issue of generalizability is usually the main concern, but I don't think this is really a problem. My own view, as you already know and can see elsewhere in this book, is a Popperian one, seeing knowledge generated by testing hypotheses. Since any single (valid) instance can falsify a hypothesis, a single case study can have as much value, and be as valid, as a huge-scale experiment. The specificity and context-bound-ness (if you'll pardon the clumsy term) are both valuable in this. If a case does not support a hypothesis because of particular circumstances, this helps us to identify limiting conditions for the validity of the hypothesis (like water not boiling at 100°C at other than 1 atmosphere pressure). Thus, instead of trying to avoid the problems of context, context is a valuable element in case study.

*MB:* I think we need to start with my concept of fuzzy generalization because it has implications for your Popperian stance. In essence, I am suggesting that instead of the potential users of research asking 'What works?', they should ask 'What *may* work, *and in what circumstances may this apply*?' The tentativeness that Karl Popper taught us to demand of empirical statements should, in my view, be built into the statements themselves. Thus, instead of the absolute predictive statement: 'Do *x* in *y* circumstances and *z will* be the result', I advocate the fuzzy prediction: 'Do *x* in *y* circumstances and *z may* be the result'. I then look for a BET (best estimate of trustworthiness), which is a *professional* assessment of how likely it is that the statement will be found to be true in particular instances. This professional assessment is not empirically justifiable, but arises from the researcher's experience in the field and reading of the literature. It is an informed expression of intuition.

*JP:*    Can you give an example?

*MB:*    Yes. On the basis of extensive research, Andrew Pollard advanced the fuzzy prediction that, 'If teachers are strongly constrained in their professional work, they are likely to become disenchanted and this probably affects recruitment and retention' (Pollard, 2001, p. 16). And he added, by way of a BET, a comment which implied that this statement is highly likely to be true: he suggested that this statement is sufficiently fundamental to be worthy of the attention of government.

*JP:*    I have a problem with this. Suppose that a substantial case study reports on a school where strong constraints on the teachers are associated with high levels of job satisfaction. In Popperian terms, Andrew's generalization should fall – or at least be modified to embrace the circumstances which seem to have operated in this new case study.

*MB:*    I disagree. It isn't the fuzzy generalization which necessarily needs to be changed. It could be that the BET is changed from 'highly likely to be true' to 'likely to be true in most cases'. However, if several other case studies showed the same phenomena then I agree that the fuzzy generalization should be rewritten – in order to lead to a BET of a high order of probability. A BET that said, 'This fuzzy generalization is unlikely to be true' would serve no useful purpose!

*JP:*    This looks like a major challenge to Popperian theory.

*MB:*    Not necessarily. It adapts Popperian theory to the complexity of social science where, typically, situations have a large number of variables. I can illustrate this in relation to policy by rewriting a couple of sentences from your own Chapter 4 (which I think gives a fascinating and important account of your contribution to policy studies). You say (p. 56):

> Policy statements can all be put into the form: 'If we do this, then that will happen'. Examples might be: 'If we teach children this way, they will learn better' . . . 'If we relate teachers' pay to their performance they will work harder and feel valued' . . .

Now I would want to put these policy statements into fuzzy form, viz.:

> Policy statements can all be put into the form: 'If we do this, then that *may* happen'. Examples might be: 'If we teach children this way, they *may* learn better'; 'If we relate teachers' pay to their performance they *may* work harder and feel valued'.

**JP:**    But I go on to say, 'These are propositional statements: they are either true or false.' By making them tentative, or 'fuzzy' as you call it, you destroy the opportunity of testing them from a Popperian stance.

**MB:**    Ah. If each of these fuzzy statements also has a BET (best estimate of trustworthiness), your testing of these statements can result in a refinement of the BET. If you like, it can enable the researcher to make a closer approximation to the trustworthiness of the statement. And that seems to me to be in accord with Popper.

**JP:**    I can see that it has something to do with, if you like, the *spirit* of Popper, in that it permits testing, and I think it illustrates the complexity of social problems. But I also think that a purist Popperian would argue that there are a number of other implicit propositional statements in the problem situation that are being overlooked – such as 'The effect of performance-related pay depends on the personality of the teacher' or 'The effect of performance-related pay depends on the culture of the school' – which affect the outcome of the policy.

**MB:**    Yes, but can I come back to the issue of social science situations having a large number of variables? This is in marked contrast to many natural science situations, in say chemistry or physics above the atomic level, but not dissimilar to sciences like epidemiology or meteorology where predictions about the onset of disease or of rain storms always have an element of uncertainty – that is, are fuzzy. You referred earlier to the boiling point of water being affected by the atmospheric pressure. What else is expected to affect it? Dissolved substances, yes – but little else. But put it in a social context and there are many variables. I could even argue that the perceptions of the observer are relevant – as in the proverb 'A watched pot never boils'!

*JP:*    You may be surprised to learn that I agree with your point about the complex circumstances of much social science – but I would go further. I think it reveals yet another one of those misconceptions that have so bedevilled social science. You make the contrast between the study of complex social phenomena and atomic level physical science. That kind of science is a very specialist area. I would suggest that *most* of the phenomena that are thought to be the subject of physical science are as complex as social phenomena, but we have allowed ourselves to believe that classical laboratory-based chemistry and physics are the archetypes. They study the very few phenomena it is possible to isolate, and thus eliminate the effects of extraneous variables. Most physical phenomena that we are interested in, and which affect us on a daily basis, are much more complex, as you point out, and the sciences of them offer few laws comparable with those of classical physics. If you think about it, the classical laws of physics are rarely useful in isolation. They *contribute* to our understanding of complex physical phenomena, but the phenomena are so complex and there are so many variables that, as with meteorology, we cannot describe or predict *precisely* what will happen.

This connects with what I think is another misconception about the natural and social sciences. It concerns the distinction between these and engineering. The kind of things that interest me ('what works in what circumstances') are answers to what some Popperians call 'How to?' questions, rather than 'Why?' or 'What is the case?' questions. 'How to?' questions are the domain of engineering, rather than science, yet we expect social science to offer answers to them. In this regard, policy is better addressed as a question of engineering than of science. Policy is a social artefact, just as a bridge is a physical artefact, and both have to be constructed within constraints of time, resources and current knowledge. Of course, 'science' makes a contribution, in providing tested knowledge about isolated aspects of the phenomenon (like breaking strains for bridges), but it doesn't provide the total answer to how to build a bridge – for sometimes, regrettably, a bridge falls down.

In this context, I would point out that our discussion so far relates only to one-and-a-half of the types of case study you identify – 'evaluation' and 'theory-testing' (not theory-seeking, which you group with it). Evaluation studies are a kind of theory-testing anyway (Pratt, 1999), for they test the (often implicit) hypotheses of policy or practice ('If we do this, then that will happen, and it will be better than what happened before'). Theory-testing is, in my view, the most important use for, or type of, case study, for it is *the* one that generates *tested* knowledge.

*MB:*    I agree, and this points to the importance of replication studies. Of course, no case study can exactly replicate another, but the accumulated evidence of *similar* case studies does strengthen theoretical concepts.

*JP:*    But this is not to say that theory-seeking case studies are not interesting or useful, although for me they are merely preliminary to the 'real thing' – they are one way of generating hypotheses for testing – but then so is laying in the bath and thinking. The generation of hypotheses is an important part of the process of knowledge generation, but it is not what I mean (and what I think most thinkers about research mean) by 'research'. It is not necessarily even a rational process; indeed, the most valuable hypotheses may be the ones that arise irrationally. Who, apart from Einstein, would have (could have?) *rationally* dreamed up the idea of relativity?

*MB:*    If we return to definitions, I see research as systematic and critical enquiry; so to me the generation of, critical testing of, and rational argument about, hypotheses are all part of the process. I would use the word 'empirical' where you have used 'research' – meaning, the systematic search for data by using the senses. We may disagree here. I completely agree that the generation of hypotheses is not necessarily a rational process, and that the Archimedean approach of intuitive, unfocused thinking in a hot bath is an important contribution to the development of knowledge. Dare I suggest that the ablutionary shift in our society, from the early 1980s onwards, from baths to showers may have adversely affected the advancement of knowledge!

*JP:*    Presumably you would use surveys rather than case studies to test this hypothesis? But to return to my critique, I think a similar argument applies to 'storytelling' cases. They are useful as generators of ideas, but logically their value is as evidence about the validity of hypotheses. The accounts 'deserve to be told' because they support, illustrate or contradict our (again often implicit) hypotheses about practice.

*MB:*    I think this is a matter of audience. For the people involved in the story (or in the portrayal for picture-drawing case studies), the success of the case study is in the extent to which it provides them with new insights into their situation – and this may have been the principal aim of the case-study researcher. But if the researcher publishes the study to wider audiences, then, I agree with you, the value lies in the extent to which it illuminates issues that relate to situations outside the case. Bob Stake, in his book *The Art of Case Study Research* (Stake, 1995), which I strongly recommend, distinguishes between the case (which he represents by the Greek letter theta) and issues (represented by iota) which are embedded in a case. This leads him to distinguish between what he calls 'intrinsic' case study (where theta is the focus) and 'instrumental' case study (where iota is the focus). His classification goes one step further by describing multi-site case study as 'collective' case study (where iota is studied in several thetas).

*JP:*    All right. So, to come back to my search for a robust defence of case study as a form of research, how would you summarize your position?

*MB:*    If I may, I'll do it by way of a diagram (Figure 12.1). Taking the Lawrence Stenhouse (1975) view, I see a dichotomy between studies of singularities and studies of samples. You'll see that I've placed surveys in the latter and case studies and action researches in the former. Located in both are randomized controlled experiments.

*JP:*    Hold on. Can you explain these terms?

*MB:*    Of course. A singularity has a clear boundary around one individual site (or sometimes a few), chosen because it exhibits the phenomenon that is the focus of study. A sample is a collection of sites, chosen by a process which should ensure that the sample is representative of a much larger population of sites which can be defined by a clear boundary. For example, an enquiry into truancy in one school would be a study of a singularity, while an enquiry into truancy in all secondary schools in Barsetshire, conducted in 1 in 10 of these schools, would be a study of a sample. The study in one school might be a case study, as we have discussed earlier, or it might be an action research study in which changes in the school's approach to truancy were being tried and evaluated.

*JP:*    What about randomized controlled experiments? Why are they placed in both arenas?

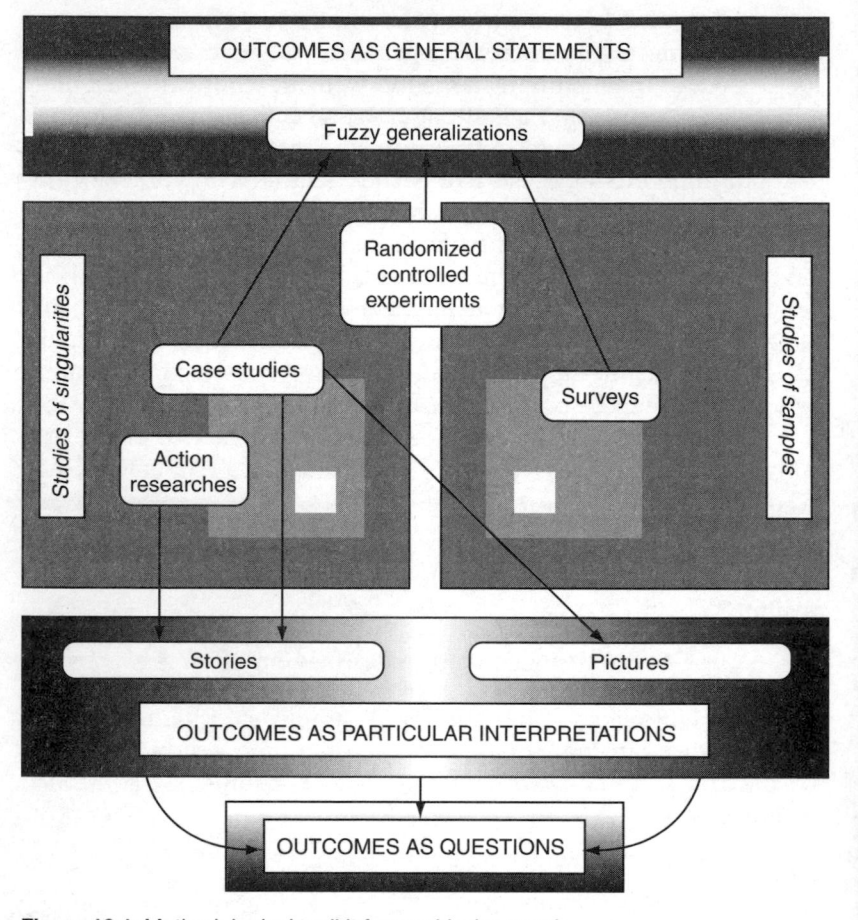

**Figure 12.1:** Methodological toolkit for empirical research

*MB:* Like an action research study, a randomized controlled experiment would entail changes in the school's approach, but there would be a control being studied (that is, a similar school) in which the approach to truancy remained unchanged. No doubt a number of experimental schools and control schools would feature in the experiment – and each of these would, of course, be a singularity. But they would have been chosen from a large population of schools by a random process, in the expectation that any findings could be applied not just to the schools under study but to all the schools in the larger population.

*JP:*    In Figure 12.1 you have various arrows leading to outcomes.

*MB:*    Yes. I have identified three different kinds of outcomes (or findings, results, conclusions, etc.) from research. These are general statements, particular interpretations or simply questions. It seems to me that case studies, randomized controlled experiments and surveys can all have the outcome of general statements, which I would choose to have expressed in the form of fuzzy generalizations (that is, 'may be' statements). Action researches can have the outcome of providing interpretations of particular situations (in the form of stories), and case studies can do the same in terms of both stories and pictures. And beyond these is the sort of outcome where the research poses questions which may stimulate practitioners or policy-makers to look deeper into their practices and policies.

*JP:*    I feel you are moving beyond the discussion of case study, but I presume this is giving a broader context to your defence of case study.

*MB:*    Indeed yes. My defence of case study is that it is one of four major forms of enquiry, each of which has a proper place in the methodological toolkit of the educational researcher. According to the circumstances of an investigation, each of these may be a valid way of seeking outcomes to critical enquiry. Forgive the pun if I say: here I rest my case.

## REFERENCES

Pollard, A. (2001) 'Possible consequences of strong constraints on teachers and pupils: some fuzzy generalizations from the PACE project', in M. Bassey, S. Hallam, A. Pollard, A. West, P. Noden and R. Stake, *Fuzzy generalization: transforming research findings into fuzzy predictions which can inform teachers', policy-makers', and researchers' discourse and action* (BERA symposium at AERA 2001), Southwell, Nottinghamshire, UK: British Educational Research Association.

Pratt, J. (1999) 'Testing policy', in J. Swann and J. Pratt (eds) *Improving Education: Realist Approaches to Method and Research*, London: Cassell, pp. 39–52.

Stake, R. E. (1995) *The Art of Case Study Research*, London: Sage.

Stenhouse, L. (1975) *An Introduction to Curriculum Research and Development*, London: Heinemann.

# Part IV

## Educational Research in Practice

# Doing good research

John Pratt, *University of East London, UK*
Joanna Swann, *King's College London, UK*

## INTRODUCTION

Various approaches to educational research have been presented in this book. In response to the questions posed in Chapter 1, researchers have explained what they do and why they do it. Our contributors do not always agree with each other, nor with us. We, the editors, have discussed some key ideas with them in the dialogues, where we have tried to draw out what we consider to be the issues raised by different approaches and their fundamental strengths and weaknesses. The main purpose of this chapter is to offer a set of principles for good research practice. Before doing this, however, we feel it will be helpful to discuss some issues of concern that have arisen from our reading of the contributors' chapters.

## CONCEPTIONS OF SCIENCE

There is a model of scientific research, largely identified with the physical sciences, which pervades discussions of educational research. Some contributors to this book react against the model – Michael Collins and Trish Johnston, in particular. Some seem to accept an aspect of it. This model goes by the name of positivism (see Glossary for a definition). The principal point we wish to make here is not just that we reject positivism, but that positivism does not accurately represent contemporary science (social and/or natural). As we noted in Chapter 1, many scientists are not positivists. When educational researchers argue, or merely assume, that scientific enquiry is inappropriate to the study of social affairs, often what they are rejecting is one particular approach to science.

We believe that there can and should be similarities of method between the natural and social sciences. As we made clear in Chapters 2 and 4, we attribute value to scientific knowledge, by which we mean testable conjectures about the world; and we consider the production of tested knowledge to be one of the main purposes of educational research. Although not all ideas about the world can be tested, we think that many ideas can be formulated for testing, and should then be tested. In particular, many aspects of educational policy and practice are associated with ideas which could be couched in a refutable – that is, testable – form. These ideas should become the focus of a science of education.

Although such a science of education could not provide us with certain and comprehensive information about 'what works', it could potentially challenge some of the assumptions on which much current policy and practice is based (Swann, 2003). If competing theories were to be rigorously tested, we would have evidence to which we could refer when deliberating whether to do one thing rather than another; we would at least have a reason to reject those theories which failed to withstand testing. The value of science both as a means of advancing knowledge and of helping us to improve practice lies only, but not insignificantly, in the method of criticism. Note also that the refutation of a theory can provide the stimulus for the creation of a new and potentially better one.

Decision-making in education is to a large extent a matter of values and politics. In this respect we agree with the arguments offered by Atkinson, Collins and Johnston. But it is of no small significance that educational decision-making also makes reference to matters of fact. All parties involved in education – as policy-makers, providers, managers, teachers, parents and students – could be well served by the development of tested knowledge about learning, teaching and the organization of education. In this respect we agree with Michael Bassey and Bill Tunmer *et al.*, although our conception of tested knowledge is somewhat different from theirs. In particular, unlike them, we do not attach value to confirming evidence. Following Karl Popper, the 'accumulated evidence of *similar* case studies' (see Bassey, p. 168) does not strengthen theoretical concepts. This is induction, and it is a myth.

The chapters by our contributors, and our dialogues with them, illustrate not only clear differences of approach – postmodern, critical theory, postpositivist, and so on – but more subtle and not insignificant differences of opinion within categories (specifically postpositivism), as well as important areas of overlap. For example, despite unresolved areas of disagreement in the dialogue between Elizabeth Atkinson and Joanna Swann, we agree with Atkinson on many issues. All three of us in our individual chapters challenge the idea that certain and secure knowledge is achievable. Although we are impressed by her account of postmodernism, we remain unconvinced by it because it seems to us that it does not go far enough. Postmodernism challenges orthodoxy and it throws up new ideas, but it does not attach value to testing these new ideas.

A further questionable aspect of the pervasive model of science is the idea that physical sciences deal with much more amenable subject matter than the social sciences, and consequently are more successful. It is not the simplicity of physical situations that makes possible the use of scientific method; rather, science has made physical situations appear simple, whereas the social sciences seem to make social situations appear complicated.[1] The model of the physical sciences that is usually implicit in discussions of social research is one of laboratory-based physics or chemistry. It is true that these endeavours have been astonishingly successful in increasing our understanding of the physical world, and have been valuable in application to technology. (Of course, they have also had some highly undesirable consequences – such as chemical weaponry.) But scientists in these fields study a very specialized and carefully controlled subset of physical phenomena, isolated in laboratories from the complications of variables with which they interact in the outside world. The laboratory-based sciences are not the counterpart to social science. Closer comparators to social science would be meteorology or astronomy, both of which address complex and uncontrollable phenomena.

We do not deny the value of non-scientific investigations of what is so – for example, exploratory or illuminative studies. But such research often, despite the denials of its protagonists, embodies elements of the hypothesis-testing approach. Similarly, we recognize the importance of research which addresses other types of theoretical problem (see p. 28). Of particular importance in education is research which addresses questions of value, such as questions of what we ought to do – ethics in education, and the ethics of education. The route to progress is similar in all types of research. It involves the formulation of a problem, the proposing of solutions, and the testing of one or more of these solutions. As in science, solutions are tested by means of critical discussion. The difference between science and non-science is this: in the latter the theories that constitute solutions are not refutable. This is not to say that matters of fact are irrelevant to questions of value. We may modify our values in light of experience when, for example, we see the implications of adopting one value position rather than another.

In our individual chapters we have emphasized a distinction between theoretical and practical problems. Whereas the former are addressed by science (and other types of enquiry), engineering addresses the latter. Of course, engineering draws on science, but it is clearly distinguishable from it; the provision of a satisfactory explanation for a phenomenon does not inevitably enable us to solve a related practical problem. In the physical world, for example, almost all of the physics relevant to weather patterns and the production of rain is known, but still we cannot avoid drought or flood. Social scientists seek to explain social phenomena, yet they are unjustly criticized for failing to solve practical social problems. Knowing that low levels of achievement at school are linked to social deprivation does not, by itself, provide a solution to the problem of how to raise levels of achievement. Although the concept of social engineering is unfashionable – and tarnished because of the atrocities committed in its name – it more accurately reflects what is often expected of the social sciences.

## PRINCIPLES FOR GOOD RESEARCH PRACTICE

Despite these critical concerns about the nature of research, and the differences of view expressed by the book's contributors and editors, there are nevertheless some themes common to all good research activity. We have drawn on our own chapters in this book, and those of our contributors, to discuss five such themes, and on this basis to suggest five principles for good research practice. The themes are: purpose, rigour, imagination, care for others, and economy. These can be remembered by means of a handy acronym: P–R–I–C–E. We are not suggesting that our contributors would agree with every aspect of the discussion, but we do think that educational researchers, whatever approach they take, should give consideration to the issues we raise. Our discussion is written with the novice researcher in mind. We have used the word 'you', when appropriate, in order to address the reader in the manner of a research supervisor advising a student.

### Purpose
All of the contributors to this book, despite their different methodological and ideological positions, have something in common. None of them is motivated purely by self-interest. Nor are they

motivated solely by the pursuit of knowledge for its own sake. Rather, they are representative of researchers who are concerned that research should be of benefit to society. Some are attempting to improve classroom practice, some are concerned with the policy context within which practice takes place. Others look to the wider socio-political issues which underlie, influence or circumscribe the organization and conduct of education.

Clearly there is no single purpose that applies to all research, though many educationists argue that educational research should be directed, in some way or other, towards the improvement of educational practice (see Bassey, p. 111 and compare with Swann, p. 12). Note also that the motivations of the individual researcher can be distinguished from the institutional purpose (if there is one) to which the research is directed.

Like many authors of textbooks for educational researchers, we advise those who are embarking on research to formulate a problem – articulated as a question – that will be central to their research programme. The core research problem stimulates other problems – research questions – and hypotheses. We also suggest that student researchers should be encouraged to recognize that good research begins with the identification of a consequential mismatch between expectation and experience (actual or anticipated) – as in, for example, 'What do you consider to be the most disappointing feature of what you've observed in classrooms?' and 'What has surprised you most about the texts you've read on formative assessment?' The identification of a mismatch may lead to the formulation of a practical problem, such as one of how to change classroom practice, or a theoretical problem, such as one of finding out more about classroom practice.

'The identification of a mismatch' and 'the formulation of a problem' are not synonymous. Mismatches have to be turned into research problems, something that often requires a good deal of thought, time and effort. The formulation of a research problem is both expectation-laden and value-impregnated. Different problems can be formulated in response to the same mismatch. A good problem will be one that is important to the researcher, worthy of investigation (a matter of value judgement), and capable of being investigated within the constraints (pertaining both to ethics and resourcing) of the situation in which the researcher is operating.

Sometimes student researchers are required by their tutors only to state the issue or issues with which they are concerned. We think the idea of an 'issue' is too vague. We encourage the formulation of problems on the grounds that it sharpens thinking and clarifies the nature of the research. You can run into difficulties if you undertake an investigation without being clear about its purpose. This is not to suggest that the initial problem cannot be refined or reformulated as the research progresses, rather that there should always be a clearly formulated problem which constitutes the focus of the study.

Formulating a research problem involves several considerations. First, and often overlooked, is *your* interest. What do *you* want to do? For many researchers (not least those contributing to this book) the stimulus for their work is something that annoys, angers or irritates them. For others it may be a burning desire to achieve a particular end, either the advancement of some area of theory or a practical benefit. Research problems are not, and should not be, conceived in isolation. There is an evolving body of disciplinary knowledge to which any research problem can be related, but being clear about what drives *you* helps to keep the research on track. The considerations brought to bear on research that has a practical problem at its core will be different from those where the main concern is with a question of what is so and why, or some other type of theoretical concern. For example, action research is often directed to problems of the kind we term 'practical'. We suggest that when initiating, planning and conducting research, researchers should be clear about the type of problem – practical or theoretical – that provides the impetus for their work (see Chapter 2, pp. 27–9 and Chapter 4, pp. 55–6).

In general, we advise the researcher to formulate just one overarching problem. Usually there is no need to have more. Indeed, if there are more the resultant study is likely to be ill-focused and confused. Sometimes, however, a research project may have more than one phase. For example, the first phase may be designed to find out more about what is the case (a theoretical problem) in a particular context, such as a school; the second may focus on how to do something about it (a practical problem). We hope we have made clear that a 'research problem' is not the same as a 'research question'. A research problem might be, 'Why can't this group of children read to the standard expected?' (theoretical problem) or 'How can I help this group of children to read to the standard I expect?' (practical problem). The research questions might include 'What help do these children get at home with reading?', 'What theories of reading are there, and what are their strengths and limitations?' These research questions may be relevant to both projects. Such questions help to focus the investigation, and help you to decide the methods that will be used. The first question might be addressed by interviewing, the second by reading books.

Some of the contributors to this book seem to be suggesting that there is only one way of doing research, or one set of issues on which educational research should focus. We reject this idea. In particular, although researchers may wish to assist under-privileged groups in society, this does not automatically entail a specific method of research. And it does not mean that this preference alters the *logic* of advancing knowledge through criticism.

The value positions and preferences of researchers should not be confused with methodological questions about how knowledge is advanced. It is clearly possible to separate philosophical and logical considerations from the choice of problem to which they are applied. This does not mean they are not connected, but that they can be – and should be – *considered* separately. As an analogy: the use to which a tool – a chisel, for example – is put is a different matter from whether that tool is of its nature good or bad. If you use it to kill people, that's bad; if you use it to carve a door, that's good. A research method is, similarly, a kind of tool that enables you to do particular kinds of things – find things out, develop new ideas and test them. Whether a research approach is good depends on what you have chosen to do and what methods you have chosen to employ to do it. The methodological question is, 'Which methods are appropriate to the research problem?'

Differences of approach, ideology or paradigm often confuse the novice researcher; they seem to imply that a researcher has to make a single choice from among them. Many research textbooks present the different paradigms as mutually exclusive. They sometimes insist that researchers should first decide on the paradigm they are employing in their research, and that this will determine the techniques they must use – as if only one view is possible, and that particular research techniques are exclusively appropriate to one paradigm. As we suggested in Chapter 1, any novice researcher who is offered a choice between quantitative and qualitative methodologies (or between the positivist and interpretivist paradigms) is, we believe, being misled. There are no exclusively quantitative or qualitative ways of doing research, only quantitative and qualitative tools and procedures. We concur with Tunmer *et al.* (p. 95) that 'scientific research can involve either quantitative or qualitative data (or both)'. And even though there are a number of distinctive approaches, they are not necessarily mutually exclusive; exponents of different approaches often collaborate on research projects. We do not claim here that it is always possible to reach agreement or resolution of all, or even many, of the differences between these approaches, but it is quite possible, and not an infrequent occurrence, to seek to test a hypothesis about an educational practice by using an interpretive approach and highly subjective qualitative data. To test, for example, whether a new teaching method results in a better pupil response may well involve exploring the feelings of pupils.

In extreme cases, it is sometimes argued that rational discussion is impossible between adherents of different approaches to research (the incommensurability thesis) or between members of different cultures. Like Popper (1994, Chapter 2), we accept that discussion between people with very different points of view may be difficult, and that agreement may be unlikely, but we think such discussion can still be valuable in the pursuit of truth. Indeed, the advancement of knowledge depends on disagreement. This is one of the ideas that the book's dialogue chapters are intended to illustrate.

*Rigour*

The contributors to this book address issues of rigour in a number of different ways. At one – technical – level, rigour means being methodical, using appropriate techniques and attending to detail. At another – logical – level, it is expressed as a concern for the validity of argument, and the soundness of evidence. We, the book's editors, are committed to research that produces, and makes reference to, ideas which have been subjected to intensive critical scrutiny. In general, this process involves the development of argumentative language, and a respect for the canons of logic – for example, one strives to avoid non sequiturs. It also involves recourse to ideas which have been tested against empirical evidence. We agree with Tunmer *et al.* that 'educational research is more than just telling stories or analysing discourses' (p. 96); it is a means by which we can generate testable and tested knowledge about how students learn in classrooms, what promotes and what inhibits learning, the consequences of policy, and so on. A concomitant of this view is that for an activity to merit the description 'research', it must not be designed with the intention of confirming existing expectations or prejudices (though it might be hoped that they are confirmed).

We think that both the generation of ideas *and* the testing of hypotheses are fundamental to educational research. While we appreciate that ideas are generated by the irony and playfulness characteristic of some postmodern approaches (discussed by Atkinson in Chapter 3), we think, as mentioned earlier, that these approaches fall short because they do not attempt to produce test-able theories. Generating novel, iconoclastic or playful interpret-ations of events and situations is one thing; what matters is whether or not the interpretations are right. In research, not all hypotheses are equal. Our knowledge of what is true is always insecure, but we can nonetheless make provisional judgements about whether a theory is false. When competing theories have been tested, there is reason to prefer those which have stood up to testing rather than those which have not. The Earth, for example, may not be perfectly spherical, but the hypothesis that it is round is much closer to the truth than the idea that it is flat.

Although we have stressed the importance of research that seeks to challenge expectations through the formulation and testing of hypotheses, we nonetheless acknowledge that many people embark on research with what they believe to be open questions. Much edu-cational research seems to be of this nature. Although there is noth-ing wrong *per se* with formulating interesting and consequential questions of what is the case, and developing ways of answering them, it seems to us that question-answering is often used in educa-tion as a substitute for hypothesis-testing. By this we mean that the researcher has expectations about what the answers to the research questions might be, but these are not made explicit. For example, a researcher might set out to address, 'What is the impact of our lit-eracy programme on children's attitudes to reading?' It may be the case that she has no conscious expectations as to what the answer will be. But if she has, there is a danger that she will merely search for evidence that will confirm her unformulated expectations (implicit hypotheses).

Our advice to student researchers who have decided to adopt an open-question approach, is to formulate their expectations about what might be found before collecting data in the field or engaging in a substantial amount of reading. They should then look for the unexpected – for answers they hadn't anticipated. Whether answer-ing open questions or testing hypotheses, it is the discovery of the unexpected that leads to learning. And it is the task of all researchers to create situations in which the unexpected may be discovered. Sometimes researchers shy away from discovering the unexpected, from discovering that their expectations are erroneous or limited. But, as argued in Chapter 2, life is a process of trial and error. The task of the researcher is not to avoid error but to discover it, and, having discovered it, to eliminate it. In the words of David Miller (1999, p. 3), 'What distinguishes human beings, and even scientists, from other beings is not a superiority in avoiding errors, but a superiority in replacing them'.

All research is flawed. We have to work within limits of time and money, sometimes of access and ethics. The evidence we collect is always partial – in both senses of the word. It is always incomplete, and in use it depends on the interpretation of the researcher. The techniques we use are never perfect. We cannot measure anything without affecting it, and rarely can we collect all the data we would wish. This is particularly true of data concerning human feelings and perceptions, but it applies equally to 'hard' data such as statistics of examination results, expenditure or student characteristics. As Popper has convincingly argued (see, for example, 1979[1972], pp. 71–3, 258–9), there is no expectation-free observation. How data are collected and handled is central to ensuring rigour. It is here that meticulousness and care become particularly important. Interviews need to be carefully conducted, questionnaires adequately piloted, and data accurately analysed. But in an important sense, these are second-order issues. More important is the choice of evidence to be sought, the method for collecting it, and the way in which the evidence is used.

Because, as noted above, evidence is always incomplete and imperfect, the way we use it should take account of this. For example, for a hypothesis to be scientific it must be susceptible to refutation by reference to empirical evidence. Whether the hypothesis is falsifiable is an unequivocal condition – either it is or it isn't – but the judgement that a theory has been falsified is not infallible. Of course, there are cases where a test seems to be definitive and the evidence conclusive, but in science as in all research the issue is one of argument and persuasion, using the evidence that is available.

One way of making a (provisional) decision about the worth of a theory, scientific or non-scientific, is to take a 'judicial' approach. The model is loosely that of a court of law. The conclusions of the analysis are based on the evidence put forward, including the testimony of the various 'witnesses'. In empirical research, possible 'witnesses' include respondents to interviews and the researcher herself (perhaps drawing on notes made in a log). What constitutes 'reasonable' depends on the content of the proposition and the circumstances in which it is applied. What counts is the strength and appropriateness of the evidence and the validity of the argument. How strong is the evidence as a foundation for these conclusions? How 'firm' a conclusion will this evidence support? The question is whether the evidence has reasonably demonstrated that a hypothesis or other proposition has stood up to the test. Popper (1972[1934], p. 415) wrote about the 'degree of corroboration' of a hypothesis being 'a measure of the rationality of *accepting*, tentatively, a problematic guess . . . that has undergone searching examinations'. For research concerned with the improvement of practice, these judgements are crucial, for they will inform decisions about future action. Decisions have to be made, and we want them to be made well. But, as in a court of law, the verdict can be mistaken. It is here that the 'public character' (Popper, 1966[1945], p. 218) of research is significant. The evidence which research produces is available for scrutiny by others. The provisional acceptance of the conclusions drawn does not rest on the 'objectivity' of the individual researcher, but on the criticism (if only potential) of others.

*Imagination*
But there is more to research than painstaking meticulousness and epistemological soundness. Good research requires imagination. Research, like learning itself, is a creative activity. It is creativity that enables research to produce *new* knowledge. The world of public knowledge – constructed out of the subjective experience of countless individuals, but not synonymous with it – is the consequence of qualities such as openness of mind, persistence, courage and, in particular, imaginative criticism:

> The process of learning, of the growth of subjective knowledge, is always fundamentally the same. It is *imaginative criticism*. This is how we transcend our local and temporal environment by trying to think of circumstances *beyond* our experience: by criticizing the universality, or the structural necessity, of what may, to us, appear (or what philosophers may describe) as the 'given' or as 'habit'; by trying to find, construct, invent, new situations – that is, *test* situations, *critical* situations; and by trying to locate, detect, and challenge our prejudices and habitual assumptions.
>
> (Popper, 1979[1972], p. 148)

As we've emphasized in our individual chapters, formulating problems is a creative process. It involves us in saying that things are not as we would wish them to be, or that we do not know what we want or need to know – as a preliminary to doing something about it. There is no formula for creating a good research problem. The researcher has to have the confidence to invent something for herself. In general, in addition to advising students to be clear about whether they are primarily concerned with changing practice or with developing theory, we also recommend that they try out different ideas and linguistic formulations – all entailing a question – and discuss them with other people as a means of clarifying their thoughts and identifying weaknesses in their formulations.

Developing a research strategy is also a creative endeavour. The purpose of the research strategy is to enable you to generate a solution to your research problem. We emphasize that the process may be iterative, with problems being reformulated as the implications of strategy become apparent. If your overriding concern is with the improvement of practice, then, as indicated above, procedures associated with action research may be (though they are not always) useful. If your problem is theoretical, you may need to formulate a set of hypotheses for testing, or a set of research questions, or a combination of both.

Remember that, as Bassey notes in Chapter 8, educational research uses and contributes to methodologies of the other social sciences. It may be useful to draw on understanding from these fields. Remember, also, that when you've developed a process for addressing your research problem, you then have to decide how you are going to analyse and interpret your findings. The research questions and hypotheses provide a framework for analysing the outcomes of your study, and will be suggestive of the way in which the research report can be structured. In thought experiments, anything can be considered. It is valuable to consider investigating a variety of hypotheses, and to be prepared to employ a variety of methods. But we suggest limiting the number of hypotheses and questions that you actually address: more isn't necessarily better.

How will the ideas with which you are concerned – your solutions to practical problems, or your hypotheses, or your answers to your research questions – be subjected to a process of rigorous criticism? As discussed in Chapter 2, we can discover error through happenstance, but we can also engage in the creative activity of finding ways to discover (and eliminate) our errors more quickly. In our view, the rationale for research is to do just this – to set up test situations and critical situations (as mentioned in the above quotation from Popper).

We have found that one way of developing tests is to ask of a hypothesis (or course of action), 'What would things look like if it were true (or if it were working)?' In the case of a hypothesis, we make a prediction and test it by observation. We test a course of action by addressing, 'To what extent, if at all, has (have) the initial problem (or problems) been solved?', 'What unintended and unexpected consequences (desirable or undesirable) have arisen?' and 'With the benefit of hindsight, might other solutions have been preferable?' (see p. 31). In order to construct a test, we have to address, 'What kinds of data are needed?'; then, 'Where are these data located?', which often leads to questions about the nature of the sample. And, finally, 'What is the best way of accessing that data?' In other words, method comes last.

The testing of hypotheses and practices is central to research, and to the improvement of policy and practice. By taking account of circumstances, and by examining our hypotheses in different contexts, it is often possible to identify the limiting conditions for success and failure. For example, a particular approach to teaching may not work when specific resources are unavailable, or with particular kinds of pupils.

Being critical about ideas in which we have a vested interest is not always easy. But, in a wider sense, as researchers we have a responsibility to search for error, to find out where theories – our own and those of others – are false, where arguments are invalid, and in what respects policies and practices have undesirable consequences. Researchers of the kind who have contributed to this book challenge not only theory, but also policy and practice. Their interest in improvement means that, almost inevitably, they will rail against the status quo in education, policy-makers in government, and even social structures and processes.

What kinds of testing is it possible to undertake in practice as a researcher? Although you might expect a country's central government to share the commitment to improvement that this book and its contributors demonstrate, your expectation may be ill-founded. The British government, for example, is reluctant to support or even acknowledge critical testing of its policies and practices. It advocates evidence-based policy, but in practice what this usually means is finding instances of where its policy seems to work. Evidence of failure is not sought, and if found this evidence is sometimes suppressed. It is in the nature of politics that politicians have a vested interest in being seen to be right.

### Care for others
Obstacles to testing come in other forms, too. It is often argued that researchers shouldn't subject children to a new approach to classroom practice if it departs radically from what has been done before.

This fails to recognize three things. First, because all knowledge is provisional, we can never be sure that existing practice is the best possible practice. Existing practice is therefore also experimental, though it is rarely treated that way. Second, practice is often not tested for its effectiveness; and even when it is, the 'test' often takes the form of searching for supporting evidence – critical evidence may be excused or explained away. Third, even when it has been tested, existing practice often continues in the face of overwhelming evidence that it is ineffective.

Formal education and formal training involve doing things to people – most often to children and young adults – and doing them on a large scale. It is surely incumbent on us, as a matter of principle, to foster rigorous systematic investigations into the consequences of what is done in the name of education or training, and to try to find ways of doing things better. This is, we think, part of the moral duty of those involved in the provision of a public service. Educational research is not an optional extra; rather, it should be construed as a core activity. In short, we think that research should be undertaken as a matter of principle – the principle of care for others. This principle is also an important one for the conduct of research itself. We do not underestimate the practical difficulties that this involves, and we would not wish to be seen as researcher-imperialists. But we believe that it is important and possible to undertake systematic yet unobtrusive investigation into the outcomes of policies and practice.

The principle of care for others has practical implications for researchers. It requires them to engage with ethical concerns in their research. Some of the book's contributors have raised these concerns: see Johnston's chapter in particular, and Box 8.3 of Bassey's chapter (also, Chapter 2, p. 12). A major consideration in research ethics is how to protect the subjects of research from breaches of confidence, undue pressure, stress, and so on. Most research projects have to be submitted to an ethics committee to ensure that they conform with widely accepted principles, such as: obtain informed consent; ensure that participation is voluntary; preserve confidentiality. (For a summary of these and other principles, see Davidson and Tolich, 1999, Appendix 7.) Johnston (in Chapter 7) makes a strong case for taking ethical issues further, arguing, largely on ideological grounds, that the research subjects should be both involved in the research and have ownership of it. Such involvement is, in our view, morally sound, and it generates (and may result from) new ways of looking at the issues. In this sense, ethics works.

The key questions raised by Johnston (pp. 107–8) centre around the relationship between the researcher and the researched. Consideration of these questions raises further questions about the choice and design of the research and the methods to be employed. But, in our view, while it is important to consider the involvement of the researched in research, as a way of recognizing both their dignity and potential contribution, it is also important that researchers maintain their independence. We think the researcher should be responsible for ensuring the integrity of the research. The idea of 'ownership' of research by its subjects, if by this is meant total control, is problematical, because, as research is an enterprise involving more than one set of interests, ownership must necessarily be joint. Research should not be driven by the prejudices of the researched, any more than the researched should be victims of the prejudices of the researcher (or those who commission the research, or make use of the research findings).

Ethical issues also arise for many researchers because of their dependence on funding agencies. Those who pay the piper, so to speak, have a right to make stipulations about the organization and conduct of the work they fund. A funding agency may also reserve the right to edit a research report, or restrict its circulation, if dissemination of its content is not in its interest. But researchers cannot allow a funding agency to specify what the findings of the research should be, for then it ceases to be properly tested knowledge. Researchers should be wary of engaging in research where pressures and stipulations of this kind prevail (see British Educational Research Association, 1992). A process with either prescribed or proscribed conclusions can hardly be called research, and if the findings of a research project are in the public interest they should be made public.

In summary, ethical considerations are important for both moral and practical reasons. The politico-ethical nature of research is often a messy business; all the more reason for the researcher to formulate and develop a view about what is and what is not ethical practice. Reference to guidelines such as those of research organizations may help here. See also, for interesting and useful discussion, Ivan Snook (1999) on the ethics and politics of social research:

> The modern tendency to make research subordinate to politics need not lead to the conclusion that a research ethic is

impossible. Instead it should lead to the conclusion that those preparing to be researchers should understand the ethics and the politics of research as well as the technical elements.

(Ibid., p. 81)

*Economy*

Research is time-consuming and it can be expensive. It is always time-consuming for the researcher(s), and often for the subjects of the research – for instance, when they are interviewed or asked to complete a questionnaire. We advise researchers – specifically novice researchers, who have yet to learn the hard way about how long it takes to complete procedures (longer than you'd expect!) and how much they cost (travel and printing, for example) – to take seriously the question of how to make their research economical.

This is not an easy business. Research can be a long and winding road. But a concern with what is feasible within the unavoidable constraints of time and money is important. In the first place, it is important to remember that research is a way of finding out what is *not* already known. For example, it's not research – or at least not good research – to discover that children at your school who come from an impoverished socio-economic background have lower standards of attainment, for this relationship is widely known and reported in the literature. Discovering this would just be a case of learning something that could more easily be learned by reading a book. A better research question might focus on investigating whether children from similar socio-economic backgrounds in your school perform differently from each other, or how the advice from research about effective measures to improve performance of pupils like these can be implemented in your school.

This is where a literature search comes in. Many research students regard the literature search as a bit of a chore. It's what academics make you do, because it's the currency that academics trade in, and it's a way of checking whether you've read any of the books on the reading list. But a literature search should be functional. There's no point in reading all those books and articles for the sake of it. An important function of reading, as Tunmer *et al.* point out in Chapter 6 (p. 95), is to develop a solid understanding of theoretical issues, of the kind discussed in this book, in the philosophy of science. Another function is to find out what is already known about the topic that interests you, so that you can go on to do something useful. A good literature search concisely summarizes the established findings in the research area and establishes the boundaries, so to speak, of what is (conjecturally) known, and where existing findings cease to inform. It establishes the theoretical framework for your own research problem, and shows that it is worth researching.

Often, there is no need to rehearse the literature at length, though this depends on the area and on the function of the literature review. There is little value in copying out extensive quotations, or paraphrasing at length what is written better in the original – though there are plenty of original texts for which a paraphrase is clearer! In our experience as assessors of research reports, you get credit for what *you* think, not what other people have said. It's also worth remembering that you are more likely to be accurately informed about the work of a particular author if you read primary rather than secondary sources. Secondary sources may help you to understand complex texts, and may offer valuable critiques of the primary source, but they are no substitute for the original. We have noted earlier (in Chapters 1 and 2) the frequent misrepresentations of Popper by otherwise apparently competent academics. Popper's work is not unique in this respect. Reading the original helps to avoid such errors. Reading others' critiques helps to engage with the issues raised.

Fieldwork is particularly time-consuming and expensive. Don't plan extensive fieldwork if the information you need is already available in published texts (in books, journal articles, on the Internet, etc.). This is not to say that there is no value in learning to conduct interviews, for example; but any interviews you conduct should serve some clear purpose in the context of your research problem and strategy. That's not to say that you shouldn't conduct large- (or even small-) scale surveys, but we advise you to select carefully the questions to ask. Even modest surveys generate thousands of bits of information (20 questions to 150 respondents = 3000 answers and any number of cross-tabulations). It is also often useful to engage in participant or non-participant observation in order to get a better feel for the type of setting to which your research problem refers; but, again, you should only do as much of this as is necessary in the service of your specific project. Don't get sidetracked by concerns which, though they may be of interest, are nonetheless outwith the focus of your study. Of course, deciding what is necessary isn't easy; often it only becomes clear when the research has been completed.

Economy is not to be sought just for economic reasons. Other things being equal, the easiest, quickest and cheapest methods are, of course, preferable, but economic working is both an aim and an outcome of good research. Apt and relevant formulation of the problem to be solved, the hypotheses to be tested and the research questions to be addressed, lead to the identification of specific kinds of data to be sought. All too often data lie unused and unanalysed.

Finally, bear in mind that your research report will be read – by yourself (perhaps at a later date) and by the people who are to evaluate your research (tutors, examiners, or the funding body, if there is one). Make it easier for readers by avoiding unnecessary jargon, and by writing in a style that makes the ideas in your report as accessible as you can make them. Follow Quine and Ullian's dictum that 'whatever there is to be said can, through perseverance, be said clearly' (1970, quoted by Tunmer *et al.* on pp. 93 and 96 of this volume). What is clear is, of course, audience-related. Differentiation of reports for different audiences may be appropriate. By being economical with time at earlier stages in the project, you will be in a better position to ensure that you have sufficient time to devote to the analysis of your research outcomes and the writing of your report.

## SUMMARY OF PRINCIPLES FOR GOOD RESEARCH PRACTICE

The P–R–I–C–E of research is as follows:

- *Purpose*: When initiating, planning and conducting research, be clear about (a) the purposes that you wish the research to serve, and (b) the type of problem (practical or theoretical) which provides the impetus for your work. Remember that the methods you adopt should be determined by the nature of the problem, not the other way round.
- *Rigour*: Be prepared to subject ideas – your own and those of others – to rigorous critical scrutiny. This requires being methodical, using appropriate techniques and attending to detail. It involves a 'judicial' approach to the validity of argument and the soundness of evidence. Remember that the advancement of knowledge requires the discovery and elimination of error.
- *Imagination*: Be aware that research is a creative activity. You will need to use your imagination in order to invent problems, solutions and tests. Remember, in particular, that research problems don't exist until they have been formulated.
- *Care for others*: Exercise a moral duty of care for others in the planning, conduct and writing up of your research. Remember that a course of action may fulfil explicit and worthy aspirations,

but it may also have unintended consequences which do untold damage to the well-being of various individuals and groups.

- *Economy*: Research is time-consuming and can be expensive. Aim for economy of effort, time and resources – for both you and those who are participating in your research. Remember that reading the literature may save you from wasting time doing fieldwork to find out what is already known.

## NOTE

1. We are grateful to David Turner for this formulation.

## REFERENCES

British Educational Research Association (1992) *Ethical Guidelines*, Southwell, UK: British Educational Research Association: http://www.bera.ac.uk/guidelines.html (accessed 5 May 2002).

Davidson, C. and Tolich, M. (eds) (1999) *Social Science Research in New Zealand: Many Paths to Understanding*. Auckland, New Zealand: Pearson Education.

Miller, D. (1999) 'The only way to learn', English text of a lecture delivered to the 10th Congreso Nacional de Filosofía, Huerta Grande, Córdoba, Argentina, 24–27 November.

Popper, K. R. (1966) *The Open Society and its Enemies, Volume 2 – The High Tide of Prophecy: Hegel, Marx, and the Aftermath*, London: Routledge and Kegan Paul (first edition 1945).

Popper, K. R. (1972) *The Logic of Scientific Discovery*, London: Hutchinson (first published in German in 1934) (first English edition 1959).

Popper, K. R. (1979) *Objective Knowledge: An Evolutionary Approach*, Oxford, UK: Oxford University Press (first edition 1972).

Popper, K. R. (1994) *The Myth of the Framework: In Defence of Science and Rationality*, ed. M. A. Notturno, London: Routledge.

Quine, W. V. and Ullian, J. S. (1970) *The Web of Belief*, New York: Random House.

Snook, I. (1999) 'The ethics and politics of social research', in C. Davidson and M. Tolich (eds) *Social Science Research in New Zealand: Many Paths to Understanding*, Auckland, New Zealand: Pearson Education, pp. 69–81.

Swann, J. (2003) 'How science can contribute to the improvement of educational practice', *Oxford Review of Education*, June (in press).

# Glossary: a Popperian view of some important research terms and their usage

Joanna Swann, *King's College London*, UK
John Pratt, *University of East London*, UK

Here we provide definitions and brief accounts of some terms (listed in alphabetical order) that are used in discussions of research methodology. The selection is not meant to be comprehensive; rather, we have chosen terms which have been found to be problematic, particularly by novice researchers. Terms with specialist meanings which are not directly relevant to educational research have mostly been excluded. The content of the glossary reflects our own philosophical position, and is not intended as a substitute for wider reading.

***action research***    A term which came into widespread use following the work of Kurt Lewin (1946). Action research has various meanings. In general, it 'denotes that a project includes both action to change a specific situation and also research designed to understand the situation better, or to monitor the change, or both' (Finch, 1986, p. 189). Some accounts of action research lay stress on its collaborative implications:

> There are two essential aims of all action research: to *improve* and to *involve*. Action research aims at improvement in three areas: firstly, the improvement of a *practice*; secondly, the improvement of the *understanding* of the practice by its practitioners; and, thirdly, the improvement of the *situation* in which the practice takes place. The aim of *involvement* stands shoulder to shoulder with the aim of *improvement*. Those involved in the practice being considered are to be involved in the action

research process in all its phases of planning, acting, observing and reflecting. As an action research project develops, it is expected that a widening circle of those affected by the practice will become involved in the research process.

(Carr and Kemmis, 1986, p. 165)

Action research is well suited to professionals undertaking part-time study, but it can be problematic for full-time students, specifically for those who don't have the appropriate insider knowledge and contacts needed to study a change in a practice or situation. When student researchers cannot be party to a process of change, then the research they undertake will not be *action* research. Note that action research is a broad church – no particular methodological stance is entailed. It is sometimes lacking in rigour, hence Tyrrell Burgess's (2002, p. 3) scathing definition: 'any inquiry conducted in a school or classroom, in which the research involves and implies no action, and any action is innocent of research'. For a Popperian problem-based methodology that can be utilized for action research, see Swann (1999a and pp. 30–1 of the present volume). For a useful set of ethical 'Principles of procedure for action researchers', see Stephen Kemmis and Robin McTaggart (1988, pp. 106–8).

*argument*   (1) Discussion involving two or more different points of view, in which reasons are given for adopting one point of view rather than another. (2) Reasoning intended to persuade another or others to support one particular point of view or course of action. Deductive reasoning (which can be contrasted with inductive reasoning – cf. induction, q.v. hypothetico-deductive method) involves reasoning from premises that are known to a conclusion that is already contained within the premises. As in:

1. All humans are mortal. (First premise)
2. Socrates is a human. (Second premise)
3. Therefore, Socrates is mortal. (Deductive conclusion)

If at least one of the premises is false, then the conclusion may be false even though the reasoning is valid. For example (from Swartz, 1980, p. XXX):

1. All snakes can fly. (First premise)
2. There is a snake in my garden today. (Second premise)
3. Therefore, the snake in my garden can fly. (Deductive conclusion)

*axiology*   A term used to describe the study of values and value judgements.

*case study*   A widely used term with a variety of meanings – see Chapter 3 of Michael Bassey's *Case Study Research in Educational Settings* (1999). Adapting the definition from *The New Oxford Dictionary of English* (1998), a case study is a process or record of research in which detailed consideration is given to the development of a particular person, group, institution, situation or practice over a period of time. Case study often figures in discussions about generalization (q.v.), in which it would be better understood as a test of a universal theory (q.v.) under specific circumstances.

*causality*   The relation between cause and effect (q.v. explanation).

*confirming evidence*   Evidence that appears to support an expectation (q.v.), assumption, hypothesis (q.v.), or other explicit theory. Confirming evidence may encourage the development of an idea, because it fulfils a need for a feeling of security; but it may also lead to complacency and, ultimately, torpor. The Popperian view is that we do not learn from situations in which our expectations remain unchallenged; we learn only from those in which they are shown to be false or, at least, inadequate (for discussion, see Petersen, 1992). (qq.v. corroboration, induction, verification)

*corroboration*   Commonly viewed as a process in which a general theory, or other account of an event or state of affairs, is confirmed (qq.v. confirmation, induction). Alternatively, for Karl Popper, corroboration is 'an evaluating *report of past performance* ... it has to do with a situation that may lead us to prefer some theories to others. *But it says nothing whatever about future performance, or about the "reliability" of a theory*' (Popper, 1979[1972], p. 18).

*critical rationalism*   The view that

> a rationalist approach to scientific knowledge can be unhesitatingly maintained provided that we surrender completely the doctrine that identifies rationality with justification, whether conclusive or inconclusive. What is rational about scientific activity is not that it provides us with reasons for its conclusions, which it does not, but that it takes seriously the use of

reason – deductive logic, that is – in the criticism and appraisal of those conclusions.

(Miller, 1994, p. ix)

Karl Popper, with his *Logic of Scientific Discovery* (1972a[1934]), is regarded as the founding father of critical rationalism (qq.v. argument, rationalism).

*critical theory* An umbrella term for a range of approaches to research, which, like postpositivism (cf.) and interpretivism (cf.), developed as a critical response to positivism (cf.), specifically logical positivism. Most contemporary critical theory is rooted in, or at least heavily influenced by, the work of Jürgen Habermas, one of the later members of the Frankfurt School (see in particular: Habermas, 1971a, 1971b, 1984[1981], 1987[1981]). He asserted the existence of three interdependent forms of scientific enquiry: *empirical-analytic*, concerned with prediction and control; *historical hermeneutic*, concerned with understanding; and *critical theory*, concerned with emancipation (freedom from domination). In pursuit of emancipation, which requires both self-reflection and the analysis of power relationships, the critical theorist focuses on 'interpretive understanding of systems of belief and modes of communication using the methods of historical-hermeneutic science; the critical evaluation of these; and the investigation of their causes by the methods of empirical-analytic science' (Blaikie, 1993, p. 55). (See Chapter 5.)

*data* Plural of datum, meaning accumulated pieces of information. Not identical with 'evidence', which data become only if related to a problem or question.

*effectiveness* A term researchers should use with care. It refers to the ability to produce the desired result, but is often confused with efficiency (cf.).

*efficiency* The relationship between inputs and outputs. Note that the desirability of the output is irrelevant to this measure, and thus it should not be confused, as it often is, with effectiveness (cf.). Efficiency is also often muddled in use by relating inputs to other inputs (rather than outputs), as in the use of student:teacher ratios as a measure of efficiency.

*empirical* Widely used to describe research or evidence that involves observation or data collection, but it also has more precise technical meanings (q.v. empiricism).

*empiricism*   Used loosely to refer to the idea that knowledge and sensory experience are inextricably linked, in that knowledge is thought to start with experience (naïve empiricism), or be justified by experience (an implication of pragmatism), or, in the Popperian view, be criticized by experience (cf. rationalism). Many theorists mistakenly use the term more narrowly to refer to naïve empiricism. Note the following from Karl Popper (1972b[1963], p. 406):

> I am an empiricist of sorts, in so far as I hold that 'most of our theories are false anyway' . . . and that we learn from experience – that is, from our mistakes – how to correct them. But I also hold that our senses are not sources of knowledge, in any authoritative sense. There is no such thing as *pure* observation or *pure* sense-experience: all perception is interpretation in the light of experience: in the light of expectations, of theories. . . . there does not exist anything like a sense-datum, anything 'given' or uninterpreted which is the given material of that interpretation which leads to perception: everything is interpreted, selected, on some level or other, by our very senses themselves.

*engineering*   'The application of scientific and mathematical principles to practical ends such as the design, manufacture, and operation of efficient and economical structures, machines, processes, and systems' (*The American Heritage Dictionary of the English Language*, 2000). However, although an engineer refers to scientific theories when setting out to create the conditions by which a specified object, event or state of affairs can be achieved, science does not, and cannot, provide all the information she or he needs. Engineering typically deals with practical problems ('How can . . .?') and always involves a process of 'try it and see', usually by testing models and prototypes. Engineering may be better conceived as a matter of *exploiting* scientific knowledge than of simply applying it (Miller, 1994, p. 40). (cf. technology, qq.v. science, social engineering)

*epistemology*   The philosophical study of the nature of knowledge.

*ethics*   Moral principles that govern human activity. In research, the term is used to refer to codes to which researchers are expected to conform in order to protect their research subjects – and themselves. These codes may, on occasion, seem excessively protective – requiring, for example, signed statements of 'informed consent' from subjects who are unlikely to need them (such as politicians interviewed by a researcher). Many professional bodies produce useful ethical guidelines. Most universities require research involving human subjects – and hence educational research – to be subjected to ethical approval; some are more intelligent in their application of the practice than others.

*evaluation* A process by which the amount, value or worth of something is judged. It is important to note the element of judgement in evaluation. Simply presenting data is not an evaluation: it is the validity of the argument that counts.

*expectation* A term widely used by Karl Popper: 'as a *disposition to react, or as a preparation for a reaction,* which is adapted to (or which anticipates) a state of the environment yet to come about' (1979[1972], p. 344). He argued that 'every animal is born with expectations or anticipations, which could be framed as hypotheses; a kind of hypothetical knowledge' (ibid., p. 258). (cf. hypothesis, knowledge, theory)

*explanation* In research, an answer to a question about why something is the case – that is, a question about causality (q.v.). More specifically, an explanation is a

> *logical deduction*; a deduction whose conclusion is the *explicandum* – a statement of the thing to be explained – and whose premises consist of the *explicans* (a statement of the explaining laws and conditions). . . . Thus an explanation is always the deduction of the *explicandum* from certain premises, to be called the *explicans.*
> (Popper (1979[1972], pp. 349–50)

All explanations are conjectural or hypothetical, which means they may be false. They may also be unsatisfactory by virtue of being circular. A circular explanation is one where it is only possible to adduce the *explicandum* as evidence (ibid., p. 351). (cf. prediction, q.v. hypothetico-deductive method)

*fact* To a realist, a fact is a real state of affairs to which a true statement corresponds. There are, of course, more facts than there are uttered true statements. Also, even if a statement is true, we can't be certain that this is so (qq.v. induction, truth).

*fallibilism*    The idea that all scientific theories are potentially erroneous and should therefore be regarded as provisional.

*falsifiability*    A logical property of those universal theories which can be and have been formulated in such a way that they are susceptible to falsification by reference to empirical evidence. Falsifiability is Karl Popper's criterion of demarcation between scientific and non-scientific theories (1972a[1934], section 6). (qq.v. falsification, falsificationism, metaphysical, refutation, science)

*falsification*    The process of falsifying a theory (cf. refutation, q.v. falsifiability). Falsification involves argument, and reference to evidence which is invariably context-bound and incomplete. A decision as to whether or not a theory has been falsified is always a matter of judgement, and judgement is potentially flawed. Thus falsification is not, as is sometimes mistakenly assumed, a route to certain knowledge of what is not true (q.v. falsificationism).

*falsificationism*    The idea that a falsifiable universal theory should be admitted to science (q.v.) and then subjected to testing – that is, by the search for refuting evidence (cf. justificationism). When a theory has been refuted it may be either rejected or, in some cases, modified. A modification which makes a theory less testable (an immunizing stratagem) limits the potential for learning (Popper, 1985b; 1979[1972], p. 30). (qq.v. falsifiability, falsification, refutation)
    Note the difference between naïve falsificationism and sophisticated falsificationism. The former is the idea that falsifiable claims to knowledge can be absolutely refuted; the latter is the idea that falsifiable claims to knowledge can be refuted, but such claims remain tentative or conjectural (adapted from Phillips, 1987, p. 204).

*foundationalism*    The idea that some ideas are indubitably true, and thus provide a foundation upon which others can be developed. (cf. fallibilism)

*fuzzy generalization*    A term originating with Michael Bassey. A fuzzy generalization is

the kind of statement which makes no absolute claim to

knowledge, but hedges its claim with uncertainties. It arises when the empirical finding of a piece of research, such as

In *this* case it *has been* found that . . .

is turned into a qualified general statement like this:

In *some* cases it *may be* found that . . .

(Bassey, 1999, p. 12)

Fuzzy generalizations can, Bassey argues, provide useful guidance for practitioners (see Chapter 12). (cf. generalization)

*generalization*    An idea with general application that may or may not be universal (cf. universal theory). In this sense, generalizations, which are always conjectural, are simply general statements. However, 'generalization' is also used to refer to 'an inference drawn from specific cases' (q.v. induction). When not wishing to imply induction, the use of 'general statement' may be preferable.

*hypothesis*    (1) A tentative explanation for an observation, phenomenon, or scientific problem that can be tested by further investigation. (2) Something taken to be true for the purpose of argument or investigation; an assumption. (3) The antecedent of a conditional statement. (*The American Heritage Dictionary of the English Language*, 2000)

Karl Popper (1992b[1974], p. 52) argued that

conjecture or hypothesis must come before observation or perception: we have inborn expectations; we have latent inborn knowledge, in the form of latent expectations, to be activated by stimuli to which we react as a rule while engaged in active exploration.

(cf. expectation, knowledge, qq.v. empiricism, hypothetico-deductive method, induction, learning)

*hypothetico-deductive method*    A confusing term, commonly used to describe Karl Popper's account of scientific method. This method begins with the formulation of an explanation (q.v.) for a phenomenon. The explanation comprises a universal theory and a set of specific initial conditions.

As an illustration, a response to the question, 'Why is this child absent from school?' might be, 'The child is absent from school because he has a temperature of over 38°C'. This explanation implies 'Children with temperatures over 38°C will be absent from school' (universal theory) and 'This child has a temperature of over 38°C' (specific initial condition). From these two premises it can be deduced why the child is absent from school. Clearly, the explanation may be false; the universal theory and/or the specific initial condition may be in error. (q.v. argument)

A universal theory can be tested by using it to formulate a prediction (q.v.). A prediction has the same structure as an explanation, except that the universal theory and set of specific initial conditions are assumed to be known, and what remains to be discovered are the logical consequences, which have not yet been observed (Popper, 1979[1972], p. 352). The prediction, which is essentially a falsifiable hypothesis (q.v.), is tested by the search for evidence which contradicts it. To continue the illustration, a researcher might test the hypothesis, 'There does not exist a situation in which a child with a temperature of over 38°C will attend school'. She or he would do so by searching for children with temperatures over 38°C who are at school. If evidence which contradicts the hypothesis is found, the hypothesis may be judged to have been falsified. Knowledge of children who have temperatures of over 38°C and who have stayed at home, in no way constitutes evidence in support of the theory. (q.v. confirming evidence)

The method contrasts with induction (cf.), whereby a series of observations – each assumed to be, or treated as though they are, expectation-free – is recorded in anticipation that eventually a universal theory will emerge. But as David Miller (1994, p. 111) points out:

> most of those theories of science that are called hypothetico-deductivist are not strictly deductivist, since they lay on top of the truly scientific activities of hypothesizing and deductive testing also some process of inductive confirmation, so that . . . the best tested hypothesis at the end of the struggle with experience comes out as the best confirmed, dignified and glorified by the empirical engagement.

*illuminative*    An approach to research which avoids explicit hypothesis-testing, and seeks instead to 'illuminate' a phenomenon or situation (see Parlett and Dearden, 1981[1977]). Sometimes posed as the alternative paradigm (q.v.) to positivist research (cf. positivism). The principal data-gathering techniques are usually observation and unstructured and/or semi-structured interviews, supplemented by the collection and analysis of documents. The researcher may keep a detailed log of what is observed, and will test her or his account of events against those of participants in the situation, often cross-checking between one participant's account and another. Nonetheless, there is a danger that the researcher will overlook the extent to which the data she or he collects are affected by unstated, unexamined expectations. (q.v. induction)

*induction* This term has a variety of meanings, but in debates about research it most often refers to the idea that a universal theory (q.v.) – such as 'All swans are white'– can be derived from a series of singular observation statements (q.v.) of the kind 'This is a . . .', such as 'This is a swan and it's white'. Once such a theory has presented itself, the discovery of confirming evidence is thought to verify it (q.v. verification). If the confirming evidence is sufficiently strong, the theory may be accorded the status of a law. (cf. hypothetico-deductive method, q.v. empiricism)

The theory of induction has been the subject of critique, most notably by David Hume (1999[1748]) and Karl Popper (1972a[1934], 1972b[1963], 1979[1972], 1983, 1985a). The principal flaws in the theory can be summarized as follows:

First, it is logically invalid. As Hume pointed out, there is no logical reason to assume that the future will be like the past. No number of true singular observation statements of the kind, 'This is a swan and it's white', can entail the universal theory, 'All swans are white'.

Popper's alternative thesis of how knowledge grows and what happens when learning (q.v.) takes place was prompted by his discovery of an asymmetry between verification and falsification (q.v.): while no number of true singular observation statements can verify or prove the truth of a universal theory, one true singular observation statement can refute it. We may discover evidence which points to a universal theory being false, but no amount of evidence can demonstrate that it is true.

Second, all observation is expectation-laden and value-impregnated. No process of learning or of the growth of knowledge begins with observation (see, for example, Popper, 1979[1972]). This is so, whether or not the expectations (q.v.) are held individually or shared by many. (q.v. hypothesis)

Third, given that our expectations are fallible and also limited – we cannot observe all there is to be observed – the discovery of confirming instances does not strengthen a universal theory. Nor does a large number of confirming instances make the truth of a universal theory more probable (Popper, 1972a[1934]). If there is one black swan, it makes no difference whether you have previously found ten or ten thousand white swans; the universal theory, 'All swans are white', is false.

Many people accept that induction is a logically invalid theory, but they still believe that it accounts for what happens in practice, specifically at the psychological level. Hume, for example, thought that people are conditioned by dint of repetition to believe that similar instances will occur in the future. For a defence of Popper's thesis in the context of those who have critiqued it, see David Miller (1994, 2002).

*interpretivism*    This entails the idea that the natural sciences and social sciences are fundamentally different in nature: the former involves the study of physical entities; the latter involves the study of social phenomena, including mental states, which are not embodied in a physical form. Whereas natural scientists apply their own theoretical constructs to the world that they investigate, social scientists study a world that has already been interpreted by the actors within it. Interpretivism is often contrasted with positivism (cf.), but note that there are other non-positivist positions (cf. postpositivism).

*justificationism*    The idea that

a hypothesis has to pass tests, or be confirmed, or in some other way be touched with grace, if it is to be admitted to the realm of scientific knowledge; if it fails these tests, or is disconfirmed, or even if it fails to be confirmed, it is excluded. . . . For justificationists . . . the passing of tests is quite as important as the failing of tests, for it is precisely this that determines whether a hypothesis is admitted to the body of science. (Miller, 1994, pp. 6–7) (cf. falsificationism)

*knowledge*    Often used as a synonym for 'true belief' (or, at least, better than a guess), with scientific knowledge being regarded as 'justified true belief' (q.v. justificationism). 'Knowledge', as used by Karl Popper, is a generic term for all kinds of expectations (conscious or unconscious, inborn or acquired through development and/or learning), assumptions (explicit or implicit), and theoretical constructs (valid or invalid, true or false). Popper's broader usage takes into account that (a) we cannot be sure which of our beliefs are true, and (b) our beliefs, when entered into the public domain, exist independently of us. (q.v. worlds 1, 2, 3)

*learning*   Defined in *The New Oxford Dictionary of English* (1998) as 'the acquisition of knowledge or skills through experience, practice, study, or by being taught' and 'knowledge acquired in this way'. According to Swann (1999b, 2002), learning is what takes place when a human or other learning animal (a) experiences a mismatch (actual or anticipated) between expectation (q.v.) and experience (construed broadly to include experience of physical, personal, social and intellectual phenomena, (b) attempts to resolve the mismatch, and (c) survives, acquiring one or more new expectations in the process. 'New expectations' are those which are novel in the experience of the organism, and not wholly dependent on its genetic inheritance. In the living world in general, the discovery of mistaken (or sometimes merely inadequate) expectations leads to practical problems (q.v.) that individual organisms attempt to solve (Popper, 1992b[1974], p. 177). Although for many organisms the response to these problems is wholly an outcome of genetic inheritance and chance factors, other organisms are capable of learning. An ability to learn is a specific form of adaptability, and the ability to adapt confers evolutionary advantage. (See Chapter 2.)

Note that (a) most learning is unconscious, haphazard and implicit in situations, and (b) not all learning is 'good' learning – what we learn may be trivial and diversionary, misleading or even harmful.

*lifeworld*   '[A]ll the immediate experiences, activities, and contacts that make up the world of an individual or corporate life' (*The New Oxford Dictionary of English*, 1998). In critical theory (q.v.), the lifeworld refers to the totality of experiences of an individual, circumscribed by the objects, persons, and events encountered in the pursuit of the pragmatic objectives of living. It is a 'world' in which a person is 'wide awake', and it asserts itself as the 'paramount reality' (adapted from Schutz, 1970, p. 320). Others emphasize that there is a 'sphere of human experience where continuity of custom and tradition is sustained, where respect and loyalty for community [are] privileged, and from where a sense of belonging and security is derived' (Collins, 1998, p. 168).

*longitudinal*   In research, a study of an individual, group or institution, conducted over a lengthy period of time, for the purpose of describing or assessing change or development.

*metaphysical*   A term used to describe a theory which is about what is so in the world, but which is not falsifiable (qq.v. falsifiabilty, science). Consider, for example, 'There is a reality that we all inhabit' – the core tenet of realism – and its opposite, 'There is no reality that we all inhabit'. These theories are important because they lead to alternative conceptions of knowledge and competing ideas about how knowledge may be extended through research. Choosing between them is purely a matter of reasoning and argument; there can be no experimental evidence that we can cite either against or in favour of one or the other (Popper, 1979[1972], Chapter 2; 1985c). Some metaphysical theories become scientific because a means of testing them becomes conceivable – for example, through the development of, and access to, knowledge in a field other than that in which the theory was developed. In contrast, there are theories which have previously been scientific but are now metaphysical, in the sense that they were once testable but have been immunized against refutation. (q.v. falsificationism)

*method*   A way of doing something.

*methodology*   (1) The system of methods and principles used in a particular discipline or field of study. (2) The branch of philosophy concerned with the methods of science. More recently the term is sometimes, and rather confusingly, used in place of 'method' (cf.).

*negative existential statement*   A statement of the kind 'There does not exist a . . .', which derives from a universal theory (cf.). For example: 'You can't carry water in a sieve' (Popper, 1961, p. 61).

> There is a way of formulating scientific theories which points with particular clarity to the possibility of their falsification: we can formulate them in the form of prohibitions (or *negative existential statements*) . . . It can be shown that universal statements and negative existential statements are logically equivalent. This makes it possible to formulate all universal laws . . . as prohibitions. . . . [T]o the scientist they are a challenge to test and to falsify; they stimulate him to try to discover those states of affairs whose existence they prohibit, or deny.
>
> (Popper, 1979[1972], pp. 360–1)

*objective* (1) Statement of where you intend to get to, usually without taking into account where you are starting from. It is important to avoid confusing an objective with a statement of a problem (cf.) (see Swann, 1999a). The use of objectives – also referred to as 'targets' – is popular in education, where to many of the principal policy-makers the attainment of objectives is what matters, not whether or to what extent a policy has solved one or more (usually unstated) problems. (2) Adjective to describe an approach to ideas and evidence whereby the researcher attempts to be impartial. Whether anyone can adopt a fully impartial attitude is moot. One invariably has some kind of investment in the ideas one adopts. (3) Adjective to describe any idea that exists in the public domain (q.v. worlds 1, 2, 3).

*ontology* The study of the nature of being.

*paradigm* A term widely used in social science, following Thomas Kuhn (1970[1962]), but with a variety of meanings. Margaret Masterman (1970, pp. 61–5) identified 21 different uses of the term by Kuhn. It is probably most usefully understood to refer to a set of assumptions which a group of scientists or other theorists share, and which forms a basis for their investigations. More broadly, a paradigm is 'a representative example or pattern, especially one underlying a theory or viewpoint' (*The Oxford English Reference Dictionary*, 1996).

*policy* A purposive action. More than just a statement of actions to be taken. Ideally, though rarely, involving: the formulation of the problem to be tackled; consideration and testing of alternative solutions; the allocation of resources and monitoring of the consequences. Policy is usually discussed with reference to large entities – such as governments, local authorities or schools – but individuals also have policies (for example, regarding how they carry out their research or approach their teaching).

*Popperian* An idea associated with, or a person who has adopted various aspects of, the philosophy of Karl Popper (1902–1994). Popperian philosophers often disagree over matters of detail, and with regard to the practical implications of various theories, but they share a falsificationist epistemology (q.v. falsificationism) based on Popper's critique of induction (q.v.) and his demarcation between science (q.v.) and non-science (q.v. falsifiability).

*positivism*

> Nowadays the term 'positivist' is widely used as a generalized term of abuse. As a literal designator it has ceased to have any useful function – those philosophers to whom the term accurately applies have long since shuffled off this mortal coil, while any living social scientists who either bandy the term around, or are the recipients of it as an abusive label, are so confused about what it means that, while the word is full of sound and fury, it signifies nothing.
>
> (Phillips, 1992, p. 95)

Despite these words, Denis Phillips and other theorists have tried to make sense of the ways in which 'positivism' is used, distinguishing in particular between Comtean positivism (the term positivism is attributable to the nineteenth-century French philosopher Auguste Comte), logical positivism (a philosophical movement that developed in Austria and Germany during the 1920s), and the use of 'positivism' in common parlance (see Phillips, 1987, Chapter 4; 1992, Chapter 7; and Phillips and Burbules, 2000, Chapter 1).

Broadly speaking, positivism denotes the idea that:

1. Scientific knowledge is derived from the accumulation of data obtained theory-free and value-free from observation.
2. Anything that cannot be observed, and thus in some way measured (that is, quantified), is of little or no importance, or even, in extreme versions of positivism, non-existent.
3. Science is the pursuit of foundational knowledge (q.v. foundationalism).
4. Scientific method is applicable not only to the study of natural phenomena but also to human and social affairs.

Some theorists apply the term 'positivist' to anyone who accepts the last of these points. The way they use 'positivist' invariably fails to acknowledge the development of non-positivist science. There are many scientists and philosophers who think that there are similarities of method between the natural and social sciences, but their conception of science is non-positivist; that is, they reject points 1–3. (cf. postpositivism, qq.v. empiricism, induction)

*postmodernism*    Although there is no commonly accepted definition, postmodernism has been described as 'not so much a theory or a philosophy as a collection of loosely linked ideas which combine and recombine in numerous ways and contexts. At its centre, if it can be said to have one, is a refusal to take things for granted – an ironic, often playful, challenging of certainty' (Elizabeth Atkinson, in Chapter 3, p. 36). Postmodernists generally assume 'the breakdown of established forms of knowledge and inquiry, specifically those associated with the Enlightenment's self-confident pursuit of truth and reality: science and rationality' (Bailey, 1999, p. 31). Influential theorists include: Jean-François Lyotard, Michel Foucault and Jacques Derrida.

*postpositivism* A comparatively recent term which does not have a single agreed meaning. It is used mostly to refer to a broad range of philosophical positions regarding the nature of science (q.v.). One thing that postpositivists share is their rejection of positivism (cf.). More specifically, Phillips and Burbules (2000, Chapter 1) characterize the fundamental difference between positivists and postpositivists in terms of the rejection by the latter of foundationalism (q.v.) and their acceptance of fallibilism (q.v.). Popperian (q.v.) researchers are postpositivists of a particular kind.

*pragmatism*

> In the technical rather than everyday sense of the word, 'pragmatism' refers to a philosophical movement that developed in the USA in the second half of the nineteenth century, and continued to have an influence throughout much of the twentieth century. The central idea of pragmatism is that the meaning of a concept consists of its practical implications; and that the truth of any judgement is determined in and through practical activity, whether in the context of science or in life more generally.
>
> (Martyn Hammersley, personal communication)

Influential pragmatist philosophers include Charles S. Peirce (generally regarded as the founder of pragmatism), William James, John Dewey, and, more recently, Clarence I. Lewis, Willard van O. Quine and Hilary Putnam.

*prediction* A statement about what will happen (that is, a type of proposition, cf.), and essential to the testing of scientific theories. A prediction has the same structure as an explanation (cf.), except that the universal theory (cf.) and specific initial conditions are assumed to be known, and what remains to be discovered are the logical consequences, which have yet to be observed (Popper, 1979[1972],

p. 352). Put simply, a scientist uses a general theory about how the world is to predict that, under specific conditions, a particular circumstance can be anticipated. For this process to be scientific (in the Popperian sense) the prediction must be sufficiently precise for there to be a risk that counter-evidence could be discovered. If it is not sufficiently precise then the process is mere soothsaying. Note that the fulfilment of a prediction does not prove the truth of a universal theory. Predictions may be fulfilled for reasons which have nothing to do with the proposed universal theory and the stated initial conditions. When a prediction is not fulfilled, this indicates error; but the nature of the error may not be clear. (q.v. hypothetico-deductive method)

*preference*    A greater liking for one thing rather than another (or others). Note that choice doesn't necessarily indicate preference: one might choose an option from a menu of possibilities, but actually prefer something entirely different.

With regard to competing theories and the theoretician's perspective, Karl Popper (1985a, p. 112) wrote:

> We may *prefer* some competing theories to others on purely rational grounds. It is important that we are clear what the principles of preference or selection are.
>
> In the first place they are governed by the idea of truth. We want, if at all possible, theories which are true, and for this reason we try to eliminate the false ones.
>
> But we want more than this. We want new and interesting truth. We are thus led to the idea of *the growth of informative content*, and especially of *truth content*. That is, we are led to the following *principle of preference*: a theory with a great informative content is on the whole more interesting, even before it has been tested, than a theory with little content. Admittedly, we may have to abandon the theory with the greater content, or as I also call it, the bolder theory, if it does not stand up to tests.

With regard to competing proposals for action:

> we should view a set of competing proposals for action as a response to a practical problem, addressing:
>
> • What is the problem that these proposals are intended to solve?
> • To what extent is the problem worthwhile?
> • What are the cost implications (monetary or otherwise) of

each of the proposals, that is, as tentative solutions to the problem?

- For each proposal, if we act on it, to what extent can we expect the problem to be solved?
- For each proposal, what might be the unintended consequences, desirable or undesirable, of acting on it?
- Do we need to look for a better way of doing things?

When addressing these questions we should refer to the evidence and argument that is relevant and available to us, and then reject 'any practical proposal that does not survive critical scrutiny as well as others do' (Miller, 2002, p. 95). After that, what we decide to do can be only a matter of guesswork. We have to try it and see. If practical improvement is what we desire, each of us – working individually, as a member of a group, or as an agent of an institution – has to adopt a course of action and evaluate it. If we discover unexpected consequences (desirable or undesirable), we are then in a position to learn.

(Swann, 2003, in press)

*problem* (1) What exists when an organism experiences a sense of disequilibrium and 'desires' to change its state of affairs in an attempt to attain equilibrium. Problems of this kind can be termed practical problems – that is, problems of how to get from one state of affairs to another (Krick, 1969[1965], p. 3). (2) A mismatch between what is known and what is desired to be known. These are theoretical problems, such as those of value (what is good, what ought to be done, what is aesthetically pleasing), fact (what is so in the world and why, what was so and why, what will be so and why), and logic (what is valid and why). (See Chapter 2.)

Although mismatches are identified, problems have to be created. Invariably there is more than one way in which a mismatch can be turned into a problem, and the task of formulating problems is often not straightforward – nor is it value-free. Failure to formulate problems properly is the cause of much failure in policy (see Chapter 4), and of pointless toil in research.

*proof* Argument used to try to establish truth (q.v.), but proof is not possible in educational and other research because truth cannot be established (q.v. induction). Note the distinction between the idea of establishing truth and that of pursuing truth. We can pursue truth – that is, try to gain knowledge of the facts about reality – as a regulative ideal without assuming that certain or secure knowledge is able. 'Proof' is often used when the word 'evidence' would be appropriate. For example, 'This proves that . . .' should be replaced by 'This is evidence of/that . . .'.

*proposition* (1) A statement which is either true or false. (2) A proposal for action. (cf. theory)

*qualitative* Concerning the quality of something rather than its quantity. Often used in educational research to characterize a particular paradigm (q.v.), such as interpretivism (q.v.). This can lead to endless worries for research students who want to count things as well as assess them, for example in investigating *how many* students respond *favourably* to a particular form of teaching. (cf. quantitative)

*quantitative* Concerning the quantity of something rather than its quality. Often used in educational research to characterize a particular paradigm (q.v.), such as positivism (q.v.). Talk of the quantitative paradigm or quantitative methodology leads to the same kind of unhelpful dichotomy as the use of 'qualitative paradigm' or 'qualitative methodology'. It is better, where necessary, to refer to quantitative techniques (for example, averaging). If the terms 'qualitative' (cf.) and 'quantitative' are to be used, they should refer to procedures, as in 'quantitative procedures', rather than methodologies. There are no exclusively quantitative or qualitative methodologies.

*rationalism* Refers to a variety of views which emphasize the importance of reason in the conduct of human affairs and in the growth of knowledge. More specifically, the term is used to refer to the belief in the possibility of a priori knowledge – that is, knowledge prior to experience (see Cottingham, 1984, p. 6). Such knowledge may be regarded as infallible (classical rationalism) or fallible (modern rationalism – specifically critical rationalism, q.v.). In the past, rationalism and empiricism (cf.) were regarded as opposing philosophical positions, but, given their modern forms, this antithesis can no longer be upheld. Hence it was possible for Karl Popper to describe himself as 'an empiricist and a rationalist of sorts' (1972b[1963], p. 6).

*rationality* Generally, the use of logic or reason in thinking out a problem (often contrasted with intuition). A topic of controversy in educational (and other social) research; because people don't necessarily behave rationally, it is often said (illogically) that they can't be studied rationally. (q.v. rationalism)

*realism*   The belief that entities exist independently of being perceived (common-sense realism) or independently of our theories about them, which may or may not be accompanied by the belief that knowledge of these entities is possible (epistemological realism). (Adapted from Phillips, 1987, p. 205.)

*reductionism*   A process by which a complex set of entities, events or other phenomena is explained or analysed in terms of another that is less complex.

*refutation*   A process – one that always involves argument – by which a theory is shown to be false by the citing of evidence which contradicts it. Refutations are necessarily provisional, so there is no certainty nor security in science, neither from the accumulation of confirming evidence nor from the discovery of refuting evidence. The latter is, however, more productive for the growth of knowledge because it indicates error somewhere in our expectations. (cf. falsification, qq.v. falsifiability, falsificationism)

*relativism*   The idea that judgements about truth and/or value are relative to a particular framework or point of view (adapted from Phillips, 1987, p. 206). Relativism can lead to the conclusion, as in cultural relativism, that no one society has the right to judge another. But 'relativism happily defeats itself, since if it is true there can be no reason to accept it' (Burgess, 2002, p. 115).

*research*   Systematic investigation, as opposed to any old study. It can, however, include scrutiny only of existing evidence (such as books and other literature), as well as the testing of hypotheses and the collection of new data. A process must be systematic to count as research, and the outcomes must be presented in some publicly accessible form. Genuine research is not designed with the intention of confirming existing expectations or prejudices (though it may be hoped that it will).

*science*   The systematic study of the nature and behaviour of the universe by means of empirical investigation. For some theorists and scientists, this systematic study is concerned specifically with the pursuit of truth (q.v.). Of this group, Karl Popper and Popperians construe scientific knowledge as that body of knowledge which comprises (a) universal theories (q.v.) that have been formulated in a way which makes them susceptible to falsification (q.v.), and for which refuting evidence, if sought, has not been found; and (b) formulated problems and arguments which relate to such theories.

*significance*    If we assume a particular state of affairs, an event is statistically significant if the probability of the event occurring by chance is negligible. For example, 'The results are significant at the five per cent level' means that, assuming a particular state of affairs, the event we observe would be expected to happen less than five per cent of the time. We would therefore reject the possibility that the observed event is just a chance variation, and conclude that our original assumption about the state of affairs is incorrect. Statistical significance should not be confused with substantive significance. A one per cent chance of getting killed is highly significant for most of us. With very large samples, very small differences can be statistically significant, although they may not be important.

*singular observation statement*    A statement of the kind 'This is a . . .'. Note that one singular observation statement, if true, will refute (q.v. refutation) a universal theory (cf.). For example, 'This is a black swan', if true, falsifies 'All swans are white' (q.v. induction).

*situational analysis* and *situational logic*    Proposed by Karl Popper in his 27 theses on the logic of the social sciences (1992a[1969], p. 79), the method of objective understanding, or situational logic

> consists in analysing the *situation* of the acting person sufficiently to explain the action in terms of the situation without any further help from psychology. Objective 'understanding' consists in realizing that the action was objectively *appropriate to the situation*.

This situational logic assumes not only the existence of a physical world, but also a social world that includes social institutions as well as people. Popper further suggested that 'We might construct a theory of intended and unintended institutional consequences of purposive action' (ibid., p. 80). Purposive action refers here not only to what individuals do when they act purely for themselves, but also how they act as agents of institutions: 'Institutions do not act; rather, only individuals act, within or on behalf of institutions' (ibid.). This leads to the posing of questions such as, 'What problem was this action intended to solve?', 'Were there any unintended and undesirable consequences?' and 'Might an alternative course of action have been preferable?' (q.v. problem). (See Chapter 4.)

***social engineering*** A term used pejoratively to describe unfavoured social interventions, although *all* social policy is a form of social engineering:

> Popularized in Karl Popper's critique in his *Open Society and its Enemies* [1966a(1945), 1966b(1945)], it takes two forms. *Utopian* social engineering, associated with Plato, Hegel, Marx, and their totalitarian heirs, is committed to the wholesale transformation of society through central planning according to a comprehensive ideal plan and unlimited by any constraints from competing social institutions (e.g. the church). *Piecemeal* social engineering involves only 'searching for, and fighting against, the greatest and most urgent evils of society'. Popper's distinction aside, social engineering as a legitimate activity of government is essential to the welfare state and to all versions of socialism and communism. It is anathema to libertarianism but endorsed under constraints by modern liberalism.
>
> (*The Oxford Companion to Philosophy*, 1995)

For discussion of piecemeal versus Utopian engineering, see Popper (1985d).

A key difference between a social engineer and an engineer concerned with non-social matters, is that the former has far less critically tested knowledge upon which to draw. The consequences of social engineering can be far-reaching and difficult to ascertain; invariably some are unintended. Thus, even when a social engineer solves the practical problem (q.v.) that she or he set out to solve, the unintended consequences may be so undesirable as to cast doubt on the efficacy of the solution. (qq.v. engineering, science, situational analysis and situational logic, technology)

***technology*** The study of how the products of scientific investigation – that is, empirically tested theories about the nature and behaviour of the universe – can be used to create specified objects, events or states of affairs. 'Technology, unlike science, is not concerned with things as they are but with things as they might be' (Grove, 1989, quoted in Miller, 2002, pp. 90–1). Karl Popper (1961[1957]) illustrates the relationship of science (q.v.) to technology by noting that all scientific theories can be expressed in a technological form, asserting that something cannot happen. For example, the law of conservation of energy can be expressed as: 'You cannot build a perpetual motion machine' (ibid., p. 61). (cf. engineering, social engineering)

***test***   (1) An attempt to assess the effectiveness of a solution to a problem of either a theoretical or practical nature. With regard to theoretical problems, testing is best done by trying to find instances which will refute the theory (qq.v. induction, refutation, falsification). With regard to practical problems, testing is often inadequately done because what is tested is the extent to which the solution has been implemented, not whether it solves the original problem, and/ or because all that has been sought is evidence of success (q.v. situational analysis, situational logic). (2) What educators do to students to assess whether they have learned what they were taught; rarely to assess whether the learning and teaching were worthwhile.

***theory***   A term used in a variety of ways. The following definitions are listed in *The American Heritage Dictionary of the English Language* (2000):

1. A set of statements or principles devised to explain a group of facts or phenomena, especially one that has been repeatedly tested or is widely accepted and can be used to make predictions about natural phenomena.
2. The branch of a science or art consisting of its explanatory statements, accepted principles, and methods of analysis, as opposed to practice . . .
3. A set of theorems that constitute a systematic view of a branch of mathematics.
4. Abstract reasoning; speculation . . .
5. A belief or principle that guides action or assists comprehension or judgment . . .
6. An assumption based on limited information or knowledge; a conjecture.

In Karl Popper's work, 'theory' is used to refer to explicit statements of all kinds, including general and singular statements, and also to implicit assumptions and unstated expectations (cf.) – that is, ideas which could in principle be formulated as statements but have yet to be given linguistic expression.

***truth***   That which is consistent with the facts about reality. (qq.v. fact, realism, science) *universal theory*   A theory (cf.) or, more specifically, a statement (cf. proposition) which purports to describe a general feature of the world, such as 'All swans are white', 'All five-year-old children enjoy stories about animals'. The term may be used when describing all people, objects or events in the world, and when describing all members of a specific group. Thus one can formulate universal theories about, for example, 'all schools' and 'all schools in England'. All universal theories are general theories, but not all general theories are universal: for example, 'Most schools in England are state schools' is a general but not universal theory. (cf. generalization)

*values*   Ideas about what is good, including moral and aesthetic principles and standards. All ideas about what is worthwhile and desirable are value-impregnated; as too is research – for example, in the formulation of the research problem and even in the way evidence is interpreted.

*verification*   Commonly used to refer to additional evidence in support of a claim, hypothesis or other theory. Note, however, that no amount of supporting evidence makes the truth of a universal theory any more probable (qq.v. confirming evidence, induction). For Karl Popper and Popperians, the task of the scientist is characterized by the formulation and testing (that is, by the search for refuting evidence) of theories which are falsifiable (q.v.). (qq.v. falsificationism, justificationism)

*world 1, world 2, world 3*   These terms originate with Karl Popper's 3-world thesis (Popper, 1979[1972]). He posited the existence of: world 1 (physical objects and processes); world 2 (subjective experience); world 3 (objective knowledge). The world of objective knowledge, a human construct that is no less real than the other two worlds, comprises formulated problems, descriptions, hypotheses, explanations and arguments. Many of these ideas are embedded in human artefacts (books, musical scores, paintings, films, etc.), social practices and institutions. Ideas in the public domain exist independently of the people who created them; they can be criticized, modified and developed by anyone who has access to them.

## REFERENCES

Bailey, R. (1999) 'The abdication of reason: postmodern attacks upon science and reason', in J. Swann and J. Pratt (eds) *Improving Education: Realist Approaches to Method and Research*, London: Cassell, pp. 30–8.

Bassey, M. (1999) *Case Study Research in Educational Settings*, Buckingham, UK: Open University Press.

Blaikie, N. (1993) *Approaches to Social Enquiry*, Cambridge, UK: Polity Press.

Burgess, T. (2002) *The Devil's Dictionary of Education*, London: Continuum.

Carr, W. and Kemmis, S. (1986) *Becoming Critical: Education, Knowledge and Action Research*, London: Falmer Press.

Collins, M. (1998) *Critical Crosscurrents in Education*, Malabar, FL: Krieger.

Cottingham, J. (1984) *Rationalism*, London: Paladin Books.

Finch, J. (1986) *Research and Policy: The Uses of Qualitative Methods in Social and Educational Research*, Basingstoke, UK: Falmer Press.

Habermas, J. (1971a) *Knowledge and Human Interests*, trans. J. J. Shapiro, Boston, MA: Beacon Press (first published in German in 1968).

Habermas, J. (1971b) *Toward a Rational Society: Student Protest, Science, and Politics*, trans. J. J. Shapiro, Boston, MA: Beacon Press (first published in German in 1968/1969).

Habermas, J. (1984, 1987) *Theory of Communicative Action, Volumes 1 and 2*, trans. T. McCarthy, Boston, MA: Beacon (first published in German in 1981).

Hume, D. (1999) 'An enquiry concerning human understanding', in S. M. Cahn (ed.) *Classics of Western Philosophy*, 5th edition, New York: Hackett, pp. 626–96 (Hume's text first published in 1748).

Kemmis, S. and McTaggart, R. (eds) (1988) *The Action Research Planner*, Victoria, Australia: Deakin University Press (first edition 1981).

Krick, E. V. (1969) *An Introduction to Engineering and Engineering Design*, New York: John Wiley and Sons (first edition 1965).

Kuhn, T. S. (1970) *The Structure of Scientific Revolutions*, Chicago, IL: University of Chicago Press (first edition 1962).

Lewin, K. (1946) 'Action research and minority problems', *Journal of Social Issues*, 2, pp. 34–6.

Masterman, M. (1970) 'The nature of a paradigm', in I. Lakatos and A. Musgrave (eds) *Criticism and the Growth of Knowledge*, London: Cambridge University Press, pp. 59–89.

Miller, D. (1994) *Critical Rationalism: A Restatement and Defence*, Chicago, IL: Open Court Publishing.

Miller, D. (2002) 'Induction: a problem solved', in J. M. Böhm, H. Holweg and C. Hoock (eds) *Karl Poppers kritischer Rationalismus heute*, Tuebingen, Germany: Mohr Siebeck, pp. 81–106. Also available at: www.warwick.ac.uk/philosophy/dm-Induction.pdf (accessed 3 December 2002).

Parlett, M. and Dearden, G. (eds) (1981) *Introduction to Illuminative Evaluation: Studies in Higher Education*, Guildford, UK: Society for Research into Higher Education (first published 1977).

Petersen, A. F. (1992) 'On emergent pre-language and language evolution and transcendent feedback from language production on cognition and emotion in early man', in J. Wind, B. Chiarelli and B. Bichakjian (eds) *Language Origin: A Multidisciplinary Approach*, Dordrecht, The Netherlands: Kluwer Academic Publishers, pp. 449–64.

Phillips, D. C. (1987) *Philosophy, Science, and Social Inquiry: Contemporary Methodological Controversies in Social Science and Related Applied Fields of Research,* Oxford, UK: Pergamon Press.

Phillips, D. C. (1992) *The Social Scientist's Bestiary: A Guide to Fabled Threats to, and Defenses of, Naturalistic Social Science,* Oxford, UK: Pergamon Press.

Phillips, D. C. and Burbules, N. C. (2000) *Postpositivism and Educational Research,* Lanham, MD: Rowman and Littlefield.

Popper, K. R. (1961) *The Poverty of Historicism,* London: Routledge and Kegan Paul (first edition 1957).

Popper, K. R. (1966a) *The Open Society and its Enemies, Volume 1 – The Spell of Plato,* London: Routledge and Kegan Paul (first edition 1945).

Popper, K. R. (1966b) *The Open Society and its Enemies, Volume 2 – The High Tide of Prophecy: Hegel, Marx, and the Aftermath,* London: Routledge and Kegan Paul (first edition 1945).

Popper, K. R. (1972a) *The Logic of Scientific Discovery,* London: Hutchinson (first published in German in 1934) (first English edition 1959).

Popper, K. R. (1972b) *Conjectures and Refutations: The Growth of Scientific Knowledge,* London: Routledge (first edition 1963).

Popper, K. R. (1979) *Objective Knowledge: An Evolutionary Approach,* Oxford, UK: Oxford University Press (first edition 1972).

Popper, K. R. (1983) *Realism and the Aim of Science,* from W. W. Bartley III (ed.) *Postscript to the Logic of Scientific Discovery,* London: Hutchinson.

Popper, K. R. (1985a) 'The problem of induction (1953, 1974)', in D. Miller (ed.) *Popper Selections,* Princeton, NJ: Princeton University Press, pp. 101–17.

Popper, K. R. (1985b) 'The problem of demarcation (1974)', in D. Miller (ed.) *Popper Selections,* Princeton, NJ: Princeton University Press, pp. 118–30.

Popper, K. R. (1985c) 'Metaphysics and criticizability (1958)', in D. Miller (ed.) *Popper Selections,* Princeton, NJ: Princeton University Press, pp. 209–19.

Popper, K. R. (1985d) 'Piecemeal social engineering (1944)', in D. Miller (ed.) *Popper Selections,* Princeton, NJ: Princeton University Press, pp. 304–18.

Popper, K. R. (1992a) 'The logic of the social sciences', in idem, *In Search of a Better World: Lectures and Essays from Thirty Years,* trans. L. J. Bennett, with additional material by M. Mew; revised trans. K. R. Popper and M. Mew, London: Routledge (first published in German in 1969) (first published in English in 1976).

Popper, K. R. (1992b) *Unended Quest: An Intellectual Autobiography,* London: Routledge. (First published as 'Autobiography of Karl Popper', in P. A. Schilpp (ed.) (1974) *The Philosophy of Karl Popper, Book 1,* La Salle, IL: Open Court Publishing, pp. 1–204.)

Schutz, A. (1970) *On Phenomenology and Social Relations,* ed. H. R. Wagner, Chicago, IL: University of Chicago Press.

Swann, J. (1999a) 'Making better plans: problem-based versus objectives-based planning', in J. Swann and J. Pratt (eds) *Improving Education: Realist Approaches to Method and Research,* London: Cassell, pp. 53–66.

Swann, J. (1999b) 'What happens when learning takes place?' *Interchange,* 30 (3), pp. 257–82.

Swann, J. (2002) 'Understanding and pursuing learning: the importance of the logic of learning', unpublished paper, King's College London. (Revised version of Swann, J. (2001) 'Understanding and pursuing learning: the value of the logic of learning', paper presented at the annual conference of the British Educational Research Association, University of Leeds, 13–15 September.)

Swann, J. (2003) 'How science can contribute to the improvement of educational practice', *Oxford Review of Education*, 29 (2) (in press).

Swartz, R. (1980) 'Introduction: towards a fallibilistic educational perspective', in R. M. Swartz, H. J. Perkinson and S. G. Edgerton, *Knowledge and Fallibilism: Essays on Improving Education*, New York: New York University Press, pp. IX–LV.

# Contributors

**Elizabeth Atkinson** is a Reader in Social and Educational Inquiry at the University of Sunderland, where she treads a fine line between delivering and critiquing government education policy: an uncomfortable position which she has described in her writing. Her research and writing have focused on a wide range of educational and social issues, including educational policy and practice, identity and othering, sexuality and education, social justice and social change, and postmodern approaches to educational research. Her writing offers a critique of recent UK government initiatives in education, aiming to deconstruct assumptions underlying the rhetoric of 'improvement', 'standards' and 'what works', and offering a postmodern uncertainty about educational and social 'truths'. Elizabeth is UK editor of the *International Journal of Qualitative Studies in Education*, and is on the editorial board of the *International Journal of Gay and Lesbian Issues in Education*. Her current research focus is exploring the meaning of 'diversity' in educational contexts.

**Michael Bassey** is an Emeritus Professor of Education at Nottingham Trent University and Academic Secretary of the British Educational Research Association. For the latter he edits *Research Intelligence* (four times a year) and the weekly website gossip column on educational research (www.bera.ac.uk). He is an academician of the Academy of Learned Societies for the Social Sciences. Among his books *Case Study Research in Educational Settings* (Open University Press, 1999) and *Creating Education through Research* (Kirklington Moor Press, 1995) are pertinent to his contribution to this volume. He passionately believes that the education system in England is currently being grossly damaged by political interference and that educational policy should be determined by politicians, teachers and researchers working together and exploring intelligent visions of possible futures. To this end he believes case study is a vital element of the empirical researcher's methodological toolkit.

**James W. Chapman** is Professor of Educational Psychology and Head of the Department of Learning and Teaching in the College of Education at Massey University, New Zealand. He received his PhD in Educational Psychology from the University of Alberta in 1979, specializing in learning disabilities, cognitive-motivation factors in achievement, and developmental psychology. His research interests include the development of achievement-related self-perceptions, the structure and assessment of academic self-concept, and intervention strategies for children with reading difficulties. He has published book chapters and journal articles on student self-perceptions, learning disabilities, language and literacy development, reading difficulties, and intervention strategies, and has served on the editorial boards of the *Journal of Learning Disabilities*, *Learning Disability Quarterly*, and the *Canadian Journal of Special Education*. He is a Fellow of the International Academy for Research in Learning Disabilities, and in 1999 he was awarded the Dina Feitelson Research Award by the International Reading Association.

**Michael Collins** is a Professor of Education at the University of Saskatchewan, Canada. He has experience as a schoolteacher and adult educator in the UK, Canada and the USA. His interest in critical pedagogy is reinforced by practical off-campus commitments, including political activism, as well as academic work. In addition to three single-authored books, he has contributed chapters to a number of edited texts, and is widely published in academic journals and research conference proceedings.

**Patricia Maringi G. Johnston** is indigenous to Aotearoa/New Zealand and is of Ngaiterangi and Te Arawa iwi (tribal) affiliations. She is Professor and Head of Postgraduate Studies at Te Whare Wananga o Awanuiarangi (an indigenous University), New Zealand. Her areas of interest include Maori education, education policy, research issues, 'politics of difference', representation, colonial history, discourses of race/racism and ethnicity. In her 'spare' time she is involved in Maori educational initiatives such as Maori Total Immersion schooling (Kura Kaupapa Maori) and iwi developments.

**John Pratt** is Professor in the Centre for Institutional Studies at the University of East London, and was Head of the Centre until 2001. Prior to that he took a degree in engineering (which has proved to be more relevant to research into education policy than you might think) at Birmingham University, and was a researcher at the London School of Economics. The Centre, which he co-founded with Tyrrell Burgess in 1970, takes a Popperian approach to public policy and institutions, and its name derives from Popper's views about the social sciences. He has been involved in a variety of innovative education programmes, including independent study and masters programmes in public and community service. He has undertaken numerous research studies into policy, particularly in higher education, and has been a consultant for local, national and international organizations. His publications include the definitive analysis of the polytechnic policy in Britain (*The Polytechnic Experiment 1965–1992*, Society for Research into Higher Education and Open University Press, 1997), and OECD (Organisation for Economic Co-operation and Development) policy reviews of higher education in Austria and Finland. He edits the journal *Higher Education Review*.

**Jane E. Prochnow** is a Senior Lecturer in the Department of Learning and Teaching in the College of Education at Massey University, New Zealand. Her particular interest is in theories and strategies for working with children with difficult behaviour. Her background is in educational psychology and applied behaviour analysis. Her research has been in the areas of suspension, teachers' classroom needs for inclusion, and attitudinal, literacy and motivational variables related to disordered behaviour. She was involved in evaluating the Severe Behaviour Initiative strand of the Special Education 2000 initiative in New Zealand.

**Joanna Swann** is a Popperian philosopher of education. Her background is in primary school teaching, educational support services, higher education lecturing and educational research. In the UK she has lectured in education and teaching studies on pre-service courses for primary school teachers, and at Massey University, New Zealand, she taught educational research methods and methodology at masterate and doctoral levels. In 1999 she co-edited (with John Pratt) *Improving Education: Realist Approaches to Method and Research*. Her research interests are in the field of learning and method in education. In March 2001 she became a Research Fellow in the Department of Education and Professional Studies, King's College London, working on 'Learning how to learn – in classrooms, schools and networks', a project funded by the Economic and Social Research Council as part of its Teaching and Learning Research Programme.

**William E. Tunmer** is Professor of Educational Psychology in the Department of Learning and Teaching in the College of Education at Massey University, New Zealand. He received his PhD in Experimental Psychology from the University of Texas at Austin in 1979, specializing in the areas of theoretical linguistics, experimental psycholinguistics, and cognitive development. From 1980 to 1988 he held the positions of research fellow, lecturer, and senior lecturer at the University of Western Australia. In 1988 he took up a professorship at Massey University, where he served as Head of Department and Dean of the Faculty of Education. He has published books, book chapters and journal articles on language and literacy development, reading difficulties and intervention strategies, and has served on the editorial boards of *Reading Research Quarterly*, *Reading and Writing*, and *Language and Education*. In 1999 he was awarded the Dina Feitelson Research Award by the International Reading Association.

# Index

action research 13, 23, 25, 29, 30-1,
    169-71, 180, 186, 194-5
Adorno, T. 73
Agger, B. 80, 81
*American Heritage Dictionary of the English
    Language* 198, 201, 216
argument 14, 15, 16-17, 28, 29, 30, 81, 92,
    108, 114-15, 128, 131, 132, 133, 135,
    137, 139, 149, 150, 152, 154-5, 158,
    159, 163, 168, 182, 184, 187, 192, 195,
    199, 200, 201, 206, 211, 213, 214, 217
    *see also* language, argumentative
Arthurs, J. 25, 34
Atkinson, E. 5, 36, 38, 39, 41, 42, 43, 44,
    45, 46, 48, 129, 130, 136, 137, 138,
    139-40, 149, 176, 177, 182, 209
axiology 196

Bacon, F. 15-16, 32
Bailey, R. 23, 32, 52, 65, 209, 218
Ball, S. 39, 48
Barrett, S. 62, 65
Barrett, W. 75, 81
Bassey, M. 5, 6, 12, 112, 113, 116, 119,
    120, 121, 122, 176, 179, 186, 188, 196,
    200-1, 218
Benhabib, S. 81, 82
Bernhardt, D. 78, 82
Bernstein, R. J. 70, 73, 82
Bhabha, H. K. 38, 43, 48
bicultural context, research in   Chapter 7,
    Chapter 11
binary oppositions 35, 36-7, 38, 43
Blaikie, N. 197, 218
Blid, H. 79, 82
Bordo, S. 38, 48
Bourne, J. 38, 48
Bricmont, J. 91, 93-4, 97
British Educational Research Association
    116, 122, 189, 193

Britzman, D. P. 44, 48
Burbules, N. C. 6, 7, 208, 209, 219
Burgess, T. 13, 18, 23, 24, 28, 32, 55, 57, 58,
    59, 60, 64, 65, 66, 128, 140, 195, 213,
    218
Butler, J. 38, 39, 48

Cahoone, L. 44, 48
Callinicos, A. 81, 82
capitalism 67-9, 71, 73-4, 75, 80, 81, 131,
    142, 147, 151
Carr, W. 195, 218
case study 5, 6, 23, 26, Chapter 8, 196,
    144, Chapter 12, 176, 196
    different types of 113-14, 116-18,
    167-9, 171
    *see also* storytelling case study
    (studies)
causality 73, 115, 196, 199
    *see also* explanation(s)
certainty, *see* uncertainty
Chapman, J. W. 5, 87, 96, 97
civil society 71, 75-7
Cizek, G. 93, 96
Clandinin, D. J. 91, 96
Clay, M. M. 86, 89, 96
Cole, M. 46, 48-9, 129, 140
colleges 59, 60, 61, 145
    of advanced technology (CATs) 58, 59,
    60, 62
    of education 58, 63
    of higher education 58, 63
Collins, M. 5, 75, 76, 77, 79, 81, 82, 143,
    145, 147, 151, 175, 176, 205, 218
colonialism 38, 98-9, 131, 152-3, 155, 158,
    159, 161-3
    *see also* postcolonialism
Comte, A. 208
Connelly, F. M. 91, 96
contingency 42, 130, 135

corporatization 68–70, 71–2, 75, 142, 151
corroboration 185, 196
Cottingham, J. 212, 218
Council for National Academic Awards
　(CNAA) 24, 64
Cox, R. W. 101, 105, 109
creative activity 3, 20–1, 23, 29, 30, 31, 40,
　41, 46, 57, 58, 61, 64, 73, 87, 104, 108,
　127, 128, 134, 138, 139, 145, 150, 162,
　176, 183, 185, 186, 192, 198, 211, 215,
　217
　*see also* imagination
critical rationalism 196–7, 212
critical theory 5, Chapter 5, 93, 105,
　Chapter 10, 176, 197, 205
criticism 14, 15, 16, 20, 21, 23–4, 27, 36, 39,
　46, 53, 54, 91, 130, 131, 135, 159, 185,
　187, 188, 192, 198, 211
　research as a critical activity 3, 26, 29,
　　30, 43, 95, 111–12, 129, 133, 134, 139,
　　145, 150, 154, 158, 168, 171, 176, 177,
　　181, 185, 186
　　*see also* critical theory; ideology
　　critique
　*see also* critical rationalism; error, trial
　　and
curriculum 68, 69–70, 73, 74, 77–8, 80,
　142, 143, 147, 151
　national (for schools) 26, 27, 35, 56, 138
　*see also* student-initiated curricula;
　　teacher education/training,
　　national curriculum for

data 45, 52, 53, 58, 60, 61, 63, 65, 79, 84, 86,
　89, 92, 94, 95, 99, 101, 103, 108, 117,
　119, 120, 168, 181–2, 183, 184, 187,
　192, 197, 198, 199, 202–3, 208, 213
Davidson, C. 188, 193
Dearden, G. 202, 218
deconstruction 36–7, 38–9, 42, 43, 46, 60,
　80–1, 129, 131, 138
Deleuze, G. 36, 43, 49
democracy 41, 68, 71, 72, 129, 151
　participatory 74–5, 76, 79, 142, 143,
　　144, 146
Denzin, N. K. 116, 123
Department of Education and
　Science (England and Wales) 59, 60,
　65
Department for Education and Skills
　(England and Wales) 115
Derrida, J. 36, 42, 49, 80, 209
Desforges, C. 12, 32
Dewey, J. 209
dialogue 71, 74–5, 79, 141, 143, 146, 176
Dimitriades, G. 42, 49

discourse in research 41, 43, 45, 68, 91,
　93–4, 96, 130, 131, 135, 137, 138, 143,
　146–8, 182
diversity 4, 27, 30, 37, 44, 59, 62, 129,
　137–9, 162
Donmoyer, R. 115

Eccles, J. C. 21, 32
Ecclestone, K. 25, 34
Edelman, G. 23, 32
Edgerton, S. G. 34
Education Group II 70, 82
Education Reform Act (1988) (England
　and Wales) 27
Education Review Office (ERO) (New
　Zealand) 88, 89, 95, 96
effectiveness 12, 21, 62, 84, 86–7, 89, 111,
　128, 134, 148, 149–50, 188, 190, 197,
　216
efficiency 89, 197
　cult of 72–5, 78, 151
Ehri, L. C. 87, 96
Eisenhart, M. 92, 96
Eisner, E. W. 84, 96
Elley, W. B. 90, 97
empiricism 96, 198, 212
engineering 167, 198
　social 178, 215
Enlightenment 40, 209
epistemology 7, 18, 20, 46, 51, 52, 56, 90,
　92, 144, 162, 164, 185, 198, 207, 213
Epstein, D. 45, 49
error 6, 16, 17, 23, 29, 30, 128, 135, 139,
　183–4, 186, 187, 191, 192, 202, 210,
　213
　trial and 15, 18, 19–23, 134, 154, 183
　*see also* mismatch(es) between
　　expectation and experience
Escobar, M. 97
ethics 12, 26–7, 29, 37, 38–9, 41, 46, 54,
　74–5, 78, Chapter 7, 115, 116, 117,
　118, 119, 141, 156–7, 177, 179, 184,
　187–90, 192–3, 198–9
　communicative ethic 79, 146
　questions concerned with 107–8, 118,
　　136
　*see also* social justice
evaluation 11, 23, 28, 29, 56, 59, 63, 92,
　113, 115, 117–18, 120, 129, 132, 133,
　135, 136, 137, 138, 142, 147, 167–8,
　169, 192, 196, 197, 199, 211
evidence 16, 18, 30, 35, 52, 54, 78, 90, 115,
　133, 142, 148, 149, 168, 182, 184, 192,
　197, 199, 203, 206, 207, 211, 212, 213,
　217
　collected 112, 114, 147, 184, 213

evidence (*continued*)
  confirming/supporting 16, 18, 22, 26,
    30, 152, 176, 183, 184–5, 187, 188, 196,
    202–3, 213, 217
  empirical 14, 114, 184, 200
  evidence-based policy/practice 41,
    44–5, 55, 64, 136, 187
  refuting/counter 14, 59, 137, 188, 200,
    202, 210, 213, 214
  in testing policy/practice/theory 59,
    64, 61, 158, 176, 184–5, 216
  *see also* hypothesis(es), testing of
expectation(s) 13, 15, 18, 26, 85, 127, 128,
    129, 130, 131, 133, 134, 144, 145, 150,
    158, 170, 179, 182, 183, 184, 187, 196,
    198, 199, 202, 203, 204, 213, 216
  place in learning 16–17, 19–20, 22, 201,
    205
  *see also* mismatch(es) between
    expectation and experience
expense of research 51, 61, 190–2 *see also*
  principles for good research
  practice, economy
explanation(s) 15, 55, 57, 61, 62, 86, 93, 99,
    101, 178, 199, 201–2, 209, 216, 217

*Fachhochschulen* 64
*Fachhochschulrat* 64
fact(s) 14, 19, 26, 28, 47, 72, 94, 128, 132–4,
    137, 139, 150, 176, 177, 199–200, 211,
    216
fallibilism 144–5, 200, 209, 212
  *see also* knowledge, conjectural nature
    of; realism, fallibilist
falsifiability 86, 164, 184, 200, 206, 217
  *see also* negative existential
    statement(s)
falsification 14, 17, 184, 200, 202, 203, 214
falsificationism 200, 207
Farnham, D. 62, 65
feminism 35, 38–9, 43, 80, 81, 130, 154–5
Feral, J. 155, 163
Fergusson, D. M. 88, 96
Finch, J. 194, 218
Fine, M. 43, 49
Flax, J. 38, 49
Fletcher, J. M. 97
Flew, A. 53, 65
Foster, P. 123
Foucault, M. 40, 41, 49, 80, 137, 209
foundationalism 18, 129, 200, 208, 209
Frankfurt School 67, 72, 73, 74, 75, 81,
    141, 197
Freire, P. 79, 82
Fudge, C. 62, 65
Fukuyama, F. 68, 82

Fullan, M. 78, 82
Further and Higher Education Act (1992)
  (England and Wales) 64

Gage, N. L. 92, 96
gender differences in academic
  achievement 87–9, 95
generalization 5, 52, 58, 86, 93, 115–16,
    119, Chapter 12, 196, 201
  fuzzy 117, 119, 164–6, 170, 171, 200–1
Giddens, A. 68, 82
Gillham, B. 116, 123
Gilligan, C. 154, 163
Giroux, H. A. 35, 49
globalization 37, 68, 69, 70, 71–2, 76, 131
Gomm, R. 115, 123
Goodson, I. 39, 49
Gough, P. B. 87, 91–2, 96
Gouthro, P. 76, 82
government, *see* policy, government
governmentality 42
Grace, P. 99, 110
Gramsci, A. 41, 49, 100
grand narratives 39, 40, 47
Greaney, K. T. 97
Griffin, C. 82
Guattari, F. 36, 49
Guba, E. G. 115, 116, 123

Habermas, J. (Habermasian) 41, 49, 67,
    71, 72, 74, 75, 76, 79, 81, 82, 146, 147,
    197, 218
Halliday, J. 23, 32
Hammersley, M. 123, 209
Hargreaves, D. 136, 140
Hartnett, A. 28, 32
Hartsock, N. 38, 49
Hegel, G. W. F. (Hegelian) 67, 70, 82, 144,
    215
hegemony 37, 41–2, 100, 146, 155
  counter- 71, 75, 77–9, 100, 144
Heidegger, M. 78, 82
Heshusius, L. 90, 91, 97
Hirst, P. H. 14, 32
Holford, J. 70, 82
Honeychurch, K. G. 38, 49
hooks, b. 99, 110
Hoover, W. 87, 97
Horkheimer, M. 73
Horton, S. 62, 65
Horwood, L. J. 88, 96
Howe, K. 92, 96
Hume, D. 16, 17, 18, 32, 53, 203, 204, 218
hypothesis (hypotheses) 15, 20, 21, 29,
    53–4, 96, 153, 179, 183, 196, 199, 201,
    202, 217

generation of 53, 60, 168
prohibitive 26
    *see also* negative existential
    statement(s)
testable 25–6, 59, 63, 87, 89, 93, 202
testing of 51, 54, 57, 86, 93, 158–9, 164,
    168, 177, 182, 183, 184–5, 186, 187,
    192, 202, 204, 213
hypothetico-deductive method 201–2

identity 35, 36, 37, 38–9, 42–4, 46, 81, 99,
    154
ideology critique 68, 69–70, 72, 73–5, 76,
    77–8, 80, 142, 146–8
Illich, I. 76, 82
illuminative research 202–3
imagination 39, 63, 178, 185–7, 192
improvement of practice through
    research 5, Chapter 2, 84, 111, 116,
    128–9, 133, 135, 137, 139, 142–4, 147,
    149, 150, 160, 176, 179, 185, 194–5,
    211
incommensurability thesis 182
    *see also* incompatibility thesis
incompatibility thesis 90–3, 95
    *see also* incommensurability thesis
indigenous research 5, 100, 101, 155,
    161–2
induction 15–18, 53, 176, 201, 202, 203–4,
    207
Ingram, D. 72, 82, 144, 151
International Council for Adult
    Education 80
International Monetary Fund (IMF) 71,
    72
interpretation(s) 37, 39, 45, 46, 47, 52–4,
    60, 67, 78, 81, 90, 98, 107, 114, 117,
    144, 155, 170, 171, 183, 184, 186, 198,
    217
interpretivism 4, 90–3, 181–2, 197, 204,
    212
irony 36, 47, 127, 182, 208–9
Iverson, A. 87, 96

James, R. 13, 32
James, W. 209
Jarvis, P. 82
Jay, M. 72, 82
Johnson, R. 45, 49
Johnston, P. M. G. 5, 98, 99, 100, 103, 104,
    108, 110, 149, 161, 163, 175, 176,
    188–9
justificationism 204

Keelan, T. 103, 110
Kemmis, S. 195, 218

knowledge 14, 15, 24, 35, 36, 38, 40, 56,
    57, 61, 72, 80, 84, 85, 87, 88, 101, 102,
    103, 130, 131, 135, 151, 163, 180, 195,
    198, 199, 202, 204–5, 212, 213, 216
conjectural nature of 6, 14, 20, 29, 53,
    56, 70, 128, 139, 177, 183, 185, 200,
    201
    *see also* realism, fallibilist
context-bound/contingent/locally
    embedded 42, 52, 93, 135, 152
craft 121–2
different kinds of 52, 54, 108, 138, 149,
    158–9, 209
growth of 3, 5, 7, 11, 13, 15–19, 22, 23,
    24, 39, 46, 51, 54, 55, 69, 79, 100, 111,
    132, 134, 154, 160, 164, 168, 176, 178
reference will probably be moved to
    179, 181, 182, 185, 192, 205, 206, 211,
    212, 213
    *see also* induction
as bricolage 36
as a human construct 52, 163
Maori 99, 101, 102, 106, 154, 156, 162
objective 15, 21, 30, 130, 217
ownership of 45, 98, 131–2
partial nature of 42
provisional nature of 42, 51, 54, 188
scientific 14, 54, 132, 196, 198, 204, 208,
    214 *see also*: knowledge, tested;
    science
tested 54, 158, 167–8, 176, 182, 189, 215
    *see also* uncertainty
Krick, E. V. 28, 32, 211, 218
Kuhn, T. 207, 218

language 25, 26, 35, 36, 39, 42, 44, 45, 46,
    74, 92, 132, 135
argumentative 14, 21, 24, 182
    *see also* argument
clarity of 93–4, 96, 192
descriptive 14, 21
literacy 25, 26, 28, 41, 86, 88, 89, 91–2,
    94–5, 108, 135, 183
    national strategy (England) 45, 127,
    132, 136, 137, 138
    *see also* learning to read; Literacy
    Experts Group (New Zealand);
    Literacy Taskforce (New Zealand);
    Reading Recovery
Maori 101, 102, 157–8, 162
research on reading 5, 84–7, 89–90,
    94–5, 133–5, 180, 183
    *see also*: discourse; writing sous-rature
Lather, P. 38, 39, 42, 49, 104, 110
learning Chapter 2, 46, 56, 63, 68, 70, 71,
    72, 74, 77, 78, 79, 81, 90, 111, 119, 128,

learning (*continued*)
130, 133, 134, 136, 137, 138, 139, 143,
145, 146, 148, 150, 151, 166, 176, 182,
185, 196, 198, 203, 204, 205, 211, 216
inhibitions/impediments to 23, 56, 78,
88, 89, 130, 200
lifelong 70, 143
logic of 13, 18–26, 31 n 1, 132, 150
model(s) of 36, 45
to read 84–7, 88–90
*see also* language, literacy; language,
research on reading; problem(s) in
reading
in research 3, 22, 29–30, 95–6, 183, 185,
190, 191
style(s) 88–9, 95
theory (theories) 5, 7, 17, 74, 133
*see also* gender differences in academic
achievement
Levi-Strauss, C. 37
Lewin, K. 194, 218
Lewis, C. I. 209
lifeworld 75–7, 143, 205
Lincoln, Y. S. 115, 116, 123
Lindblad, S. 42, 50
Lindblom, C. E. 62, 65
Literacy Experts Group (New Zealand)
94–5
Literacy Taskforce (New Zealand) 94–5
literature search and review 190–1, 193
Locke, M. 58, 63, 65
longitudinal research 87, 89, 205–6
Lukács, G. 67, 83
Lyon, G. R. 85, 96
Lyotard, J.-F. 40, 49, 52, 65, 209

McCarthy, C. 42, 49
McCarthy, T. 73, 83
McLeod, J. 100, 110
MacLure, M. 38, 39, 40, 43, 44, 47, 49, 50
McTaggart, R. 195, 218
McWilliam, E. 40, 50
Magee, B. 7, 57, 63, 65
Maori Chapter 7, Chapter 11
Kaupapa Maori 102, 105
principles of accountability 102–3
*see also* knowledge, Maori; language,
Maori
Marcuse, H. 74, 83
marginality 37, 38, 41, 42–3, 44, 78, 80,
100, 103–4, 106, 130–1, 137–8, 157
Marx, K. (Marxism) 41, 43, 46, 67, 68, 70,
75, 81, 83, 129, 130, 141, 144, 147, 149,
151, 215
Masterman, M. 207, 218
Mayer, R. E. 84, 89, 90, 92, 93, 96

method(s) (research) 5, Chapter 2, 36, 39,
47, 51–2, 53, 61, 65, 73, 80, 84, 86, 90,
92, 93, 98, 101, 102, 106, 107, 116, 131,
134–5, 144, 145, 152, 153, 156, 162,
Chapter 13, 206, 208, 214
scientific 54, 72, 92, 162, 175–6, 177,
197
*see also* hypothetico-deductive
method; qualitative methods/
research; quantitative methods/
research
methodology, definition of 206
Miller, D. 13, 32, 183, 193, 197, 198, 202,
204, 211, 215, 218
Ministry of Education (New Zealand) 94,
95, 96
mismatch(es) between expectation and
experience 12, 19, 20, 29, 145, 179,
205
Morrow, R. A. 143, 151
Muller, J. 71, 83

Naish, M. 28, 32
negative existential statement(s) 25, 206
New Labour 58, 68
*New Oxford Dictionary of English* 196, 205
Nicholson, L. 38, 50
Nørretranders, T. 19, 32
North East London Polytechnic 23
Nottinghamshire Local Education
Authority 120
numeracy 41
national strategy for (England) 45, 127,
136, 138

objectives 23, 77, 101, 114, 136, 205, 207
objectivity 45, 52–4, 59, 69, 72, 91–2, 98,
101, 108, 158–9, 185, 207, 214
*see also* knowledge, objective
observation 16–18, 52–4, 86, 92, 107,
111–12, 116, 167, 179, 184, 186, 191,
195, 198, 201, 202, 203, 208, 209,
214
*see also* singular observation
statement(s)
Oetzi 18
Office for Standards in Education
(Ofsted or OFSTED) (England and
Wales) 112, 142–3
ontology 207
Organisation for Economic Co-operation
and Development (OECD) 52, 65
Owen, W. 63
*Oxford Companion to Philosophy* 215
*Oxford English Reference Dictionary* 207
Ozga, J. 55, 65

230    *Index*

Pakeha 99–100, 102, 103, 104, 105, 106,
    154, 155–6, 157, 160
paradigm(s) 3–4, 7, 36, 37, 39, 44, 45, 46,
    52–3, 61, 90–1, 102, 136, 159, 181, 202,
    207, 212
Parlett, M. 202, 218
Parliamentary Select Committee on
    Science and Education Inquiry into
    the Teaching of Reading (New
    Zealand) 95
participatory research 79–80, Chapter 7,
    Chapter 11, 189
    *see also* action research
performance-related pay 56, 112–15, 166
Perkinson, H. J. 23, 32–3, 34
Peters, R. S. 14, 32
Petersen, A. F. 22, 33, 196, 218–19
Phillips, D. C. 6, 7, 200, 208, 209, 213, 219
philosophy of education 13–14, 130
Pierce, C. S. 209
Plato 215
policy 29, Chapter 4, 73, 74, 104, 139, 148,
    166, 167, 179, 207, 211, 215
    government 27, 41, 55, 57–62, 63, 64,
        68, 71, 73, 78, 93, 112, 127, 129, 137,
        138, 141–3
    higher education 57–62, 64
    impact of research on 12, 61, 62–4, 68,
        77, 94–5, 115, 121–2, 176
    policy-maker(s) 35, 45, 55, 63, 77, 116,
        119, 121, 171, 176, 187, 207
    research on 5, 28, 39, 40, 42, 43, 44, 46,
        Chapter 4, 74, 75, 79, 80, 146, 165,
        188
    testing policy 30, 55, 57, 58, 59, 60,
        61, 62, 64, 137, 138, 168, 176, 182,
        187
politics 37, 46, 60, 62, 64, 67–8, Chapter 5,
    102, 104–5, 109, 113, 122, 130, 139,
    Chapter 10, 154, 155, 156, 159–60,
    176, 179, 187, 189, 190
    politicians 27, 43, 45, 58, 64, 137, 199
    *see also* power
Pollard, A. 165, 171
polytechnics 58, 60, 62, 63, 64
Popkewitz, T. S. 42, 50
Popper, K. R. (and Popperian) Chapter 1,
    Chapter 2, Chapter 4, 130, 133, 135,
    140, 164–7, 176, 182, 184–5, 186, 191
positivism (and positivists) 3–4, 6, 52–3,
    72–5, 77–8, 80, 90–2, 141, 144, 175,
    181, 197, 204, 208, 209, 212
postcolonialism 35, 38, 40, 43, 44, 46, 130,
    131
    *see also* colonialism
postmodernism 5, Chapter 3, 52, 53, 60,

80–1, 93–4, 95, Chapter 9, 141, 145,
    147, 149, 176–7, 182, 208–9
postmodernity 37
postpositivism 6–7, 176, 197, 209
post-structuralism 37–8, 80–1
power 27, 35, 40–2, 43, 45, 46, 53, 64, 67,
    72, 73, 76, 80, 93, 98, 100, 102, 105,
    108–9, 130, 132, 139, 146, 147, 149,
    150, 155, 157, 162, 197
    empowerment 46, 80, 103–5, 129, 132,
        135, 137, 139, 142, 157, 160
    *see also* politics; hegemony
pragmatism 198, 209
Pratt, J. 5, 7, 8, 28, 33, 52, 56, 57, 58, 59, 60,
    65–6, 144, 145, 168, 171
prediction 36, 39, 47, 57, 61, 88, 136, 186,
    197, 202, 209–10, 216
    fuzzy 165–7
    *see also* negative existential
        statement(s)
preference 24, 29, 31, 42, 55, 60, 128, 137,
    146, 159, 181, 183, 187, 191, 196, 201,
    210–11, 215
principles for good research practice (the
    P-R-I-C-E of research)
    care for others 187–90, 192–3
    *see also* ethics
    economy 190–2, 193
    imagination 185–7, 192
    *see also* imagination
    purpose 178–82, 192
    rigour 182–5, 192
Pring, R. 4, 8
problem(s) 14, 15, 22, 39, 53, 54, 57, 61, 70,
    101, 113, 115, 136, 144, 145, 152, 153,
    158, 162, 164, 181, 197, 201, 207, 211,
    212
    formulation of 12, 20–1, 24, 29, 31,
        58–9, 60, 99, 134, 145–6, 177, 179–80,
        185, 186, 192, 207, 211, 214, 217
    practical 27–9, 31 n 2, 55–6, 139, 145,
        149, 151, 178, 179–80, 186, 192, 205,
        210, 211, 216
    social 53, 60, 111, 166, 178, 215
    problem-based methodology 23, 25,
        30–1, 51, 54–63, 64–5, 186–7, 195
    in reading 84, 85, 87
    research problem 179, 180, 181, 185,
        186, 191, 217
    situation 62–3, 137, 166, 214–5
    solving 12, 19–22, 26, 27, 30, 31, 44,
        51, 56, 58–9, 64, 77, 79, 86, 101, 105,
        112, 135, 139, 149, 177, 186, 192,
        211, 216
    theoretical 27–9, 31 n 2, 55–6, 177,
        179–80, 186, 192, 211, 216

Prochnow, J. E. 5, 87, 95, 96, 97
proof 17, 53, 133, 211–12
proposition(s) 52, 53, 55, 57, 60, 92, 152,
    154, 166, 184–5, 209, 212
psychology 12, 13, 17, 86, 94, 104, 111,
    145, 204, 214
    behavioural 77
    social 36, 149
purpose of research 3, 11–12, 22, 29, 35,
    44, 51–2, 69–70, 84, 93, 100, 101, 104,
    111, 127, 145, 168, 178–82, 186, 192,
    213
    action research 29, 194–5
    policy research 55, 57, 61
Putnam, H. 209

qualitative methods/research 3–4, 52, 61,
    84, 86, 90, 92, 93, 95, 116, 144, 145,
    181–2, 212
quantitative methods/research 3–4, 61,
    84, 86, 90, 92, 95, 181, 212
queer theory 35, 38, 43, 130
Quine, W. V. O. 93, 96, 97, 192, 193, 209

Rabinow, P. 40, 50
rationalism 93, 212
    *see also* critical rationalism
rationality 20, 31 n 1, 62, 63, 71, 81,
    114–15, 128, 141, 143, 148, 168, 182,
    185, 196, 209, 210, 212–13
    instrumental/technical 72–5, 77, 78
    scientific 98, 101, 109, 158, 161
reading, *see* language, literacy; language,
    research on reading; Literacy
    Experts Group; Literacy Taskforce;
    problem(s) in reading; Reading
    Recovery
Reading Recovery 86–7, 89, 95, 133
realism 7, 199–200, 206, 213
    fallibilist 5, 6, 52, Chapter 9
reality 14–15, 36, 39, 42, 44, 52, 53, 57, 60,
    62, 72, 75, 78, 79, 80, 81, 91, 92, 127,
    129, 130, 132–3, 139, 155, 205, 209,
    211, 216, 217
    *see also* realism
Reason, P. 153, 163
reductionism 77, 104, 136, 213
reflective practice 35, 43–4, 52, 71, 72–3,
    74, 75, 77, 143–4, 195, 197
refutation 14, 17, 18–19, 25–6, 59, 176,
    177, 184, 200, 203, 206, 213
relativism (relativists) 11, 52–4, 55, 59, 71,
    81, 91, 93, 145, 147, 213
    *see also* truth, relativist view of
research, definition of 3, 213
Rorty, R. 40, 50

Rowan, J. 153, 163
Rustin, M. 59, 66
Ryan, H. 97

Said, E. 101, 110, 153, 163
St Pierre, E. A. 37, 38, 39, 42, 44, 50, 138,
    140
Sartre, J.-P. 78, 83
Scheurich, J. J. 39, 50
Schick, C. 80, 83
Schofield, J. W. 115
School for Independent Study 23, 24
Schutz, A. 205, 219
science 4, 14, 15, 23, 53, 54, 70, 73, 86, 119,
    132, 145, 152, 162, 175–8, 181, 184,
    197, 198,*200, 201, 202, 204, 206, 208,
    209, 210–11, 213–14, 215, 216
    anti-science attitude 89–94
    in educational research 5, 24–7, 29,
        Chapter 6, 121, 128, 131, 176
    and non-science 4, 14, 90, 177, 184, 200,
        207
        *see also* theory, definition of,
            metaphysical
    philosophy of 4, 95, 190
    social science(s) 4, 46, 52, 62, 72, 73, 77,
        80, 89, 93, 121, 122, 165, 166–7, 175–6,
        177, 178, 186, 204, 207, 208, 214
        *see also* knowledge, scientific;
            method(s) (research), scientific;
            positivism; postpositivism;
            rationality, scientific
Secretary of State for Education
    (England and Wales) 27
Shaywitz, B. A. 97
Shaywitz, S. E. 89, 97
Shore, C. 62, 66
significance 214
Simon, H. 120
Simon, H. A. 62, 66
singular observation statement(s) 16, 17,
    203, 214
situational analysis and situational logic
    62–3, 214
Smith, J. 90, 97
Smith, J. K. 90, 91, 97
Smith, J. W. A. 90, 97
Smith, L. 99, 100, 101, 102, 107, 108, 110,
    160, 163
Snook, I. 189, 193
social justice 35, 37, 46, 76, 81, 129
    *see also* ethics
Sokal, A. 91, 93, 94, 97
Spear-Swerling, L. 85, 88, 97
Spivak, G. 38, 43, 50
Stahl, S. 88, 97

Stake, R. E.  115, 116, 123, 169, 171
Stanovich, K. E.  85, 97
Stenhouse, L.  169, 171
Stephenson, J.  24, 33–4
Sternberg, R. J.  85, 88, 97
storytelling  91, 93, 96, 162, 171
  case study (studies)  117, 118, 120, 168, 171
  *see also* grand narratives
Street, B. V.  91, 97
Stronach, I.  38, 39, 40, 43, 44, 45, 50
student-initiated curricula  20, 24, 128, 138, 150
subjective ideas and experience  11, 15, 21, 36, 53, 54, 72, 94, 127, 130, 182, 185, 217
Swann, J.  5, 7, 8, 13, 16, 18, 19, 20, 22, 23, 24, 25, 26, 27, 28, 29, 32, 34, 52, 55, 66, 128, 133, 134, 138, 140, 154, 158, 176, 177, 179, 193, 195, 205, 207, 211, 219–20
Swartz, R.  23, 34, 195, 220

Taylor, D.  91, 97
teacher education/training  27, 41, 45, 120
  national curriculum for (UK)  41, 127
Teacher Training Agency  136
technology  73, 177, 215–16
test, definition of  216
theory, definition of  216
  metaphysical  206
  universal  14, 16, 17, 18, 196, 200, 201–2, 203–4, 206, 209–10, 214, 217
  *see also* expectation(s); generalization; proposition(s)
Tierney, W. G.  38, 50
*Times Educational Supplement*  118
Tolich, M.  188, 193
Trinh, T. M.  38, 43, 50
trustworthiness  113, 116, 117, 118, 119, 121
  best estimate of (BET)  119, 165, 166
truth  20, 25, 28, 38, 39, 45, 91, 99, 112, 119, 129, 130, 132, 134, 136, 139, 152, 165–6, 177, 183, 186, 200, 201, 202, 203, 204, 210, 212, 214, 216–17
  as consensus  133
  as correspondence  92
  to fact  14, 199–200

pragmatic view of  209
pursuit of  12, 15–18, 52–3, 128, 134–5, 139, 182, 209, 211, 213
  regimes of  40–1, 45, 137
  relativist view of  213
Tunmer, W. E.  5, 6, 87, 89, 92, 96, 97, 133, 134, 176, 181, 190, 192
Turner, D.  193

Ullian, J. S.  93, 96, 97, 192, 193
uncertainty  6, 14–15, 17, 35–6, 38, 39, 42, 43, 45, 46, 53, 127, 128, 166, 176, 200, 201, 209, 211, 213
  *see also* knowledge, conjectural nature of
university (universities)  3, 57, 58, 60, 62, 68–70, 71, 77, 80, 90, 145, 147, 151, 153, 160, 199

value(s) in learning and research  11–12, 19, 20, 26, 28, 30, 36, 52, 53, 58, 70, 72, 90, 108, 109, 111, 128, 130, 131–2, 134, 139, 143, 150, 153, 154, 158, 159, 160, 164, 168, 169, 176, 177–8, 179, 181, 191, 196, 199, 203, 208, 211, 213, 217
  *see also* ethics
verification  16, 17, 53, 86, 92, 203, 217

Waitere-Ang, H.  98, 104, 108, 110, 161, 163
Walker, R.  100, 104, 110, 157, 163
Warde, I.  70, 83
Weber, M. (Weberian)  73–4, 75
Welton, M.  75, 83, 143, 151
Western framework(s)  98, 101, 106, 109, 152–4, 158–9
'what works'  29, 41, 44, 57, 128, 136–7, 155, 164, 167, 176
Woods, T.  37, 38, 50
World Bank  71, 72
world 1, world 2, world 3  15, 217
Wright, S.  62, 66
writing sous-rature  42

Yarmol-Franko, K.  80, 83
Yin, R. K.  116, 123